UNWIN BOOKS

My Philosophical Development

A survey such as this by one of the world's leading thinkers, of nearly seventy years of his own philosophical work, is clearly as important as it is fascinating. It is a masterpiece of philosophical autobiography.

'My philosophical development,' wrote Russell, 'may be divided into various stages according to the problems with which I have been concerned and the men whose work has influenced me. There is only one constant pre-occupation: I have throughout been anxious to discover how much we can be said to know and with what degree of certainty or doubtfulness. I wanted certainty in the kind of way people wanted religious faith.'

'Bertrand Russell is not only the most brilliant philosopher of this century: he is also one of the most self-critical. These qualities come out clearly in his philosophical auto-biography . . . Russell tells this story with his usual economy, wit and elegance . . .' – A. J. Ayer

' . . . beside being a philosopher, he is a ready and graceful writer with opinions of his own on most topics. He has an acute, inventive and original intelligence; he has given a fresh turn to almost every important philosophical problem; he is the remarkably unsolemn and unpretentious doyen of contemporary English philosophy . . .' – *Birmingham Post*

'Bertrand Russell is the greatest philosopher today: he is also one of the most remarkable human beings that the twentieth century – an age already rich in genius and personal fulfilment – has produced. It is therefore only to be expected that a book from his hand that describes the progress of his opinions over a period of seventy years, should be a work of immense fascination and distinction. *My Philosophical Development* will not disappoint.' – *The Observer*

Photograph: Lotte Meitner-Graf

My
Philosophical
Development

BERTRAND RUSSELL

UNWIN BOOKS

First published in 1959
Second impression 1959
Third impression 1969
Unwin Books edition 1975

© George Allen & Unwin Ltd, 1959

ISBN 0 04 192030 9

UNWIN BOOKS
George Allen & Unwin Ltd
Ruskin House, 40 Museum Street
London W.C.1

Printed in Great Britain
in 9 point Plantin type
by Cox & Wyman Ltd
London, Reading and Fakenham

Prefatory Note

MR ALAN WOOD, whose book *The Passionate Sceptic* won widespread and well-deserved applause, was intending to write a more technical examination of my philosophy, but at the time of his death only a small part of this work had been completed. This small part included an Introduction, and this Introduction has seemed to those who have read it to be of value, and, therefore, worth publishing. On this ground, it is being printed at the end of the present volume. If it had become available sooner, it would have been put at the beginning of the volume, but it came too late for this to be possible. I think readers may find it advisable to turn to it first, as it admirably clarifies various things that might otherwise cause misunderstanding. It is deeply to be regretted that Mr Wood did not live to complete the work.

B.R.

Contents

EPISTLE TO THE COLOSSIANS: II. 8

Beware lest any man spoil you through philosophy and vain deceit.

EPISTLE TO TITUS: I. 12–13

One of themselves, even a prophet of their own, said, 'the Cretians are always liars, evil beasts, slow bellies'. This witness is true.

Chapter 1

Introductory Outline

My philosophical development may be divided into various stages according to the problems with which I have been concerned and the men whose work has influenced me. There is only one constant pre-occupation: I have throughout been anxious to discover how much we can be said to know and with what degree of certainty of doubtfulness. There is one major division in my philosophical work: in the years 1899–1900 I adopted the philosophy of logical atomism and the technique of Peano in mathematical logic. This was so great a revolution as to make my previous work, except such as was purely mathematical, irrelevant to everything that I did later. The change in these years was a revolution; subsequent changes have been of the nature of an evolution.

My original interest in philosophy had two sources. On the one hand, I was anxious to discover whether philosophy would provide any defence for anything that could be called religious belief, however vague; on the other hand, I wished to persuade myself that something could be known, in pure mathematics if not elsewhere. I thought about these problems during adolescence, in solitude and with little help from books. As regards religion, I came to disbelieve first in free will, then in immortality, and finally in God. As regards the foundations of mathematics, I got nowhere. In spite of strong bias towards empiricism, I could not believe that 'two plus two equals four' is an inductive generalisation from experience, but I remained in doubt as to everything beyond this purely negative conclusion.

At Cambridge I was indoctrinated with the philosophies of Kant and Hegel, but G. E. Moore and I together came to reject both these philosophies. I think that, although we agreed in our revolt, we had important differences of emphasis. What I think at first chiefly interested Moore was the independence of fact from knowledge and the rejection of the whole Kantian apparatus of *a priori* intuitions and categories, moulding experience but not the outer world. I agreed enthusiastically with him in this respect, but I was more concerned than he was with certain purely logical matters. The most important of these and the one which has dominated all my subsequent philosophy, was what I called 'the doctrine of external relations'. Monists had maintained that a relation between two terms is always, in reality, composed of properties of the two separate terms and of the whole which they compose, or, in ultimate strictness, only of this last. This view seemed to me to make mathematics inexplicable. I came to the conclusion that relatedness does not imply any corresponding complexity in the related terms and is, in general, not equivalent to any property of the whole which they compose. Just after developing this view in my book on *The Philosophy of Leibniz*, I became aware of Peano's work in mathematical logic, which led me to a new technique and a new philosophy of mathematics. Hegel and his disciples had been in the habit of 'proving' the impossibility of space and time and matter, and generally everything that an ordinary man would believe in. Having become convinced that the Hegelian arguments against this and that were invalid, I reacted to the opposite extreme and began to believe in the reality of whatever could not be *dis*proved – e.g. points and instants and particles and Platonic universals.

When, however, after 1910, I had done all that I intended to do as regards pure mathematics, I began to think about the physical world and, largely under Whitehead's influence, I was led to new applications of Occam's razor, to which I had become devoted by its usefulness in the philosophy of arithmetic. Whitehead persuaded me that one could do physics without supposing points and instants to be part of the stuff of the world. He considered – and in this I came to agree with him – that the stuff of the physical world could consist of events, each occupying a finite amount of space-time. As in all uses of Occam's razor, one was not obliged to deny the existence of the entities with which one dispensed, but one was enabled to abstain from ascertaining it. This had the advantage of diminishing the assumptions required for the interpretation of whatever branch of knowledge was in question. As regards the physical world, it is impossible to prove that there are not point-instants, but it is possible to prove that physics gives no reason whatever for supposing that there are such things.

At the same time, that is to say in the years from 1910 to 1914, I became interested, not only in what the physical world is, but in how we come to know it. The relation of perception to physics is a problem which has occupied me intermittently ever since that time. It is in relation to this problem that my philosophy underwent its last substantial change. I had regarded perception as a two-term relation of subject and object, as this had made it comparatively easy to understand how perception could give knowledge of something other than the subject. But under the influence of William James, I came to think this view mistaken, or at any rate an undue simplification. Sensations, at least, even those that are visual or auditory, came to seem to me not in their own nature relational occurrences. I do not, of course, mean to say that when I see something there is no relation between me and what I see; but what I do mean to say is that the relation is much more indirect than I had supposed and that everything that happens in me when I see something could, so far as its logical structure is concerned, quite well occur without there being anything outside me for me to see. This change in my opinions greatly increased the difficulty of problems involved in connecting experience with the outer world.

There was another problem which began to interest me at about the same time – that is to say, about 1917. This was the problem of the relation of language to facts. This problem has two departments: the first concerned with vocabulary; the second, with syntax. The problem had been dealt with by various people before I became interested in it. Lady Welby wrote a book about it and F. C. S. Schiller was always urging its importance. But I had thought of language as transparent – that is to say, as a medium which could be employed without paying attention to it. As regards syntax, the inadequacy of this view was forced upon me by the contradictions arising in mathematical logic. As regards vocabulary, linguistic problems arose for me in investigating the extent to which a behaviouristic account of knowledge is possible. For these two reasons, I was led to place much more emphasis than I had previously done on the linguistic aspects of epistemology. But I have never been able to feel any sympathy with those who treat language as an autonomous province. The essential thing about language is that it has meaning – i.e. that it is related to something other than itself, which is, in general, non-linguistic.

My most recent work has been connected with the problem of non-demonstrative inference. It used to be supposed by empiricists that the justification of such inference rests upon induction. Unfortunately, it can be proved that induction by simple enumeration, if conducted without regard to common sense, leads very much more often to error than the truth. And if a principle needs common sense before it can be safely used, it is not the sort of principle that can satisfy a logician. We must, therefore, look for a principle other than induction if we are to accept the broad outlines of science, and of common sense in so far as it is not refutable. This is a very large problem and I cannot pretend to have done more than indicate lines along which a solution may be sought.

Ever since I abandoned the philosophy of Kant and Hegel, I have sought solutions of philosophical problems by means of analysis; and I remain firmly persuaded, in spite of some modern tendencies to the contrary, that only by analysing is progress possible. I have found, to take an important example, that by analysing physics and perception the problem of the relation of mind and matter can be completely solved. It is true that nobody has accepted what seems to me the solution, but I believe and hope that this is only because my theory has not been understood.

Chapter 2

My Present View
of the World

The view to which I have been gradually led is one which has been almost universally misunderstood and which, for this reason, I will try to state as simply and clearly as I possibly can. I am, for the present, only endeavouring to state the view, not to give the reasons which have led me to it. I will, however, say this much by way of preface: it is a view which results from a synthesis of four different sciences – namely, physics, physiology, psychology and mathematical logic. Mathematical logic is used in creating structures having assigned properties out of elements that have much less mathematical smoothness. I reverse the process which has been common in philosophy since Kant. It has been common among philosophers to begin with how we know and proceed afterwards to what we know. I think this a mistake, because knowing how we know is one small department of knowing what we know. I think it a mistake for another reason: it tends to give to knowing a cosmic importance which it by no means deserves, and thus prepares the philosophical student for the belief that mind has some kind of supremacy over the non-mental universe, or even that the non-mental universe is nothing but a nightmare dreamt by mind in its un-philosophical moments. This point of view is completely remote from my imaginative picture of the cosmos. I accept without qualification the view that results from astronomy and geology, from which it would appear that there is no evidence of anything mental except in a tiny fragment of space-time, and that the great processes of nebular and stellar evolution proceed according to laws in which mind plays no part.

If this initial bias is accepted, it is obviously to theoretical physics that we must first look for an understanding of the major processes in the history of the universe. Unfortunately, theoretical physics no longer speaks with that splendid dogmatic clarity that it enjoyed in the seventeenth century. Newton works with four fundamental concepts: space, time, matter and force. All four have been swept into limbo by modern physicists. Space and time, for Newton, were solid, independent things. They have been replaced by space-time, which is not substantial but only a system of relations. Matter has had to be replaced by series of events. Force, which was the first of the Newtonian concepts to be abandoned, has been replaced by energy; and energy turns out to be indistinguishable from the pale ghost which is all that remains of matter. Cause, which was the philosophical form of what physicists called force, has also become decrepit. I will not admit that it is dead, but it has nothing like the vigour of its earlier days.

For all these reasons, what modern physics has to say is somewhat confused. Nevertheless, we are bound to believe it on pain of death. If there were any community which rejected the doctrines of modern physics, physicists employed by a hostile government would have no difficulty in exterminating it. The modern physicist, therefore, enjoys powers far exceeding those of the Inquisition in its palmiest days, and it certainly behoves us to treat his pronouncements with due awe. For my part, I have no doubt that, although progressive changes are to be expected in physics, the present doctrines are likely to be nearer to the truth than any rival doctrines now before the world. Science is at no moment quite right, but it is seldom quite wrong, and has, as a rule, a better chance of being right than the theories of the unscientific. It is, therefore, rational to accept it hypothetically.

It is not always realised how exceedingly abstract is the information that theoretical physics has to give. It lays down certain fundamental equations which enable it to deal with the logical structure of events, while leaving it completely unknown what is the intrinsic character of the events that have the structure. We only know the intrinsic character of events when they happen to us. Nothing whatever in theoretical physics enables us to say anything about the intrinsic character of events elsewhere. They may be just like the events that happen to us, or they may be totally different in strictly unimaginable ways. All that physics gives us is certain equations giving abstract properties of their changes. But as to what it is that changes, and what it changes from and to – as to this, physics is silent.

The next step is an approximation to perception, but without passing beyond the realm of physics. A photographic plate exposed to a portion of the night sky takes photographs of separate stars. Given similar photographic plates and atmospheric conditions, different photographs of the same portion of the sky will be closely similar. There must, therefore, be some influence (I am using the vaguest word that I can think of) proceeding from the various stars to the various photographic plates. Physicists used to think that this influence consisted of waves, but now they think that it consists of little bundles of energy called photons. They know how fast a photon travels and in what manner it will, on occasion, deviate from a rectilinear path. When it hits a photographic plate, it is transformed into energy of a different kind. Since each separate star gets itself photographed, and since it can be photographed anywhere on a clear night where there is an unimpeded view of the sky, there must be something happening, at each place where it can be photographed, that is specially connected with it. It follows that the atmosphere at night contains everywhere as many separable events as there are stars that can be photographed there, and each of these separable events must have some kind of individual history connecting it with the star from which it has come. All this follows from the consideration of different photographic plates exposed to the same night sky.

Or let us take another illustration. Let us imagine a rich cynic, disgusted by the philistinism of theatregoers, deciding to have a play performed, not before live people, but before a collection of cine-cameras. The cine-cameras – supposing them all of equal excellence – will produce closely similar records, differing according to the laws of perspective and according to their distance from the stage. This again shows, like the photographic plate, that at each cine-camera a complex of events is occurring at each moment which is closely related to the complex of events occurring on the stage. There is here the same need as before of separable influences proceeding from diverse sources. If, at a given moment, one actor shouts, 'Die, Varlet!' while another exclaims, 'Help! Murder!' both will be recorded, and therefore something connected with both must be happening at each cine-camera.

To take yet another illustration: suppose that a speech is recorded simultaneously by a number of gramophones, the gramophone records do not in any obvious way resemble the original speech, and yet, by a suitable mechanism, they can be made to reproduce something exceedingly like it. They must, therefore, have something in common with the speech. But what they have in common can only be expressed in rather abstract language concerning structure. Broadcasting affords an even better illustration of the same process. What intervenes between an orator and a man listening to him on the radio is not, on the face of it, at all similar either to what the orator says or to what the listener hears. Here, again, we have a causal chain in which the beginning resembles the end, but the intermediate terms, so far as intrinsic qualities are concerned, appear to be of quite a different kind. What is preserved throughout the causal chain, in this case as in that of the gramophone record, is a certain constancy of structure.

These various processes all belong purely to physics. We do not suppose that the cine-cameras have minds, and we should not suppose so even if, by a little ingenuity on the part of their maker, those in the stalls were made to sneer at the moments when those in the pit applauded. What these physical analogies to perception show is that in most places at most times, if not in all places at all times, a vast assemblage of overlapping events is taking place, and that many of these events, at a given place and time, are connected by causal chains with an original event which, by a sort of prolific heredity, has produced offspring more or less similar to itself in a vast number of different places.

What sort of picture of the universe do these considerations invite us to construct ? I think the answer must proceed by stages differing as to the degree of analysis that has been effected. For present purposes I shall content myself by treating as fundamental the notion of 'event'. I conceive each event as occupying a finite amount of space-time and as overlapping with innumerable other events which occupy partially, but not wholly, the same region of space-time. The mathematician who wishes to operate with point-instants can construct them by means of mathematical logic out of assemblages of overlapping events, but that is only for his technical purposes, which, for the moment, we may ignore. The events occurring in any given small region of space-time are not unconnected with events occurring elsewhere. On the contrary, if a photographic plate can photograph a certain star, that is because an event is happening at the photographic plate which is connected by what we may call heredity with the star in question. The photographic plate, in turn, if it is photographed, is the origin of a fresh progeny. In mathematical physics, which is only interested in exceedingly abstract aspects of the matters with which it deals, these various processes appear as paths by which energy travels. It is because mathematical physics is so abstract that its world seems so different from that of our daily life. But the difference is more apparent than real. Suppose you study population statistics, the people who make up the items are deprived of almost all the characteristics of real people before they are recorded in the census. But in this case, because the process of abstraction has not proceeded very far, we do not find it very difficult to undo it in imagination. But in the case of mathematical physics, the journey back from the abstract to the concrete is long and arduous, and, out of sheer weariness, we are tempted to rest by the way and endow some semi-abstraction with a concrete reality which it cannot justly claim.

There is a possibility of a further stage of analysis in which events are no longer the ultimate raw material. But I will not consider this in the present discussion.

We have seen that, for purely physical reasons, events in many different places and times can often be collected into families proceeding from an original progenitor as the light from a star proceeds from it in all directions. The successive generations in a single branch of such a family have varying degrees of resemblance to each other according to circumstances. The events which constitute the journey of the light from a star to our atmosphere change slowly and little. That is why it is possible to regard them as the voyage of single entities called photons, which may be thought of as persisting. But when the light reaches our atmosphere, a series of continually odder and odder things begins to happen to it. It may be stopped or transformed by mist or cloud. It may hit a sheet of water and be reflected or refracted. It may hit a photographic place and become a black dot of interest to an astronomer. Finally, it may happen to hit a human eye. When this occurs, the results are very complicated. There are a set of events between the eye and the brain which are studied by the physiologist and which have as little resemblance to the photons in the outer world as radio waves have to the orator's speech. At last the disturbance in the nerves, which has been traced by the physiologist, reaches the appropriate region in the brain; and then, at last, the man whose brain it is sees the star. People are puzzled because the seeing of the star seems so different from the processes that the physiologist discovered in the optic nerve, and yet it is clear that without these processes the man would not see the star. And so there is supposed to be a gulf between mind and matter, and a mystery which it is held in some degree impious to try to dissipate. I believe, for my part, that there is no greater mystery than there is in the transformation by the radio of electro-magnetic waves into sounds. I think the mystery is produced by a wrong conception of the physical world and by a Manichaean fear of degrading the mental world to the level of the supposedly inferior world of matter.

The world of which we have been speaking hitherto is entirely an inferred world. We do not perceive the sort of entities that physics talks of, and, if it is of such entities that the physical world is composed, then we do not see the eye or the optic nerve, for the eye and the optic nerve, equally, if the physicist is to be believed, consist of the odd hypothetical entities with which the theoretical physicist tries to make us familiar. These entities, however, since they owe their credibility to inference, are only defined to the degree that is necessary to make them fulfil their inferential purpose. It is not necessary to suppose that electrons, protons, neutrons, mesons, photons, and the rest have that sort of simple reality that belongs to immediate objects of experience. They have, at best, the sort of reality that belongs to 'London'. 'London' is a convenient word, but every *fact* which is stated by using this word could be stated, though more cumbrously, without using it. There is, however, a difference, and an important one, between London and the electrons: we can see the various parts of which London is composed, and, indeed, the parts are more immediately known to us than the whole. In the case of the electron, we do not perceive it and we do not perceive anything that we know to be a constituent of it. We know it only as a hypothetical entity fulfilling certain theoretical purposes. So far as theoretical physics is concerned, anything that fulfils these purposes can be taken to *be* the electron. It may be simple or complex; and, if complex, it may be built out of any components that allow the resultant structure to have the requisite properties. All this applies not only to the inanimate world but, equally, to the eyes and other sense organs, the nerves, and the brain.

But our world is not wholly a matter of inference. There are things that we know without asking the opinion of men of science. If you are too hot or too cold, you can be perfectly aware of this fact without asking the physicist what heat and cold consist of. When you see other people's faces, you have an experience which is completely indubitable, but which does not consist of seeing the things which theoretical physicists speak of. You see other people's eyes and you believe that they see yours. Your own eyes as visual objects belong to the inferred part of the world, though the inference is rendered fairly indubitable by mirrors, photographs and the testimony of your friends. The inference to your own eyes as visual objects is essentially of the same sort as the physicist's inference to electrons, etc.; and, if you are going to deny validity to the physicist's inferences, you ought also to deny that you know you have visible eyes – which is absurd, as Euclid would say.

We may give the name 'data' to all the things of which we are aware without inference. They include all our observed sensations – visual, auditory, tactile, etc. Common sense sees reason to attribute many of our sensations to causes outside our own bodies. It does not believe that the room in which it is sitting ceases to exist when it shuts its eyes or goes to sleep. It does not believe that its wife and children are mere figments of its imagination. In all this we may agree with common sense; but where it goes wrong is in supposing that inanimate objects resemble, in their intrinsic qualities, the perceptions which they cause. To believe this is as groundless as it would be to suppose that a gramophone record resembles the music that it causes. It is not, however, the *difference* between the physical world and the world of data that I chiefly wish to emphasise. On the contrary, it is the possibility of much closer resemblances than physics at first sight suggests that I consider it important to bring to light.

I think perhaps I can best make my own views clear by comparing them with those of Leibniz. Leibniz thought that the universe consisted of monads, each of which was a little mind and each of which mirrored the universe. They did this mirroring with varying degrees of inexactness. The best monads had the least confusion in their picture of the universe. Misled by the Aristotelian subject-predicate logic, Leibniz held that monads do not interact, and that the fact of their continuing to mirror the same universe is to be explained by a pre-established harmony. This part of his doctrine is totally unacceptable. It is only through the causal action of the outer world upon us that we reflect the world in so far as we do reflect it. But there are other aspects of his doctrine which are more in agreement with the theory that I wish to advocate. One of the most important of these is as to space. There are for Leibniz (though he was never quite clear on this point) two kinds of space. There is the space in the private world of each monad, which is the space that the monad can come to know by analysing and arranging data without assuming anything beyond data. But there is also another kind of space. The monads, Leibniz tells us, reflect the world each from its own point of view, the differences of points of view being analogous to differences of perspective. The arrangement of the whole assemblage of points of view gives us another kind of space, different from that in the private world of each monad. In this public space, each monad occupies a point or, at any rate, a very small region. Although in its private world there is a private space which from its private point of view is immense, the whole of this immensity shrinks into a tiny pin-point when the monad is placed among other monads. We may call the space in each monad's world of data 'private' space, and the space consisting of the diverse points of view of diverse monads 'physical' space. In so far as monads correctly mirror the world, the geometrical properties of private space will be analogous to those of physical space.

Most of this can be applied with little change to exemplify the theory that I wish to advocate. There is space in the world of my perceptions and there is space in physics. The whole of the space in my perceptions, for me as for Leibniz, occupies only a tiny region in physical space. There is, however, an important difference between my theory and that of Leibniz, which has to do with a different conception of causality and with consequences of the theory of relativity. I think that space-time order in the physical world is bound up with causation, and this, in turn, with the irreversibility of physical processes. In classical physics, everything was reversible. If you were to start every bit of matter moving backwards with the same velocity as before, the whole history of the universe would unroll itself backwards. Modern physics, starting from the Second Law of Thermodynamics, had abandoned this view not only in thermodynamics but also elsewhere. Radioactive atoms disintegrate and do not put themselves together again. Speaking generally, processes in the physical world all have a certain direction which makes a distinction between cause and effect that was absent in classical dynamics. I think that the space-time order of the physical world involves this directed causality. It is on this ground that I maintain an opinion which all other philosophers find shocking: namely, that people's thoughts are in their heads. The light from a star travels over intervening space and causes a disturbance in the optic nerve ending in an occurrence in the brain. What I maintain is that the occurrence in the brain *is* a visual sensation. I maintain, in fact, that the brain consists of thoughts – using 'thought' in its widest sense, as it is used by Descartes. To this people will reply 'Nonsense! I can see a brain through a microscope, and I can see that it does not consist of thoughts but of matter just as tables and chairs do.' This is a sheer mistake. What you see when you look at a brain through a microscope is part of your private world. It is the effect in you of a long causal process starting from the brain that you say you are looking at. The brain that you say you are looking at is, no doubt, part of the physical world; but this is not the brain which is a datum in your experience. *That* brain is a remote effect of the physical brain. And, if the location of events in physical space-time is to be effected, as I maintain, by causal relations, then your percept, which comes after events in the eye and optic nerve leading into the brain, must be located in your brain. I may illustrate how I differ from most philosophers by quoting the title of an article by Mr H. Hudson in *Mind* of April 1956. His article is entitled, 'Why we cannot witness or observe what goes on "in our heads".' What I maintain is that we *can* witness or observe what goes on in our heads, and that we cannot witness or observe anything else at all.

We can approach the same result by another route. When we were considering the photographic plate which photographs a portion of the starry heavens, we saw that this involves a great multiplicity of occurrences at the photographic plate: namely, at the very least, one for each object that it can photograph. I infer that, in every small region of space-time, there is an immense multiplicity of overlapping events each connected by a causal line to an origin at some earlier time – though, usually, at a very slightly earlier time. A sensitive instrument, such as a photographic plate, placed anywhere, may be said in a sense to 'perceive' the various objects from which these causal lines emanate. We do not use the word 'perceive' unless the instrument in question is a living brain, but that is because those regions which are inhabited by living brains have certain peculiar relations among the events occurring there. The most important of these is memory. Wherever these peculiar relations exist, we say that there is a percipient. We may define a 'mind' as a collection of events connected with each other by memory-chains backwards and forwards. We know about one such collection of events – namely, that constituting ourself – more intimately and directly than we know about anything else in the world. In regard to what happens to ourself, we know not only abstract logical structure, but also qualities – by which I mean what characterises sounds as opposed to colours, or red as opposed to green. This is the sort of thing that we cannot know where the physical world is concerned.

There are three key points in the above theory. The first is that the entities that occur in mathematical physics are not part of the stuff of the world, but are constructions composed of events and taken as units for the convenience of the mathematician. The second is that the whole of what we perceive without inference belongs to our private world. In this respect, I agree with Berkeley. The starry heaven that we know in visual sensation is inside us. The external starry heaven that we believe in is inferred. The third point is that the causal lines which enable us to be aware of a diversity of objects, though there are some such lines everywhere, are apt to peter out like rivers in the sand. That is why we do not at all times perceive everything.

I do not pretend that the above theory can be proved. What I contend is that, like the theories of physics, it cannot be disproved, and gives an answer to many problems which older theorists have found puzzling. I do not think that any prudent person will claim more than this for my theory.

Chapter 3

First Efforts

I began thinking about philosophical questions at the age of fifteen. From then until I went to Cambridge, three years later, my thinking was solitary and completely amateurish, since I read no philosophical books, until I read Mill's *Logic* in the last months before going to Trinity. Most of my time was taken up by mathematics, and mathematics largely dominated my attempts at philosophical thinking, but the emotional drive which caused my thinking was mainly doubt as to the fundamental dogmas of religion. I minded my theological doubts, not only because I had found comfort in religion, but also because I felt that these doubts, if I revealed them, would cause pain and bring ridicule, and I therefore became very isolated and solitary. Just before and just after my sixteenth birthday, I wrote down my beliefs and unbeliefs, using Greek letters and phonetic spelling for purposes of concealment. The following are some extracts from these reflections.

'Eighteen eighty-eight. March three. I shall write about some subjects, especially religious ones, which now interest me. I have, in consequence of a variety of circumstances, come to look into the very foundations of the religion in which I have been brought up. On some points my conclusions have been to confirm my former creed, while others I have been irresistibly led to such conclusions as would not only shock my people, but have given me much pain. I have arrived at certainty in few things, but my opinions, even where not convictions, are on some things nearly such. I have not the courage to tell my people that I scarcely believe in immortality. . . .

'19th. I mean today to put down my grounds for belief in God. I may say to begin with that I do believe in God, and that I should call myself a theist if I had to give my creed a name. Now in finding reasons for believing in God I shall only take account of scientific arguments. This is a vow I have made, which costs me much to keep, and to reject all sentiment. To find the scientific grounds for a belief in God we must go back to the beginning of all things. We know that, if the present laws of nature have always been in force, the exact quantity of matter and energy now in the universe must always have been in existence, but the nebular hypothesis points to no distant date for the time when the whole universe was filled with undifferentiated nebulous matter. Hence it is quite possible that the matter and force now in existence may have had a creation which clearly could be only by divine power. But even granting that they have always been in existence, yet whence comes the cause which regulates the action of force on matter? I think they are only attributable to a divine controlling power which I accordingly call God.

'March twenty-two. In my last exercise I proved the existence of God by the uniformity of nature and the persistence of certain laws in all her ways. Now let us look into the reasonableness of the reasoning. Let us suppose that the universe we now see has, as some suppose, grown by mere chance. Should we then expect every atom to act in any given conditions precisely similarly to another atom? I think, if atoms be lifeless, there is no reason to expect them to do anything without a controlling power. If, on the other hand, they be endowed with free will, we are forced to the conclusion that all atoms in the universe have combined in the commonwealth and have made laws which none of them ever break. This is clearly an absurd hypothesis, and therefore we are forced to believe in God. But this way of proving his existence at the same time disproves miracles and other supposed manifestations of divine power. It does not, however, disprove their possibility, for, of course, the maker of laws can also unmake them. We may arrive in another way at a disbelief in miracles, for, if God is the maker of the laws, surely it would imply an imperfection in the law if it had to be altered occasionally, and such imperfection we can never impute to the divine nature, as in the Bible God repented him of the work.

'April second. I now come to the subject which personally interests us poor mortals, more, perhaps, than any other. I mean the question of immortality. This is the one in which I have been most disappointed and pained by thought. There are two ways of looking at it. First, by evolution and comparing man to animals. Second, by comparing man with God. The first is the more scientific, for we know all about the animals but not about God. Well, I hold that, taking free will first to consider, there is no clear dividing line between man and the protozoon. Therefore, if we give free will to man, we must give it also to the protozoon. This is rather hard to do. Therefore, unless we are willing to give free will to the protozoon, we cannot give it to man. This, however, is possible, but it is difficult to imagine if, as seems to me probable, protoplasm only came together in the ordinary course of nature without any special providence from God. Then we and all living things are simply kept going by chemical forces and are nothing more wonderful than a tree, which no one pretends has free will, and, even if we had a good enough knowledge of the forces acting on any-one at any time, the motives pro and con, the constitution of his brain, at any time, then we could tell exactly what he will do.

Again, from the religious point of view, free will is a very arrogant thing for us to claim, for of course it is an interruption of God's laws, for by his ordinary laws all our actions would be fixed as the stars. I think we must leave to God the primary establishment of laws which are never broken and determine everybody's doings. And not having free will we cannot have immortality.

'Monday, April 9 . . . I do wish I believed in the life eternal, for it makes me quite miserable to think man is merely a kind of machine endowed, unhappily for himself, with consciousness. But no other theory is consistent with the complete omnipotence of God of which science I think gives ample manifestations. Thus, I must either be an atheist or disbeliever in immortality. Finding the first impossible, I accept the second and let no one know. I think, however disappointing may be this view of man, it does give us a wonderful idea of God's greatness to think that he can, in the beginning, create laws which, by acting on a mere mass of nebulous matter, perhaps merely ether diffused through this part of the universé, will produce creatures like ourselves, conscious not only of our existence but even able to fathom to a certain extent God's mysteries! All this with no more intervention on his part! Now let us think whether this doctrine of want of free will is so absurd. If we talk about it to anyone they kick their legs or something of that sort. But perhaps they cannot help it, for they have something to prove and therefore that supplies a motive to them to do it. Thus, in anything we do we always have motives which determine us. Also, there is no line of demarcation between Shakespeare or Herbert Spencer and a Papuan. But between them and a Papuan there seems as much difference as between a Papuan and a monkey.

'April 14th. Yet there are great difficulties in the way of the doctrine that man has not immortality nor free will nor a soul, in short that he is nothing more than a species of ingenious machine endowed with consciousness. For consciousness, in itself, is a quality quite distinguishing men from dead matter, and if they have one thing different from dead matter why not another, free will? By free will I mean that they do not, for example, obey the first law of motion, or at least that the direction in which the energy they contain is employed depends not entirely on external circumstances. Moreover, it seems impossible to imagine that man, the great Man, with his reason, his knowledge of the universe and his ideas of right and wrong, Man with his emotions, his love and hate, and his religion, that this Man should be a mere perishable chemical compound, whose character and his influence for good or for evil depends solely and entirely on the particular motions of the molecules of his brain and that all the greatest men have been great by reason of some one molecule hitting up against some other a little oftener than in other men! Does not this seem utterly incredible, and must not any one be mad who believes in such an absurdity ? But what is the alternative ? That, accepting the evolution theory which is practically proved, apes having gradually increased in intelligence, God suddenly by a miracle endowed one with that wonderful reason which it is a mystery how we possess. Then is man, truly called the glorious work of God, is man destined to perish utterly after he has been so many ages in evolving ? We cannot say, but I prefer that idea to God's having needed a miracle to produce man and now leaving him free to do as he likes.

'April eighteenth. Accepting, then, the theory that man is mortal and destitute of free will, which is as much as ever a mere theory, as of course all these kinds of things are mere speculations, what idea can we form of right and wrong ? Many say, if you make any mention of such an absurd doctrine as predestination, which comes to much the same thing though persons don't think so, why what becomes of conscience, etc. (which they think has been directly implanted in man by God) ? Now my idea is that our conscience is in the first place due to evolution which would of course form instincts of self-preservation, and in the second place to civilisation and education, which introduces great refinements of the ideal of self-preservation. Let us take, for example, the ten commandments as illustrative of primitive morality. Many of them are conducive to the quiet living of the community which is best for the preservation of the species. Thus, what is always considered the worst possible crime, and the one for which most remorse is felt, is murder, which is direct annihilation of the species. Again, as we know, among the Hebrews it was thought a mark of God's favour to have many children, while the childless were considered as cursed of God. Among the Romans, also, widows were hated and, I believe, forbidden to remain unmarried in Rome more than a year. Now why these peculiar ideas ? Were they not simply because these objects of pity or dislike did not bring forth fresh human beings ? We can well understand how such ideas might grow up when men became rather sensible, for, if murder and suicide were common in a tribe, that tribe would die out, and hence one which held such acts in abhorrence would have a great advantage. Of course, among more educated societies, these ideas are rather modified. My own, I mean to give next time.

'April twentieth. Thus I think that primitive morality always originates in the idea of the preservation of the species. But is this a rule which a civilised community ought to follow ? I think not. My rule of life which I guide my conduct by, and a departure from which I consider as a sin, is to act in the manner which I believe to be most likely to produce the greatest happiness considering both the intensity of the happiness and the number of people made happy. I know that my grandmother considers this an impractical rule of life and says that, since you can never know the thing which will produce greatest happiness, you do much better in following the inner voice. The conscience, however, can easily be seen to depend mostly upon education (as, for example, common Irishmen do not consider lying wrong) which fact alone seems to be quite sufficient to disprove the divine nature of conscience. And, since, as I believe, conscience is merely the combined product of evolution and education, then obviously it is an absurdity to follow that rather than reason. And my reason tells me that it is better to act so as to produce maximum of happiness than in any other way. For I have tried to see what other object I could set before me, and I have failed. Not my own individual happiness in particular, but everybody's equally, making no distinction between myself, relations, friends, or perfect strangers. In real life it makes very little difference to me as long as others are not of my opinion, for obviously where there is any chance of being found out, it is better to do what one's people consider right. My reason for this view is, first, that I can find no other, having been forced as everybody must who seriously thinks about evolution to give up the old idea of asking one's conscience; next, that it seems to me that happiness is the great thing to seek after and which practically all honest public men do seek after. As an application of the theory to practical life, I will say that in a case where nobody but myself was concerned (if indeed such a case exist) I should of course act entirely selfishly to please myself. Suppose, for another instance, that I had the chance of saving a man whom I knew to be a bad man who would be better out of the world, obviously I should consult my own happiness better by plunging in after him. For, if I lost my life, that would be a very neat way of managing it, and, if I saved him, I should have the pleasure of no end of praise. But if I let him drown, I should have lost an opportunity of death and should have the misery of much blame, but the world would be better for his loss and, as I have some slight hope, for my life.

'April 29. In all things I have made the vow to follow reason, not the instincts inherited partly from my ancestors and gained gradually by selection and partly due to my education. How absurd it would be to follow these in the questions of right and wrong. For as I observed before, the inherited part can only be principles leading to the preservation of the species, or of that particular section of the species to which I belong. The part due to education is good or bad according to the individual education. Yet this inner voice, this God-given conscience which made Bloody Mary burn the Protestants, this is what we reasonable beings are to follow. I think this idea mad, and I endeavour to go by reason as far as possible. What I take as my ideal is that which ultimately produces greatest happiness of greatest number. Then I can apply reason to find out the course most conducive to this, and in my individual case however I can also go more or less by conscience owing to the excellence of my education. But it is curious how people dislike the abandonment of brutish impulse for reason. . . .

'May three. . . . There is another very strong argument which I did not insert in its place, namely, that the soul here below seems so inseparably bound up with the body, growing with it, weakened with it, sleeping with it and affecting the brain and affected in return by anything abnormal in the brain. Wordsworth's *Intimations* are humbug, for it is obvious how the soul grows with the body, not as he says perfect from the first.

'June third. It is extraordinary how few principles of dogmas I have been able to become convinced of. One after another I find my former undoubted beliefs slipping from me into the region of doubt. For example, I used never for a moment to doubt that truth was a good thing to get hold of. But now I have the very greatest doubt and uncertainty. For the search for truth has led me to these results I have put in this book, whereas, had I been content to accept the teachings of my youth, I should have remained comfortable. The search for truth has shattered most of my old beliefs and has made me commit what are probably sins where otherwise I should have kept clear of them. I do not think it has in any way made me happier; of course it has given me a deeper character, a contempt for trifles or mockery, but at the same time it has taken away cheerfulness and made it much harder to make bosom friends and, worst of all, it has debarred me from free intercourse with my people, and thus made them strangers to some of my deepest thoughts which, if by any mischance I do let them out, immediately become the subject for mockery which is inexpressibly bitter to me though not unkindly meant. Thus, in my individual case, I should say the effects of a search for truth have been more bad than good. But the truth which I accept as such may be said not to be truth, and I may be told that if I get at real truth I shall be made happier by it, but this is a very doubtful proposition. Hence I have great doubts of the unmixed advantages of truth. Certainly, truth in biology lowers one's idea of man, which must be painful. Moreover, truth estranges former friends and prevents the making of new ones, which is also a bad thing. One ought perhaps to look upon all these things as a martyrdom, since very often truth attained by one man may lead to the increase in the happiness of many others, though not to his own. On the whole I am inclined to pursue truth, though truth of the kind in this book (if that indeed be truth) I have no desire to spread, but rather to prevent from spreading.'

My mind at this time was in a state of confusion derived from an attempt to combine points of view and ways of feeling belonging to three different centuries. As the above extracts show, my thinking was,

in a crude form, along lines very similar to that of Descartes. I was
familiar with the *name* of Descartes, but I knew him only as the inventor of Cartesian co-ordinates, and was not aware that he had written
philosophy. My rejection of free will on the ground that it infringed
God's omnipotence might have led me on to a philosophy like that of
Spinoza. I was led to this seventeenth-century point of view by the
same causes which had originally produced it: namely, familiarity
with the laws of dynamics and belief that they accounted for all the
movements of matter. After a time, however, I came to disbelieve in
God, and advanced to a position much more like that of the eighteenth-
century French *Philosophes*. I agreed with them in being a passionate
believer in rationalism; I liked Laplace's calculator; I hated what I
considered superstition; and I believed profoundly in the perfectibility
of man by a combination of reason and machinery. All this was en-
thusiastic, but not essentially sentimental. I had, however, alongside of
this, a very vivid emotional attitude for which I could find no intellectual support. I regretted my loss of religious belief; I loved natural
beauty with a wild passion; and I read with sympathetic feeling, though
with very definite intellectual rejection, the sentimental apologies for
religion of Wordsworth, Carlyle and Tennyson. I did not come across
any books, except Buckle, until I read Mill's *Logic* which seemed to me
to possess intellectual integrity. But, nonetheless, I was moved by
rhetoric which I could not accept. Carlyle's 'Everlasting No' and
'Everlasting Yea' seemed to me very splendid, in spite of my thinking
that at bottom they were nonsense. Only Shelley, among the writers
whom I knew at that time, was wholly congenial to me. He was congenial to me not only in his merits, but also in his faults. His self-pity
and his atheism, alike, consoled me. I was quite unable to combine into
a harmonius total seventeenth-century knowledge, eighteenth-century
beliefs and nineteenth-century enthusiasms.

It was not only as to theology that I had doubts, but also as to mathematics. Some of Euclid's proofs, especially those that used the method
of superposition, appeared to me very shaky. One of my tutors spoke
to me of non-Euclidean geometry. Although I knew nothing of it,
except the bare fact of its existence, until many years later, I found the
knowledge that there was such a subject very exciting, intellectually
delightful, but a source of disquieting geometrical doubt. Those who
taught me the infinitesimal Calculus did not know the valid proofs of
its fundamental theorems and tried to persuade me to accept the official
sophistries as an act of faith. I realised that the calculus works in
practice, but I was at a loss to understand why it should do so. However, I found so much pleasure in the acquisition of technical skill that
at most times I forgot my doubts. And, to some extent, they were laid
to rest by a book which greatly delighted me: W. K. Clifford's *Common
Sense of the Exact Sciences*.

Although filled with adolescent misery, I was kept going in these years by the desire for knowledge and for intellectual achievement. I thought that it should be possible to clear away muddles, and that then everybody would be happy in a world where machines would do the work and justice would regulate distribution. I hoped sooner or later to arrive at a perfected mathematics which should leave no room for doubts, and bit by bit to extend the sphere of certainty from mathematics to other sciences. Gradually during these three years my interest in theology grew less, and it was with a genuine sense of relief that I discarded the last vestiges of theological orthodoxy.

Chapter 4

Excursion into Idealism

It was not until I went up to Cambridge, in October 1890, that I came across professional philosophers other than Mill, whether in their books or in person. Although during my first three years I had to give the bulk of my time to mathematics, I managed to get through a fair amount of philosophical reading and a large amount of philosophical arguing. Harold Joachim, a philosophy don at Merton and a disciple of Bradley, was our neighbour at Haslemere and became my uncle's brother-in-law. I told him of my interest in philosophy, and he very kindly gave me a list of books to read. I remember only two items in the list: one was Bradley's *Logic* which, he said, was good but hard; the other was Bosanquet's *Logic* which, he said, was better but harder. Probably to his surprise, I proceeded to read the books on his list. But my reading of philosophy was interrupted for a time by an accidental occurrence. At the beginning of 1892 I had a slight attack of influenza which left me for several months completely without energy or interest in anything whatever. My work at this time was bad, and, as I had not told anybody about the influenza and its aftermath, it was supposed that reading philosophy was what had spoilt my mathematics. James Ward, whom I had consulted as to what I should read, sent for me and told me that a Wrangler is a Wrangler. From this instance of the law of identity he drew the inference that I had better read no more philosophy till after my mathematical Tripos, with the result that I did not do so badly in it as had been feared when he gave his advice.

The mathematical teaching at Cambridge when I was an undergraduate was definitely bad. Its badness was partly due to the order of merit in the Tripos, which was abolished not long afterwards. The necessity for nice discrimination between the abilities of different examinees led to an emphasis on 'problems' as opposed to 'bookwork'. The 'proofs' that were offered of mathematical theorems were an insult to the logical intelligence. Indeed, the whole subject of mathematics was presented as a set of clever tricks by which to pile up marks in the Tripos. The effect of all this upon me was to make me think mathematics disgusting. When I had finished my Tripos, I sold all my mathematical books and made a vow that I would never look at a mathematical book again. And so, in my fourth year, I plunged with whole-hearted delight into the fantastic world of philosophy.

All the influences that were brought to bear upon me were in the direction of German idealism, either Kantian or Hegelian, with one single exception. The exception was Henry Sidgwick, the last survivor of the Benthamites. At the time, I, in common with other young people, did not give him nearly as much respect as he deserved. We called him 'Old Sidg' and regarded him merely as out of date. The two men who had most to do with teaching me were James Ward and G. F. Stout, the former a Kantian, the latter a Hegelian. Bradley's *Appearance and Reality* was published at this time, and Stout said that this book accomplished as much as is humanly possible in ontology. Neither of these two men, however, influenced me as much as McTaggart did. McTaggart had Hegelian answers to the rather crude empiricism which had previously satisfied me. He said he could prove by logic that the world is good and the soul immortal. The proof, he admitted, was long and difficult. One could not hope to understand it until one had studied philosophy for some time. I stood out against his influence with gradually diminishing resistance until just before my Moral Sciences Tripos in 1894, when I went over completely to a semi-Kantian, semi-Hegelian metaphysic.

After the Tripos, the next academic step was the writing of a Fellowship dissertation. I chose for my subject 'The Foundations of Geometry', and paid special attention to the effect of non-Euclidean geometry on Kant's transcendental aesthetic. My work on this dissertation was interspersed with work on economics and on German social democracy, which was the subject of my first book, based upon two winters in Berlin. These two winters, and a journey to America with my wife in the following year (1896), did much to cure me of Cambridge parochialism, and made me aware of German work in pure mathematics which I had not previously heard of. In spite of my earlier vow, I read a very great deal of mathematics – much of it, as I afterwards discovered, quite irrelevant to my main purpose. I read Darboux's *Theory of Surfaces*, Dini's *Theory of Functions of a Real Variable*, and several French *Cours d'Analyse*, Gauss's *General Theory of Curved Surfaces*, and Grassman's *Ausdehnungslehre*, to which I was led by Whitehead, whose *Universal Algebra*, which greatly excited me, was published shortly after this time and was largely concerned with Grassman's system. I was, however, persuaded that applied mathematics is a worthier study than pure mathematics, because applied mathematics – so, in my Victorian optimism, I supposed – was more likely to further human welfare. I read Clerk Maxwell's *Electricity and Magnetism* carefully, I studied Herzt's *Principles of Mechanics*, and I was delighted when Hertz succeeded in manufacturing electro-magnetic waves. J. J. Thompson's experimental work interested me greatly. I read, also, works that proved more relevant to my purpose, such as those of Dedekind and Cantor.

Frege, who might have helped me more, I did not know of until later.

My first philosophical book, *An Essay on the Foundations of Geometry*, which was an elaboration of my Fellowship dissertation, seems to me now somewhat foolish. I took up Kant's question, 'how is geometry possible?' and decided that it was possible if, and only if, space was one of the three recognised varieties, one of them Euclidean, the other two non-Euclidean but having the property of preserving a constant 'measure of curvature'. Einstein's revolution swept away everything at all resembling this point of view. The geometry in Einstein's General Theory of Relativity is such as I had declared to be impossible. The theory of tensors, upon which Einstein based himself, would have been useful to me, but I never heard of it until he used it. Apart from details, I do not think that there is anything valid in this early book.

However, there was worse to follow. My theory of geometry was mainly Kantian, but after this I plunged into efforts at Hegelian dialectic. I wrote a paper 'On the Relations of Number and Quantity' which is unadulterated Hegel. The gist of this paper is contained in its first two paragraphs, which are as follows:

'I wish in this paper to discuss one of the most fundamental questions of mathematical philosophy. On the view we take of this relation must depend our interpretation of the Infinitesimal Calculus and all its consequences – in a word, of all higher mathematics. The very idea of the continuum – an idea which, in philosophy as in mathematics, has become gradually more and more prominent, and has, of late especially, ousted the atomic views which were shared by Hume and Kant – must stand or fall, I think, with the relative justification of quantity in mathematics as against number. It will not be necessary, however, to deal with mathematical considerations here; it will be sufficient to consider number and quantity in their purely logical aspects. I shall use quantity, always, as equivalent to *continuous* quantity, and I shall endeavour, in the course of the paper, to make clear the meaning of the word continuous.

'My argument will be as follows: First, I shall discuss number, and show that its extensions beyond the positive integers result from a gradual absorption of the properties of the unit, and give a gradually diminishing information as to the whole. Then I shall discuss the application of number to continua, and shall endeavour to show that number *per se* gives no information as to quantity, but only comparison with an already quantitative unit. It will appear, therefore, that quantity must be sought in an analysis of the unit. Assuming quantity to be an intrinsic property of quantities, I shall discuss two hypotheses. The first regards quantity as an irreducible category, the second regards it as an immediate sense-datum. On the first hypothesis, we shall see that extensive quantities are rendered contradictory by their divisibility, and must be taken as really indivisible, and so intensive. But intensive quantity too, it will appear, must, if it be an intrinsic property of intensive quantities, be also a mere relation between them. The hypothesis that quantity is a category giving an intrinsic property will therefore have to be rejected. The hypothesis that quantity is a datum in sense will also be found to lead to contradictions. We shall be forced, therefore, to reject the view that quantity is an intrinsic property of quantities. We shall regard it, instead, as a category of comparison; there is no common property, we shall say, among things that can be treated quantitatively, except what is involved in the extraneous property that there are other qualitatively similar things with which they can be quantitatively compared. This will turn quantity into measure, in the broadest sense, and with this, I think, our previous difficulties will cease. But at the same time, every connexion with number will cease – quantity or measure, we shall say, is a wholly independent conception of comparison. But a discussion of the kind of comparison involved in measure will bring back our previous difficulties in a new form; we shall find that the terms compared, though we were no longer regarded them as quantitative, are infected with contradictions similar to those which, in the first part of the paper, will have belonged to quantity itself. I shall conclude that quantity is only applicable to classes of actual and possible immediate data, and not to any fully understood material.'

Although Couturat described this article as 'ce petit chef d'oeuvre de dialectique subtile', it seems to me now nothing but unmitigated rubbish.

I had when I was younger – perhaps I still have – an almost unbelievable optimism as to the finality of my own theories. I finished my book on the foundations of geometry in 1896, and proceeded at once to what I intended as a similar treatment of the foundations of physics, being under the impression that problems concerning geometry had been disposed of. I worked on the foundations of physics for two years, but the only thing that I published expressing my views at that time was the article on number and quantity already mentioned. I was at this time a full-fledged Hegelian, and I aimed at constructing a complete dialectic of the sciences, which should end up with the proof that all reality is mental. I accepted the Hegelian view that none of the sciences is quite true, since all depend upon some abstraction, and every abstraction leads, sooner or later, to contradictions. Wherever Kant and Hegel were in conflict, I sided with Hegel. I was much impressed by Kant's *Metaphysische Anfangsgründe der Naturwissenschaft* and made elaborate notes on it, but I remarked, 'the book is divided into four sections corresponding to the Table of Categories, and in each section three laws are found for the three corresponding categories. But the three laws are usually very artificial: two would be natural.'

Two questions specially interested me in the philosophy of physics. The first of these was the question of absolute or relative motion. Newton had an argument to show that rotation must be absolute and not relative. But, although this argument worried people and they could not find an answer to it, the arguments for the contrary view, that all motion is relative, seemed at least equally convincing. This puzzle remained unsolved until Einstein produced his Theory of Relativity. From the point of view of Hegelian dialectics it was a convenient source of antinomies: it was not necessary (so I supposed) to find a solution within physics, but to acknowledge that matter is an unreal abstraction and that no science of matter can be logically satisfactory.

The other problem which concerned me was the question whether matter consists of atoms separated by empty space, or of a plenum pervading all space. I inclined at first to the former view, of which the most logical exponent was Boscovitch. According to his view, an atom occupies only a point of space, and all interaction is action at a distance, as in the Newtonian law of gravitation. A different view, however, had resulted from Faraday's experiments and been embodied in Clerk Maxwell's great book on electricity and magnetism. This book had been the subject of Whitehead's Fellowship dissertation,[1] and Whitehead urged me to prefer its views to those of Boscovitch. In addition to empirical arguments in its favour, it had the advantage of doing away with action at a distance, which had always seemed incredible, even to Newton. When I adopted the more modern view, I gave it a Hegelian dress, and represented it as a dialectical transition from Leibniz to Spinoza, thus permitting myself to allow what I considered the logical order to prevail over that of chronology.

On re-reading what I wrote about the philosophy of physics in the years 1896 to 1898, it seems to me complete nonsense, and I find it hard to imagine how I can ever have thought otherwise. Fortunately, before any of this work had reached a stage where I thought it fit for publication, I changed my whole philosophy and proceeded to forget all that I had done during those two years. The notes I made at that time have, however, a possible historical interest, and, although they now seem to me to be misguided, I do not think that they are any more so than the writings of Hegel. Some of the more salient passages from the notes that I made in those years follow.

---

[1] On this ground, Whitehead was always regarded at Cambridge as an applied, rather than a pure, mathematician. This view persisted in spite of *Universal Algebra*, to which Cambridge paid much less attention than it deserved.

ON THE IDEA OF A DIALECTIC OF THE SCIENCES
(January 1, 1898)

It seems possible, by including space and time from the beginning, to
obtain a dialectic having a closer relation to Appearance than that of
pure Logic, and perhaps differing therefrom by more than the mere
schematisation of categories. For there may be what we might call a
chemical union between categories and sense, leading to new ideas not
obtainable by mere subsequent schematisation of pure categories. In
this dialectic, I should start from the result that quantity is a conception applicable only to immediate data as such, and yet rendering
them mediate by its application. Everything, therefore, to be derived
dialectically from quantity would differ materially from the logical
categories, none of which applies to immediate data *as such*. The
success of mathematics both sustains and is explained by the present
view. It seems possible that, in such ideas as the continuum and the
plenum, the immediacy vainly sought by logic is retained. We might
thus find a method of turning Appearance into Reality, instead of first
constructing Reality and then being confronted by a hopeless dualism.

But it is to be observed that, in such a dialectic, one must avoid, at
all stages short of the last, too rigid a demand for self-consistency.
Since a sensuous element is to be always present, we cannot retard
every contradiction as condemning our conceptions; some must be
regarded as inevitably resulting from the sensuous element. Before
such a dialectic can be constructed, therefore, a principle must be
discovered by which to distinguish avoidable from unavoidable contradictions. I believe the only unavoidable contradiction will be that
belonging to quantity, namely that two things may differ though in all
points conceptually identical, and that the difference may be a conception. This contradiction appears to derive its necessity from the
fact that differences may be given in sense.

NOTE ON TRANSITION FROM GEOMETRY TO DYNAMICS

Matter commonly thought of as defined by one or other of two properties: extension, or force. But if space *purely* relative, as discussion of
geometry suggests, extension cannot be the distinguishing mark of
matter, which has to do duty as substance. Therefore, only force
remains, i.e. atoms are to be regarded as unextended centres of force,
not inherently spatial, and localised only by their interactions. Now
force can only manifest itself by producing motion: statical conception
of equilibrium of forces only deduction from dynamical conception.
Hence geometry involves consideration of matter, and matter must be
considered primarily as that which produces motion in other matter.
We have, here, a mainly relative conception of matter, which is desir-

able: a conception, moreover, whose relativity involves contradictions if matter takes as ultimate category. We have first to discuss laws of motion, and then show that these and their view of matter involve something more, and lead us on to some other science.

Observe: For the dialectical transition from geometry to dynamics, that geometry involves opposition of different parts of figures in space, and that this involves motion, and that motion involves a more than spatial matter, for a position in space, being defined solely *by* its position, cannot move. Hence geometry impossible without moving matter. This brings us to kinematics, and hence to dynamics. For motion involves a moving matter, whose motion is only relative to other matter. The motion must have a cause, and being a reciprocal relation between bits of matter, the interactions of these bits must be the cause. This contains already the laws of motion.

SOME DEFINITIONS OF MATTER

General definition. Matter is that, in the date of the outer sense, which can be regarded, with less contradiction than any other sensational datum, as logical subject, or as substance.

I. *Kinematical definition.* Matter is that of which spatial relations are adjectives.

We saw, in geometry, that the attempt to make space a logical subject breaks down: that those axioms, which alone make a knowledge of space possible, can only be true on condition that space is a mere adjective. It must, therefore, be an adjective of *something*: and even geometry, though otherwise indifferent to matter, registers this something, in general, as a condition of its possibility. For geometry compares different parts of space: therefore its possibility involves the possibility of motion, i.e. of change of position. This does not yet, so far as geometry is concerned, introduce time, for how the change of place is effected is irrelevant – nor does it introduce any property of matter except that of being susceptible of varying spatial adjectives without loss of identity. But so much is necessary, for motion is necessary, and motion involves something more than space, since positions, being defined solely as such, are immovable. Space, in short, is immovable, and therefore, if geometry is impossible without motion, we require something which can move in space. Again space, as required for geometry, is not merely an adjective, but an adjective of relation: therefore the ultimate constituents of this kinematical matter must *contain* no space, but be localised, by their spatial relations, as points. These punctual atoms must, for the axiom of free mobility, e.g. actually move, i.e. change their spatial relations – but how they move, is here irrelevant. The atoms are only localised by the relations to each other, and these relations alone, in the manifold of their *possible* values, give space. Thus, e.g. if there were only two atoms, space would *be* only the straight line joining them: if three, the plane in which they lie.

II. *Dynamical Definition of Matter.* Matter is not only the movable, but the mover: two pieces of matter are capable of causally affecting one another in such a way as to change their spatial relations.

For we saw, in the above definition, that matter must actually move, i.e. change its spatial relations to other matter; now such a change is an event, and must, by the Law of Causation, have a cause. Moreover, if we are to be able to construct a dynamic, i.e. a science of matter in motion, considered apart from other things in the universe, we must be able to find this cause within the conceptions we already have, i.e. within matter and spatial relations. That we cannot really construct such a science independently of higher categories is proved by the antinomy of absolute motion. The cause of what appears as motion of matter must therefore really be something more complex than mere matter or force. Hence we say the motion of matter is caused by matter: any two pieces of matter have a reciprocal causal relation tending to change their spatial relation, i.e. their distance. This relation is *force*.

Force must be reciprocal (3rd law), since its effect is change of distance, which is a reciprocal relation: moreover, unless we suppose it capable of a finite effect in an infinitesimal time, which would be absurd, its effect must be to produce a finite change of spatial relation, and therefore a finite velocity, in a finite time, which gives its instantaneous effect as acceleration (fallacy!). (This is equivalent to 1st law.) Again, in order that a science of force may be possible, the force between two atoms must be a function of their spatial relation, since this alone is measurable. (This necessity may also be deduced from inverse of Law of Concomitant Variations, since spatial relation and force causally connected.) Hence Force $= f$ (distance), which is general form of law of gravitation. Since experience does not immediately confirm this, we invent a new conception, mass, and put $F = mm'f(\pi)\,(r)$. (This includes 2nd law of motion.) This assumes mass (equivalent to quantum of motion) constant for same particle at all times and places, which follows from conception of matter as substance (No!). The above gives gravitation as ultimate law of dynamics, and astronomical measure of mass as the fundamental one. Hence, for dynamics, matter consists of interrelated things, whose relations consist of (1) spatial relations, (2) causal relations (forces) tending to change the spatial relations, and themselves measured by their effects in changing these, and functionally connected with these. Their measurement, as well as the subsidiary measurement of mass, thus depends on the measurement of space and time, and thus ultimately on that of space.

DYNAMICS AND ABSOLUTE MOTION

The only way of defining a position, and hence a motion, is by reference to axes, which axes, to be perceptible, and to be capable of
supplying relata for spatial relations, must be material, or rather, must
be generated by the relations of material points. Motion can therefore
only be defined by relation to matter. But it is essential to the laws of
motion that this matter should have no *dynamical* (i.e. causal) relation
to the matter whose motion is considered or, indeed, to *any* matter.
If it *has* such a relation, the laws of motion become inapplicable, and
our equations become untrue. But the laws of motion lead to gravitation, and if this be universal, there is *no* matter without any dynamical
relation to any given matter. Hence arises an antinomy. For dynamics,
it is *geometrically* necessary that our axes should be material and
dynamically necessary that they should be *immaterial*.

How solve this antinomy? It is plain it is so fundamental as to
render a purely dynamical universe absurd – real things, in short,
must have other adjectives than space and force, whose relativity
destroys them. For practical purposes, the antinomy does not destroy
the utility of dynamics, for we can always find matter sufficiently
unrelated to any matter whose motion we are studying to make our
equations practically true. But for theory, we must replace space and
force by relations whose relativity does not render them unintelligible.
Perhaps there may be hope in restoring the pre-eminence of the *here*,
as a source of absolute position; *perhaps* we may replace force by
conation, and pass on into psychology.

NOTE ON MATTER AND MOTION

The ordinary mechanical doctrine, set forth, e.g., by Stallo, proceeds
entirely on a dualistic conception of substance and attribute, matter
and motion. It regards both as real, independent, quanta, the
latter transferable from matter to matter, but indestructible. Further it
supposes an absolute space, in which its motion takes place, and from
its absolute space it is led to affirm (1) that the elements of matter must
have extension, (2) that all communication of motion must be by
contact (a thing cannot act where it isn't). With the relativity of space,
both these axioms vanish, and are replaced by (1′) the elements of
matter contain no space, but are localised by their geometrical relations as points. (2′) All action is action at a distance, and distance itself
is an interaction. The substitution of these two propositions for the
above two removes many antinomies, e.g.: (*a*) The antinomy of in-
elastic, since indeformable, but elastic, since losing no energy by impact.
(*b*) The antinomy that the elements of mass must be quantitatively
equal, and yet in chemistry are not. For if the elements be points, any

necessary number can be collected together in any volume however small, and no experience can attain the ultimate atom. (c) The antinomy: inert, and yet acting at a distance: for on this definition of matter, its most essential quality would be to act at a distance: apart from the fact that it moves and causes motion, it would be hopelessly incomplete. This view above explains that gravity is instantaneous, and that intermediate bodies are not *opaque to it*. Does it solve antinomy of kinetic energy and potential energy ? I don't know yet. It leaves the fundamental antinomy of absolute motion, i.e. the motion of a system must be treated relatively to matter itself under the action of no forces, but the very conception of matter excludes the existence of any such matter. This is a result of the excessive relativity of the definition of matter as that which moves and is moved by another matter, which definition makes it impossible permanently to treat matter as a logical subject, as substance or as Absolute.

SHORT STATEMENT OF THE ANTINOMY OF ABSOLUTE MOTION

(1) Matter is that which moves and is moved by other matter.

(2) Motion of matter is change of spatial relation to some other matter.

(3) Change of spatial relation between matters can only be measured by some unchanging spatial relation between matters.

(4) No two matters can be known to have unchanging spatial relations unless they are free from dynamical relations to each other and to other matter.

(5) But such relations (in 1) constitute the definition of matter.
Therefore

(a) No change of spatial relation can be measured.

(b) No motion, and therefore no matter and no force can be measured.

(c) Dynamics is rendered dialectically untenable by the contradiction arising from the essential relativity of matter.

(d) Matter and motion cannot form a self-subsistent world, and cannot constitute Reality.

Note. The relativity of motion leads to an infinite regress in space, which is a precise counterpart of the equally fatal infinite regress in time introduced by causality. Motion has a double relativity, both in space and in time, leading to two infinite regresses. And it is important to observe that the antinomy does not, strictly speaking, arise on kinematical ground, but only when matter is regarded as the *cause* of motion.

Observe. The necessity of absolute motion is intimately connected with the attempt to regard mass as intrinsic. A relativity of mass would obviate its necessity. Perhaps this will yield assistance in connection with plenum.

CAN WE MAKE A DIALECTICAL TRANSITION FROM PUNCTUAL MATTER TO THE PLENUM?

The antinomy of absolute motion arises only in Kinetics, not in Kinematics. It shows therefore that the mistake lies in our conception of force, i.e. of the inter-connection of atoms. We defined elements of matter as that which moves, and is moved by, other matter. But in this definition, the elements are no longer self-subsistent at all. On the contrary, all the adjectives of any elements, except mass, consist wholly of relations to all the other elements, and mass is only exhibited in these relations. The necessary course seems, therefore, to regard our atoms either as mere adjectives of one single substance, or, if we prefer it, as the same substance appearing in different places. This comes to the same thing, for, in either case, whatever makes their particularity is only adjectival. The true view seems to be Lotze's: if M be the Whole, and A, B, become A' B' then $M = \phi (A, B, \ldots) = \phi (A', B' \ldots)$, and it is this equation which connects A and B, not any direct transient causal action. We shall now, being resolved still to regard matter as self-subsistent, say M is the one Whole, of which space and motion are mere adjectives; it is a Whole not validly analysable into simple reals, though there may, in some sense, be centres of condensation, as in the world of spirit. There may be, i.e., some adjective with a distribution over points of space, giving discrete points peculiar properties. But since all space is matter's adjective, matter will in some sense be everywhere. In some such way, a distinction between ether and gross matter might be preserved. The laws of matter will have to result somehow from the immutability of the Whole, as in the above equation $M = \phi (A, B, \ldots)$. How the principle is to be applied, may be a matter for purely empirical investigation. It seems just possible that this view would solve the antinomy of absolute motion, for there is now no matter except the one Whole, and this is eternally under no forces. But matter under no forces was precisely what we required to solve the antinomy. The principle of our dialectic appears to lie in making the Whole gradually more explicit. Our separate particles turn out, first to be related to other particles, and then to be necessarily related to *all* other particles, and finally to err in being separate particles at all. With this we pass to the plenum. The crude view of the plenum – according to which there are really different parts of matter at different places, only that there is no division between the parts – is obviously hopeless. The true view is, that the same matter, which is thus necessarily the One Whole, is present in every point of space, and is not, in the ordinary sense, extended, but contains all extension. ('Light is in the soul, she all in every part', *Samson Agonistes*.) Our principles of motion, now, will lie in the permanence of the Whole, not in the habits of monads. Thus there is a gradual increase, throughout, of the explicitness of the Whole; but how to continue this process beyond dynamics I do not know.

Observe. In connection both with the kinematics of motion in a plenum, and with the question of absolute motion (or 1st law), it is very important to consider the possibility of a *motion which is not a change.* If change only arose with *change* of motion, this would explain the 1st law, and would allow motion in a homogeneous plenum. It is to be observed that our Whole is not properly extended: space is in it, not it in space. Space must be regarded as a mere aspect of its differentiation, and time too. This will give the appearance of qualitatively different adjectives attaching to each point in space and time, but in reality space and time are abstracted from these qualitative adjectives, not vice versa. In this way, there would be differences resulting from a change either of time or place, which is all we require for the appearance of motion. It is interesting to observe that, in a sense, the whole universe is present in every point of space, as well as every point of time. (This resulted from our previous definition of matter, if a thing is where it acts, and matter acts everywhere.)

NOTE ON THE LOGIC OF THE SCIENCES

Every science works with a certain limited number of fundamental ideas, which number is smaller than that of all fundamental ideas. Now every science may be regarded as an attempt to construct a universe out of none but its own ideas. What we have to do, therefore, in a logic of the sciences, is to construct, with the appropriate set of ideas, a world containing no contradictions but those which unavoidably result from the incompleteness of these ideas. Within any science, all contradictions not thus unavoidable are logically condemnable; from the standpoint of a general theory of knowledge, the whole science, if taken as a metaphysic, i.e. as independent and self-subsistent knowledge, is condemnable. We have, therefore, first to arrange the postulates of the science so as to leave the minimum of contradictions; then to supply, to these postulates or ideas, such supplement as will abolish the special contradictions of the science in question, and thus pass outside to a new science, which may then be similarly treated.

Thus, e.g. number, the fundamental notion of arithmetic, involves something numerable. Hence geometry, since space is the only directly measurable element in sensation. Geometry, again, involves something which can be located, and something which can move – for a position, by definition, cannot move. Hence matter and physics.

I think, however, that two types of dialectical transition will have to be distinguished: the one, like the transition from number to things numerable, from space to matter, merely supplies to an abstract idea its necessary and substantive complement, while leaving, to the abstract science, full validity on its own level. In this case, there is hardly contradiction, but only incompleteness. The other kind of transition, like that from continua to discreta, or from matter to force to (?), is dialectical in the true Hegelian sense, and shows that the notion of the science in question is fundamentally self-contradictory, and must be throughout replaced by another, in any metaphysical construction of the real.

Chapter 5

Revolt into Pluralism

It was towards the end of 1898 that Moore and I rebelled against both Kant and Hegel. Moore led the way, but I followed closely in his footsteps. I think that the first published account of the new philosophy was Moore's article in *Mind* on 'The Nature of Judgement'. Although neither he nor I would now adhere to all the doctrines in this article, I, and I think he, would still agree with its negative part – i.e. with the doctrine that fact is in general independent of experience. Although we were in agreement, I think that we differed as to what most interested us in our new philosophy. I think that Moore was most concerned with the rejection of idealism, while I was most interested in the rejection of monism. The two were, however, closely connected. They were connected through the doctrine as to relations, which Bradley had distilled out of the philosophy of Hegel. I called this 'the doctrine of internal relations', and I called my view 'the doctrine of external relations'. The doctrine of internal relations held that every relation between two terms expresses, primarily, intrinsic properties of the two terms and, in ultimate analysis, a property of the whole which the two compose. With some relations this view is plausible. Take, for example, love or hate. If A loves B, this relation exemplifies itself and may be said to consist in certain states of mind of A. Even an atheist must admit that a man can love God. It follows that love of God is a state of the man who feels it, and not properly a relational fact. But the relations that interested me were of a more abstract sort. Suppose that A and B are events, and A is earlier than B. I do not think that this implies anything in A in virtue of which, independently of B, it must have a character which we inaccurately express by mentioning B. Liebniz gives an extreme example. He says that, if a man living in Europe has a wife in India and the wife dies without his knowing it, the man undergoes an intrinsic change at the moment of her death. This is the kind of doctrine that I was combating. I found the doctrine of internal relations particularly inapplicable in the case of 'asymmetrical' relations – i.e. relations which, if they hold between A and B, do not hold between B and A. Let us take again the relation *earlier*. If A is earlier than B, then B is not earlier than A. If you try to express the relation of A to B by means of adjectives of A and B, you will have to make the attempt by means of dates. You may say that the date of A is a property of A and the date of B is a property of B, but that will not help you because you will have to go on to say that the date of A is earlier than the date of B, so that you will have found no escape from the relation. If you adopt the plan of regarding the relation as a property of the whole composed of A and B, you are in a still worse predicament, for in that whole A and B have no order and therefore you cannot distinguish between 'A is earlier than B' and 'B is earlier than A'. As asymmetrical relations are essential in most parts of mathematics, this doctrine was important.

I think perhaps I can best illustrate the importance of this question by quoting part of a paper that I read to the Aristotelian Society in 1907, which deals with Harold Joachim's book on *The Nature of Truth*.

'The doctrines we have been considering may all be deduced from one central logical doctrine, which may be expressed thus: "Every relation is grounded in the natures of the related terms." Let us call this the *axiom of internal relations*. It follows at once from this axiom that the whole of reality or of truth must be a significant whole in Mr Joachim's sense. For each part will have a nature which exhibits its relations to every other part and to the whole; hence, if the nature of any one part were completely known, the nature of the whole and of every other part would also be completely known; while conversely, if the nature of the whole were completely known, that would involve knowledge of its relations to each part, and therefore of the relations of each part to each other part, and therefore of the nature of each part. It is also evident that, if reality or truth is a significant whole in Mr Joachim's sense, the axiom of internal relations must be true. Hence the axiom is equivalent to the monistic theory of truth.

'Further, assuming that we are not to distinguish between a thing and its "nature", it follows from the axiom that nothing can be considered quite truly except in relation to the whole. For if we consider "A is related to B", the A and the B are also related to everything else in the universe. When we consider merely that part of A's nature in virtue of which A is related to B, we are said to be considering A *qua* related to B; but this is an abstract and only partially true way of considering A, for A's nature, which is the same thing as A, contains the grounds of its relations to everything else as well as to B. Thus nothing quite true can be said about A short of taking account of the whole universe; and then what is said about A will be the same as what would be said about anything else, since the natures of different things must, like those of Leibniz's monads, all express the same system of relations.

'Let us now consider more closely the meaning of the axiom of internal relations and the grounds for and against it. We have, to begin with, two possible meanings, according as it is held that every relation is really *constituted* by the natures of the terms or of the whole which they compose, or merely that every relation has a *ground* in these natures. I do not observe that idealists distinguish these two meanings; indeed, speaking generally, they tend to identify a proposition with its consequences, thus embodying one of the distinctive tenets of pragmatism. The distinction of the two meanings is, however, less important than it would otherwise be, owing to the fact that both meanings lead, as we shall see, to the view that there are no relations at all.

'The axiom of internal relations in either form involves, as Mr Bradley has justly urged [cf. *Appearance and Reality*, 2nd ed., p. 519: "Reality is one. It must be single because plurality, taken as real, contradicts itself. Plurality implies relations, and, through its relations it unwillingly asserts always a superior unity"], the conclusion that there are no relations and that there are not many things, but only one thing. (Idealists would add: *in the end*. But that only means that the consequence is one which it is often convenient to forget.) This conclusion is reached by considering the relation of diversity. For if there really are two things, A and B, which are diverse, it is impossible wholly to reduce this diversity to adjectives of A and B. It will be necessary that A and B should have *different* adjectives, and the diversity of these adjectives cannot, on pain of an endless regress, be interpreted as *meaning* that they in turn have different adjectives. For if we say that A and B differ when A has the adjective "different from B" and B has the adjective "different from A", we must suppose that these two adjectives differ. Then "different from A" must have the adjective "different from 'different from B'", which must differ from "different from 'different from A'", and so on *ad infinitum*. We cannot take "different from B" as an adjective requiring no further reduction, since we must ask what is meant by "different" in this phrase, which, as it stands, derives an adjective from a relation, not a relation from an adjective. Thus, if there is to be any diversity, there must be a diversity not reducible to difference of adjectives, i.e. not grounded in the "natures" of the diverse terms. Consequently, if the axiom of internal relations is true, it follows that there is no diversity, and that there is only one thing. Thus the axiom of internal relations is equivalent to the assumption of ontological monism and to the denial that there are any relations. Wherever we seem to have a relation, this is really an adjective of the whole composed of the terms of the supposed relation.

'The axiom of internal relations is thus equivalent to the assumption that every proposition has one subject and one predicate. For a proposition which asserts a relation must always be reduced to a subject-predicate proposition concerning the whole composed to the terms of the relation. Proceeding in this way to larger and larger wholes, we gradually correct our first crude abstract judgements, and approximate more and more to the one truth about the whole. The one final and complete truth must consist of a proposition with one subject, namely, the whole, and one predicate. But since this involves distinguishing subject from predicate, as though they could be diverse, even this is not quite true. The best we can say of it is, that it is not "*intellectually* corrigible", i.e. it is as true as any truth can be; but even absolute truth persists in being not quite true. [Cf. *Appearance and Reality*, 1st ed., p. 544: "Even absolute truth seems thus to turn out in the end to be erroneous. And it must be admitted that, in the end, no possible truth is quite true. It is a partial and inadequate translation of that which it professes to give bodily. And this internal discrepancy belongs irremovably to truth's proper character. Still, the difference, drawn between absolute and finite truth, must none the less be upheld. For the former, in a word, is not intellectually corrigible."]

'If we ask ourselves what are the grounds in favour of the axiom of internal relations, we are left in doubt by those who believe in it. Mr Joachim, for example, assumes it throughout, and advances no argument in its favour. So far as one can discover the grounds, they seem to be two, though these are perhaps really indistinguishable. There is first the law of sufficient reason, according to which nothing can be just a brute fact, but must have some reason for being thus and not otherwise. [Cf. *Appearance and Reality*, 2nd ed., p. 575: "If the terms from their own inner nature do not enter into the relation, then, so far as they are concerned, they seem related for no reason at all, and, so far as they are concerned, the relation seems arbitrarily made," cf. also p. 577.] Secondly, there is the fact that, if two terms have a certain relation, they cannot but have it, and if they did not have it they would be different; which seems to show that there is something in the terms themselves which leads to their being related as they are.

'(1) The law of sufficient reason is hard to formulate precisely. It cannot merely mean that every true proposition is logically deducible from some other true proposition, for this is an obvious truth which does not yield the consequences demanded of the law. For example, $2+2 = 4$ can be deduced from $4+4 = 8$, but it would be absurd to regard $4+4 = 8$ as a reason for $2+2 = 4$. The *reason* for a proposition is always expected to be one or more *simpler* propositions. Thus the law of sufficient reason should mean that every proposition can be deduced from simpler propositions. This seems obviously false, but in any case it cannot be relevant in considering idealism, which holds propositions to be less and less true the simpler they are, so that it would be absurd to insist on starting from simple propositions. I conclude, therefore, that, if any form of the law of sufficient reason is relevant, it is rather to be discovered by examining the second of the grounds in favour of the axioms of relations, namely, that related terms cannot but be related as they are.

'(2) The force of this argument depends in the main, I think, upon a fallacious form of statement. "If A and B are related in a certain way", it may be said, "you must admit that if they were not so related they would be other than they are, and that consequently there must be something in them which is essential to their being related as they are." Now if two terms are related in a certain way, it follows that, if they were not so related, every imaginable consequence would ensue. For, if they are so related, the hypothesis that they are not so related is false, and from a false hypothesis anything can be deduced. Thus the above form of statement must be altered. We may say: "If A and B are related in a certain way, then anything not so related must be other than A and B, hence, etc." But this only proves that what is not related as A and B are must be *numerically* diverse from A or B; it will not prove difference of adjectives, unless we assume the axiom of internal relations. Hence the argument has only a rhetorical force, and cannot prove its conclusion without a vicious circle.

'It remains to ask whether there are any grounds against the axiom of internal relations. The first argument that naturally occurs to an opponent of this axiom is the difficulty of actually carrying it out. We have had one instance of this as regards diversity; in many other instances, the difficulty is even more obvious. Suppose, for example, that one volume is greater than another. One may reduce the relation "greater than" between the volumes to adjectives of the volumes, by saying that one is of such and such a size and the other of such and such another size. But then the one size must be greater than the other size. If we try to reduce this new relation to adjectives of the two sizes, the adjectives must still have a relation corresponding to "greater than", and so on. Hence we cannot, without an endless regress, refuse to admit that sooner or later we come to a relation not reducible to adjectives of the related terms. This argument applies especially to all asymmetrical relations, i.e. to such as, when they hold between A and B, do not hold between B and A. [The argument which is merely indicated above, is set forth fully in my *Principles of Mathematics*, §§212–16.]

'A more searching argument against the axiom of internal relations is derived from a consideration of what is meant by the "nature" of a term. Is this the same as the term itself, or is it different? If it is different, it must be related to the term, and the relation of a term to its nature cannot, without an endless regress, be reduced to something other than a relation. Thus if the axiom is to be adhered to, we must suppose that a term is not other than its nature. In that case, every true proposition attributing a predicate to a subject is purely analytic, since the subject is its own whole nature, and the predicate is part of that nature. But in that case, what is the bond that unites predicates into predicates of one subject? Any casual collection of predicates might be supposed to compose a subject, if subjects are not other than the system of their own predicates. If the "nature" of a term is to consist of predicates, and at the same time to be the same as the term itself, it seems impossible to understand what we mean when we ask whether S has the predicate P. For this cannot mean: "Is P one of the predicates enumerated in explaining what we mean by S ?" and it is hard to see what else, on the view in question, it could mean. We cannot attempt to introduce a relation of *coherence* between predicates, in virtue of which they may be called predicates of one subject; for this would base predication upon a relation, instead of reducing relations to predications. Thus we get into equal difficulties whether we affirm or deny that a subject is other than "its nature". [On this subject, cf. my *Philosophy of Leibniz*, §§21, 24, 25.]

'Again, the axiom of internal relations is incompatible with all complexity. For this axiom leads, as we saw, to a rigid monism. There is only one thing, and only one proposition. The one proposition (which is not merely the only *true* proposition, but the *only* proposition) attributes a predicate to the one subject. But this one proposition is not quite true, because it involves distinguishing the predicate from the subject. But then arises the difficulty: if predication involves difference of the predicate from the subject, and if the one predicate is *not* distinct from the one subject, there cannot, even, one would suppose, be a *false* proposition attributing the one predicate to the one subject. We shall have to suppose, therefore, that predication does not involve difference of the predicate from the subject, and that the one predicate is identical with the one subject. But it is essential to the philosophy we are examining to deny absolute identity, and retain "identity in difference". The apparent multiplicity of the real world is otherwise inexplicable. The difficulty is that "identity in difference" is impossible, if we adhere to strict monism. For "identity in difference" involves many partial truths, which combine, by a kind of mutual give and take, into the one whole of truth. But the partial truths, in a strict monism, are not merely not quite true: they do not subsist at all. If there were such propositions, whether true of false, that would give plurality. In short, the whole conception of "identity in difference" is incompatible with the axiom of internal relations; yet without this conception, monism can give no account of the world, which suddenly collapses like an opera-hat. I conclude that the axiom is false, and that those parts of idealism which depend upon it are therefore groundless.

'There would seem, therefore, to be reasons against the axiom that relations are necessarily grounded in the "nature" of their terms or of the whole composed of the terms, and there would seem to be no reason in favour of this axiom. When the axiom is rejected, it becomes meaningless to speak of the "nature" of the terms of a relation: relatedness is no longer a proof of complexity, a given relation may hold between many different pairs of terms, and a given term may have many different relations to different terms. "Identity in difference" disappears: there is identity and there is difference, and complexes may have some elements identical and some different, but we are no longer obliged to say of any pair of objects that may be mentioned that they are both identical and different – "in a sense", this "sense" being something which it is vitally necessary to leave undefined. We thus get a world of many things, with relations which are not to be deduced from a supposed "nature" or scholastic essence of the related things. In this world, whatever is complex is composed of related simple things, and analysis is no longer confronted at every step by an endless regress. Assuming this kind of world, it remains to ask what we are to say concerning the nature of truth.'

I first realised the importance of the question of relations when I was working on Leibniz. I found – what books on Leibniz failed to make clear – that his metaphysic was explicitly based upon the doctrine that every proposition attributes a predicate to a subject and (what seemed to him almost the same thing) that every fact consists of a substance having a property. I found that this same doctrine underlies the systems of Spinoza, Hegel and Bradley, who, in fact, all developed the doctrine with more logical rigour than is shown by Leibniz.

But it was not only these rather dry, logical doctrines that made me rejoice in the new philosophy. I felt it, in fact, as a great liberation, as if I had escaped from a hot-house on to a wind-swept headland. I hated the stuffiness involved in supposing that space and time were only in my mind. I liked the starry heavens even better than the moral law, and could not bear Kant's view that the one I liked best was only a subjective figment. In the first exuberance of liberation, I became a naïve realist and rejoiced in the thought that grass is really green, in spite of the adverse opinion of all philosophers from Locke onwards. I have not been able to retain this pleasing faith in its pristine vigour, but I have never again shut myself up in a subjective prison.

Hegelians had all kinds of arguments to prove this or that not 'real'. Number, space, time, matter, were all professedly convicted of being self-contradictory. Nothing was real, so we were assured, except the Absolute, which could think only of itself since there was nothing else for it to think of and which thought eternally the sort of things that idealist philosophers thought in their books.

All the arguments used by Hegelians to condemn the sort of things dealt with by mathematics and physics depended upon the axiom of internal relations. Consequently, when I rejected this axiom, I began to believe everything the Hegelians disbelieved. This gave me a very full universe. I imagined all the numbers sitting in a row in a Platonic heaven. [Cf. my *Nightmares of Eminent Persons*, 'The Mathematician's

Nightmare'.] I thought that points of space and instants of time were actually existing entities, and that matter might very well be composed of actual elements such as physics found convenient. I believed in a world of universals, consisting mostly of what is meant by verbs and prepositions. Above all, I no longer had to think that mathematics is not quite true. Hegelians always maintained that it is not quite true that two and two are four, but they did not mean by this that two and two are 4·00001 or some such figure. What they did mean, though not what they said, was that the Absolute can find better things to occupy its mind than doing sums, but they did not like to put the matter in such simple language.

As time went on, my universe became less luxuriant. In my first rebellion against Hegel, I believed that a thing must exist if Hegel's proof that it cannot is invalid. Gradually, Occam's razor gave me a more clean-shaven picture of reality. I do not mean that it could prove the non-reality of entities which it showed to be unnecessary; I mean only that it abolished arguments in favour of their reality. I still think it impossible to disprove the existence of integers or points or instants or the Gods of Olympus. For aught I know these may all be real, but there is not the faintest reason to think so.

I was very much occupied, in the early days of developing the new philosophy, by questions which were largely linguistic. I was concerned with what makes the unity of a complex, and, more especially, the unity of a sentence. The difference between a sentence and a word puzzled me. I saw that the unity of a sentence depends upon the fact that it contains a verb, but it seemed to me that the verb means exactly the same thing as the corresponding verbal noun, although the verbal noun no longer possesses the capacity of binding together the parts of the complex. I worried about the difference between *is* and *being*. My mother-in-law, a famous and forceful religious leader, assured me that philosophy is only difficult because of the long words that it uses. I confronted her with the following sentence from notes I had made that day: 'What *is* means is and therefore differs from *is*, for "*is* is" would be nonsense.' It cannot be said that it is long words that make this sentence difficult. As time went on, I ceased to be troubled by such problems. They arose from the belief that, if a word means something, there must be some thing that it means. The theory of descriptions which I arrived at in 1905 showed that this was a mistake and swept away a host of otherwise insoluble problems.

Although I have changed my opinion on various matters since those early days, I have not changed on points which, then as now, seemed of most importance. I still hold to the doctrine of external relations and to pluralism, which is bound up with it. I still hold that an isolated truth may be quite true. I still hold that analysis is not falsification. I still hold that any proposition other than a tautology, if it is true, is true in virtue of a relation to *fact*, and that facts in general are independent of experience. I see nothing impossible in a universe devoid of experience. On the contrary, I think that experience is a very restricted and cosmically trivial aspect of a very tiny portion of the universe. On all these matters my views have not changed since I abandoned the teachings of Kant and Hegel.

Chapter 6

Logical Technique in Mathematics

The division of universities into faculties is, I suppose, necessary, but it has had some very unfortunate consequences. Logic, being considered to be a branch of philosophy and having been treated by Aristotle, has been considered to be a subject only to be treated by those who are proficient in Greek. Mathematics, as a consequence, has only been treated by those who knew no logic. From the time of Aristotle and Euclid to the present century, this divorce has been disastrous. It was at the International Congress of Philosophy in Paris in the year 1900 that I became aware of the importance of logical reform for the philosophy of mathematics. It was through hearing discussions between Peano of Turin and the other assembled philosophers that I became aware of this. I had not previously known his work, but I was impressed by the fact that, in every discussion, he showed more precision and more logical rigour than was shown by anybody else. I went to him and said, 'I wish to read all your works. Have you got copies with you?' He had, and I immediately read them all. It was they that gave the impetus to my own views on the principles of mathematics.

Mathematical logic was by no means a new subject. Leibniz had made some attempts at it, but had been thwarted by respect for Aristotle. Boole had published his *Laws of Thought* in 1854 and had developed a whole calculus dealing mainly with class-inclusion. Pierce had developed a logic of relations, and Schröder had published a work in three big volumes summarising all that had previously been done. Whitehead devoted the first portion of his *Universal Algebra* to Boole's calculus. Most of the above works were already familiar to me, but I had not found that they threw any light on the grammar of arithmetic. I still have the MS. of what I wrote on this subject just before my visit to Paris and I find, on re-reading it, that it does not make even a beginning of solving the problems which arithmetic presents to logic.

The enlightenment that I derived from Peano came mainly from two purely technical advances of which it is very difficult to appreciate the importance unless one had (as I had) spent years in trying to understand arithmetic. Both these advances had been made at an earlier date by Frege, but I doubt whether Peano knew this, and I did not know it until somewhat later. Although it is difficult, I must do my best to explain what these advances were and why they were important. I will begin with what they were.

The first advance consisted in separating propositions of the form 'Socrates is mortal' from propositions of the form 'All Greeks are mortal'. In Aristotle and in the accepted doctrine of the syllogism (which Kant thought forever incapable of improvement), these two forms of proposition are treated as indistinguishable or, at any rate, as not differing in any important way. But, in fact, neither logic nor arithmetic can get far until the two forms have been seen to be completely different. 'Socrates is mortal' attributes a predicate to a subject which is named. 'All Greeks are mortal' expresses a relation of two predicates – viz. 'Greek' and 'mortal'. The full statement of 'All Greeks are mortal' is 'For all possible values of x, if x is Greek, x is mortal'. We have here, instead of a subject-predicate proposition, a connection of two propositional functions, each of which becomes a subject-predicate proposition when a value is assigned to the variable x. The statement, 'All Greeks are mortal', says nothing about Greeks in particular, but is a statement about everything in the universe. The statement 'if x is Greek, x is mortal' is just as true when x is not Greek as when x is Greek. Indeed, it is true if there are no Greeks at all. 'All Lilliputians are mortal' is true, although there are no Lilliputians. The statement, 'All Greeks are mortal', unlike the statement, 'Socrates is mortal', names no one and expresses only and solely a connection of predicates. It cannot be proved by enumeration, since (to repeat) the x in question is not confined to the x's that are Greeks, but extends over the whole universe. But, although it cannot be proved by enumeration, it can nevertheless be known. I do not know whether there are any winged horses, and certainly I have never come across one, but nevertheless I can know that all winged horses are horses. In short, every statement containing the word *all* involves propositional functions, but does not involve any particular value of these functions.

The second important advance that I learnt from Peano was that a class consisting of one member is not identical with that one member. 'Satellite of the Earth', for instance, is a class and it has only one member, namely, the Moon. But to identify a class with its only member is to introduce utterly insoluble problems into the logic of collections and, therefore, of numbers, since it is to collections that numbers apply. The impropriety of identifying 'Satellite of the Earth' with the Moon is easily seen when it has once been pointed out. The phrase, 'Satellite of the Earth', would not alter its meaning if a second satellite were discovered; nor would it be destitute of meaning for a person who understood astronomy but did not know that the Earth had a satellite. Statements about the Moon, on the other hand, if we may take 'The Moon' as a name, are meaningless except to those who are aware of the Moon. To others, 'The Moon' would be a meaningless noise unless it were explained to be equivalent to the phrase. 'The only satellite of the Earth'; and if this explanation were substituted, statements about the Moon would not have the meaning that they have for you and me when we say, 'The Moon is bright tonight'. The man who substitutes a description is in the region of a connection of concepts, not in direct contact with the world of sense as is the man who says, 'The Moon is bright'. In this respect, the distinction with which we are now concerned has a certain analogy with our previous distinction between 'Socrates is mortal' and 'All Greeks are mortal'.

The reader may be disposed to think that the above distinctions are mere scholastic pedantry. I must now try to explain why this is not the case.

The philosophy of arithmetic was wrongly conceived by every writer before Frege. The mistake that all of them made was a very natural one. They thought of numbers as resulting from counting, and got into hopeless puzzles because things that are counted as one can equally well be counted as many. Take, say, the question, 'How many football clubs are there in England?' In answering this question, you treat each club as one, but you may just as well ask: 'How many members has such and such a football club?' In that case, you treat the club as many. And, if Mr A is a member of one of these clubs, although he counted as one before, you may ask just as legitimately, 'How many molecules make up Mr A?' And, then, Mr A counts as many. It is obvious, therefore, that what makes anything one from the point of view of counting is not its physical constitution but the question, 'Of what is this an instance?' The number that you arrive at by counting is the number of some collection, and the collection has whatever number it does have before you count it. It is only *qua* many instances of something that the collection is many. The collection itself will be an instance of something else, and *qua* instance counts as one in enumeration. We are thus forced to face the question, 'What is a collection?' and 'What is an instance?' Neither of these is intelligible except by means of propositional functions. A propositional function is an expression containing a variable and becoming a proposition as soon as a value is assigned to the variable. For example, 'x is a man' is a propositional function. If, in place of x, we put Socrates or Plato or anybody else, we get a proposition. We can also replace x by something that is not a man and we still get a proposition, though in this case a false one. A propositional function is nothing but an expression. It does not, by itself, represent anything. But it can form part of a sentence which does say something, true or false: 'x was an Apostle' says nothing, but 'there are twelve values of x for which "x was an Apostle" is true' is a complete sentence. Similar considerations apply to the concept *instance*. When we consider something as an instance, we are considering it as a possible value of a variable in a propositional function. If I say, 'Socrates is an instance of *Man*', I mean Socrates is a value of x for which 'x is a man' is true. The Scholastics had a maxim to the effect that *one* and *being* are convertible terms. This maxim, so long as it was believed, made it impossible to define 1. The truth is that *being* is a useless word, and that the kind of things to which this useless word is applied by those who mistakenly use it are just as apt to be many as to be one. *One* is a characteristic, not of things, but of certain propositional functions, namely, of those propositional functions which have the following property: there is an x which makes the function true and which is such that, if y makes the function true, y is identical with x. This is the definition of unitary functions, and the number 1 is the property of being unitary which certain functions possess. Similarly, a null-function is one which is false for all values of x, and 0 is the property of being a null-function.

The older theories of number always got into difficulties over 0 and 1, and it was Peano's capacity of dealing with these difficulties that first impressed me. But it was a good many years before I drew the full consequences of the new point of view. It is convenient in mathematics to think of 'classes', and for a long time I thought it necessary to distinguish between classes and propositional functions. Ultimately, however, I came to the conclusion that this distinction is unnecessary except as a technical device. The phrase 'propositional function' sounds perhaps unnecessarily formidable. For many purposes one can substitute the word 'property'. Thus, we may say that each number is a property of certain properties, but, except in ultimate analysis, it is perhaps easier to continue to use the word 'class'.

The definition of numbers to which I was led by the above considerations had been formulated by Frege sixteen years earlier, but I did not know this until a year or so after I had re-discovered it. I defined 2 as the class of all couples, 3 as the class of all trios, etc. A couple is defined as a class of which there are members x and y, x is not identical with y, and if z is a member of the class, then z is identical with x or with y. A number, in general, is a set of classes having the property which is called 'similarity'. This is defined as follows: Two classes are similar if there is a way of coupling their terms one to one. For example, in a monogamous country, you can know that the number of married men is the same as the number of married women, without having to know how many there are of either (I am excluding widows and widowers). Again, if a man has not lost a leg, you may be pretty sure that the number of his right-hand shoes is the same as the number of his left-hand shoes. If every member of a company has a chair to sit on and there are no empty chairs, the number of chairs must be the same as the number of people sitting on them. In all these cases there is what is called a one-one relation between the terms of one class and the terms of another, and it is the existence of such a one-one relation which is defined as similarity. The number of any class is defined as all the classes that are similar to it.

This definition has various advantages. It deals with all the problems that had previously arisen concerning 0 and 1. 0 is the class of those classes that have no members – i.e. it is the class whose only member is a class having no members. 1 is the class of those classes that have the property of consisting of whatever is identical with some term x. A second advantage of the definition is that it gets over difficulties concerning the one and the many. Since the terms counted are counted as instances of a propositional function, the unity involved is only that of the propositional function, which in no way conflicts with the plurality of instances. But much more important than either of these two advantages is the fact that we get rid of numbers as metaphysical entities. They become, in fact, merely linguistic conveniences with no more substantiality than belongs to 'etc.' or 'i.e.'. Kronecker, in philo-sophising about mathematics, said that 'God made the integers and the mathematicians made the rest of the mathematical apparatus'. By this he meant that each integer had to have an independent being, but other kinds of numbers need not have. With the above definition of numbers this prerogative of the integers disappears and the primitive apparatus of the mathematician is reduced to such purely logical terms, as *or*, *not*, *all* and *some*. This was my first experience of the use-fulness of Occam's razor in diminishing the number of undefined terms and unproved propositions required in a given body of know-ledge.

The above definition of numbers offers a further advantage which is of profound importance, and that is that it puts an end to difficulties concerning infinite numbers. While numbers were derived from count-ing, which takes terms one by one, it was difficult to conceive to the numbers of collections which could not be exhaustively enumerated one at a time. You cannot, for example, come to an end of the finite numbers by counting: however long you go on, there are always larger numbers to come. Therefore, so long as numbers were derived from counting, it seemed impossible to speak of the number of finite numbers. Now, however, it appears that counting is only one way of discovering how many terms there are in a collection, and is only applicable to such collections as happen to be finite. The logic of counting, as fitted into the new theory, is as follows: suppose, for example, that you are counting pound notes. By an act of will, you establish a one-one relation between the several notes and the numbers 1, 2, 3, etc., until there are no notes left. You then know, in accordance with our definition, that the number of notes is the same as the number of numbers that you have mentioned, and, if you have begun with 1 and gone on without skipping, the number of numbers that you have mentioned is the last number that you have mentioned. You cannot apply this process to infinite collections because life is not long enough. But, as counting is no longer essential, that need cause you no concern.

Having defined the whole numbers as above, there is no difficulty in the extension that mathematics requires. Rational fractions are relations between whole numbers which are derived from multiplication. Real numbers are sets of rational numbers consisting of everything above zero until a certain point. For example, the square-root of two is all rational numbers whose square is less than two. This definition, of which I believe I was the inventor, puts an end to a puzzle which had perplexed mathematicians ever since the time of Pythagoras. Complex numbers can be regarded as couples of real numbers, using 'couple' in the sense in which there is a first term and a second term – i.e. in which the order of the terms is essential.

In addition to the matters that I have already mentioned, there were other things that delighted me in the work of Peano and his disciples. I like the way in which they developed geometry without the use of figures, thus displaying the needlessness of Kant's *Anschauung*, and I liked Peano's curve that filled a whole area. But before coming across Peano I had been filled with the importance of relations, and I therefore set to work almost at once supplementing what he had done by a symbolic treatment of the logic of relations. It was at the end of July that I met him, and it was in September that I wrote a paper on the logic of relations which was published in his journal. I spent October, November and December of that same year on *The Principles of Mathematics*. Parts III, IV, V and VI of that book are almost exactly as I wrote them during those months. Parts I, II and VII, however, I re-wrote later. I finished this first draft of *The Principles of Mathematics* on the last day of the nineteenth century – i.e. 31st December, 1900. The months since the previous July had been an intellectual honeymoon such as I have never experienced before or since. Every day I found myself understanding something that I had not understood on the previous day. I thought all difficulties were solved and all problems were at an end. But the honeymoon could not last, and early in the following year intellectual sorrow descended upon me in full measure.

Chapter 7

Principia Mathematica: Philosophical Aspects

Throughout the years from 1900 to 1910 both Whitehead and I gave the bulk of our time to what ultimately became *Principia Mathematica*. Although the third volume of this work was not published until 1913, our part in it (apart from proof-reading) was finished in 1910 when we took the whole manuscript to the Cambridge University Press. *The Principles of Mathematics*, which I finished on 23rd May, 1902, turned out to be a crude and rather immature draft of the subsequent work, from which, however, it differed in containing controversy with other philosophies of mathematics.

The problems with which we had to contend were of two sorts: philosophical and mathematical. Broadly speaking, Whitehead left the philosophical problems to me. As for the mathematical problems, Whitehead invented most of the notation, except in so far as it was taken over from Peano; I did most of the work concerned with series and Whitehead did most of the rest. But this only applies to first drafts. Every part was done three times over. When one of us had produced a first draft, he would send it to the other, who would usually modify it considerably. After which, the one who had made the first draft would put it into final form. There is hardly a line in all the three volumes which is not a joint product.

The primary aim of *Principia Mathematica* was to show that all pure mathematics follows from purely logical premises and uses only concepts definable in logical terms. This was, of course, an antithesis to the doctrines of Kant, and initially I thought of the work as a parenthesis in the refutation of 'yonder sophistical Philistine', as Georg Cantor described him, adding for the sake of further definiteness, 'who knew so little mathematics'. But as time went on, the work developed in two different directions. On the mathematical side, whole new subjects came to light, involving new algorithms making possible the symbolic treatment of matters previously left to the diffuseness and inaccuracy of ordinary language. On the philosophical side, there were two opposite developments, one pleasant and the other unpleasant. The pleasant one was that the logical apparatus required turned out to be smaller than I had supposed. More especially, classes turned out to be unnecessary. In *The Principles of Mathematics* there is a lot of discussion about the distinction between a class as one and a class as many. The whole of this discussion, along with a great many complicated arguments contained in that book, proved unnecessary. The consequence was that the work in its final form appeared to lack that philosophic profundity of which obscurity is the most easily recognisable feature.

The unpleasant aspect was indubitably very unpleasant. It appeared that, from premisses which all logicians of no matter what school had accepted ever since the time of Aristotle, contradictions could be deduced, showing that *something* was amiss but giving no indication as to how matters were to be put right. It was the discovery of one such contradiction, in the spring of 1901, that put an end to the logical honeymoon that I had been enjoying. I communicated the misfortune to Whitehead, who failed to console me by quoting, 'never glad confident morning again'.

I was led to this contradiction by considering Cantor's proof that there is no greatest cardinal number. I thought, in my innocence, that the number of all the things there are in the world must be the greatest possible number, and I applied his proof to this number to see what would happen. This process led me to the consideration of a very peculiar class. Thinking along the lines which had hitherto seemed adequate, it seemed to me that a class sometimes is, and sometimes is not, a member of itself. The class of teaspoons, for example, is not another teaspoon, but the class of things that are not teaspoons, is one of the things that are not teaspoons. There seemed to be instances which are not negative: for example, the class of all classes is a class. The application of Cantor's argument led me to consider the classes that are not members of themselves; and these, it seemed, must form a class. I asked myself whether this class is a member of itself or not. If it is a member of itself, it must possess the defining property of the class, which is to be not a member of itself. If it is not a member of itself, it must not possess the defining property of the class, and therefore must be a member of itself. Thus each alternative leads to its opposite and there is a contradiction.

At first I thought there must be some trivial error in my reasoning. I inspected each step under a logical microscope, but I could not discover anything wrong. I wrote to Frege about it, who replied that arithmetic was tottering and that he saw that his Law V was false. Frege was so disturbed by this contradiction that he gave up the attempt to deduce arithmetic from logic, to which, until then, his life had been mainly devoted. Like the Pythagoreans when confronted with incommensurables, he took refuge in geometry and apparently considered that his life's work up to that moment had been misguided. For my part, I felt that the trouble lay in logic rather than in mathematics and that it was logic which would have to be reformed. I was confirmed in this view by discovering a recipe by means of which a strictly infinite number of contradictions could be manufactured.

Philosophers and mathematicians reacted in various different ways to this situation. Poincaré, who disliked mathematical logic and had accused it of being sterile, exclaimed with glee, 'it is no longer sterile, it begets contradiction'. This was all very well, but it did nothing towards the solution of the problem. Some other mathematicians, who disapproved of Georg Cantor, adopted the March Hare's solution: 'I'm tired of this. Let's change the subject.' This, also, appeared to me inadequate. After a time, however, there came to be serious attempts at solution by men who understood mathematical logic and realised the imperative necessity of a solution in terms of logic. The first of these was F. P. Ramsey, whose early death unfortunately left his work incomplete. But during the years before the publication of *Principia Mathematica*, I did not have the advantage of these later attempts at solution, and was left virtually alone with my bewilderment.

There were older paradoxes, some of them known to the Greeks, which raised what seemed to me similar problems, though writers subsequent to me considered them to be of a different sort. The best known of these was the one about Epimenides, the Cretan, who said that all Cretans are liars, and caused people to ask whether he was lying when he said so. This paradox is seen in its simplest form if a man says, 'I am lying'. If he is lying, it is a lie that he is lying, and therefore he is speaking the truth; but if he is speaking the truth, he is lying, for that is what he says he is doing. Contradiction is thus inevitable. This contradiction is mentioned by St Paul,[1] who, however, is not interested in its logical aspects but only in its demonstration that the heathen are wicked. But such ancient puzzles could be dismissed by mathematicians as having nothing to do with their subject, though they could not well ignore the questions whether there is a greatest cardinal or a greatest ordinal, both of which landed them in contradictions. The contradiction about the greatest ordinal was discovered by Burali-Forti before I discovered my contradiction, but the matter in his case was much more complex, and I had therefore allowed myself to suppose that there was some unimportant error in the reasoning. In any case, his contradiction, being much less simple than mine, seemed *prima facie* less devastating. In the end, however, I had to admit that it was just as serious.

In *The Principles of Mathematics* I did not profess to have found a solution. I said in the preface to that work: 'For publishing a work

[1] Titus i. 20.

containing so many unsolved difficulties, my apology is, that investigation revealed no near prospect of adequately resolving the contradiction discussed in Chapter X, or of acquiring a better insight into the nature of classes. The repeated discovery of errors in solutions which for a time had satisfied me caused these problems to appear such as would have been only concealed by any seemingly satisfactory theories which a slightly longer reflection might have produced; it seemed better, therefore, merely to state the difficulties, than to wait until I had become persuaded of the truth of some almost certainly erroneous doctrine.' And at the end of the chapter discussing the contradiction, I say: 'No peculiar philosophy is involved in the above contradiction, which springs directly from common sense, and can only be solved by abandoning some common-sense assumption. Only the Hegelian philosophy, which nourishes itself on contradictions, can remain indifferent, because it finds similar problems everywhere. In any other doctrine, so direct a challenge demands an answer, on pain of a confession of impotence. Fortunately, no other similar difficulty, so far as I know, occurs in any other portion of *The Principles of Mathematics*.' In an appendix at the end of the book I suggested the doctrine of types as affording a possible solution. I ultimately became convinced that the solution is to be found by this doctrine, but at the time when I wrote *The Principles of Mathematics* I had developed only a crude form of the doctrine, and in this form it was inadequate. The conclusion I came to at that time is expressed in the last paragraph of the book: 'To sum up: it appears that the special contradiction of Chapter X is solved by the doctrine of types, but that there is at least one closely analogous contradiction which is probably not soluble by this doctrine. The totality of all logical objects, or of all propositions, involves, it would seem, a fundamental logical difficulty. What the complete solution of the difficulty may be, I have not succeeded in discovering; but as it affects the very foundations of reasoning, I earnestly commend the study of it to the attention of all students of logic.'

When *The Principles of Mathematics* was finished, I settled down to a resolute attempt to find a solution of the paradoxes. I felt this as almost a personal challenge and I would, if necessary, have spent the whole of the rest of my life in an attempt to meet it. But for two reasons I found this exceedingly disagreeable. In the first place, the whole problem struck me as trivial and I hated having to concentrate attention upon something that did not seem intrinsically interesting. In the second place, try as I would, I could make no progress. Throughout 1903 and 1904, my work was almost wholly devoted to this matter, but without any vestige of success. My first success was the theory of descriptions, in the spring of 1905, of which I will speak presently. This was, apparently, not connected with the contradictions, but in time an unsuspected connection emerged. In the end, it became entirely clear to me that some form of the doctrine of types is essential. I lay no stress upon the particular form of that doctrine which is embodied in *Principia Mathematica*, but I remain wholly convinced that without *some* form of the doctrine the paradoxes cannot be resolved.

While I was looking for a solution, it seemed to me that there were three requisites if the solution was to be wholly satisfying. The first of these, which was absolutely imperative, was that the contradictions should disappear. The second, which was highly desirable, though not logically compulsive, was that the solution should leave intact as much of mathematics as possible. The third, which is difficult to state precisely, was that the solution should, on reflection, appeal to what may be called 'logical common sense' – i.e. that it should seem, in the end, just what one ought to have expected all along. Of these three conditions, the first is of course universally acknowledged. The second, however, is rejected by a large school which holds that great portions of analysis are not valid as they stand. The third condition is not regarded as essential by those who are content with logical dexterity. Professor Quine, for example, has produced systems which I admire greatly on account of their skill, but which I cannot feel to be satisfactory because they seem to be created *ad hoc* and not to be such as even the cleverest logician would have thought of if he had not known of the contradictions. On this subject, however, an immense and very abstruse literature has grown up, and I will say no more about its finer points.

Without going into difficult technical details, it is possible to explain the broad principles of the theory of types. Perhaps the best way of approaching the theory is by examination of what is meant by a 'class'. Let us start with a homely illustration. Suppose, at the end of dinner, your host offers you a choice of three different sweets, urging you to have any one or two or all three, as you may wish. How many courses of conduct are open to you? You may refuse all of them. That is one choice. You may take one of them. This is possible in three different ways and therefore gives you three more choices. You may choose two of them. This again is possible in three ways. Or you may choose all three, which gives you one final possibility. The total number of possibilities is thus eight, i.e. 2^3. It is easy to generalise this procedure. Suppose you have n objects before you and you wish to know how many ways there are of choosing none or some or all of the n. You will find that the number of ways is 2^n. To put it in logical language: a class of n terms has 2^n sub-classes. This proposition is still true when n is infinite. What Cantor proved was that, even in this case, 2^n is greater than n. Applying this, as I did, to all the things in the universe, one arrives at the conclusion that there are more classes of things than there are things. It follows that classes are not 'things'. But, as no one quite knows what the word 'thing' means in this statement, it is not very easy to state at all exactly what it is that has been proved. The conclusion to which I was led was that classes are merely a convenience in discourse. I was already somewhat bewildered on the subject of classes at the time when I wrote *The Principles of Mathematics*. I expressed myself, however, in those days, in language which was more realistic (in the scholastic sense) than I should now think suitable. I said in the preface to that work:

'The discussion of indefinables – which forms the chief part of philosophical logic – is the endeavour to see clearly, and to make others see clearly, the entities concerned, in order that the mind may have that kind of acquaintance with them which it has with redness or the taste of a pineapple. Where, as in the present case, the indefinables are obtained primarily as the necessary residue in a process of analysis, it is often easier to know that there must be such entities than actually to perceive them; there is a process analogous to that which resulted in the discovery of Neptune, with the difference that the final stage – the search with a mental telescope for the entity which has been inferred – is often the most difficult part of the undertaking. In the case of classes, I must confess, I have failed to perceive any concept fulfilling the conditions requisite for the notion of *class*. And the contradiction discussed in Chapter X proves that something is amiss, but what this is I have hitherto failed to discover.'

I should now phrase the matter somewhat differently. I should say that, given any propositional function, say fx, there is a certain range of values of x for which this function is 'significant' – i.e. either true or false. If a is in this range, then fa is a proposition which is either true or false. In addition to substituting a constant for the variable x, there are two other things that may be done with a propositional function: one is to assert that it is always true; and the other, that it is sometimes true. The propositional function, 'if x is human, x is mortal' is always true; the propositional function, 'x is human' is sometimes true. There are thus three things that can be done with a propositional function: the first is to substitute a constant for the variable; the second is to assert all values of the function; and the third is to assert some values or at least one value. The propositional function itself is only an expression. It does not assert or deny anything. A class, equally, is only an expression. It is only a convenient way of talking about the values of the variable for which the function is true.

As regards the third of the above three requisites which a solution should fulfil, I advanced a theory which does not seem to have commended itself to other logicians, but which still seems to me sound. This theory was as follows: When I assert all values of a function fx, the values that x can take must be definite if what I am asserting is to be definite. There must be, that is to say, some totality of possible values of x. If I now proceed to create new values defined in terms of that totality, the totality appears to be thereby enlarged and therefore the new values referring to it will refer to that enlarged totality. But, since they must be included in the totality, it can never catch up with them. The process is like trying to jump on to the shadow of your head. We can illustrate this most simply by the paradox of the liar. The liar says, 'everything that I assert is false'. This is, in fact, an assertion which he makes, but it refers to the totality of his assertions and it is only by including it in that totality that a paradox results. We shall have to distinguish between propositions that refer to some totality of propositions and propositions that do not. Those that refer to some totality of propositions can never be members of that totality. We may define first-order propositions as those referring to no totality of propositions; second-order propositions, as those referring to totalities of first-order propositions; and so on, *ad infinitum*. Thus our liar will now have to say, 'I am asserting a false proposition of the first order which is false'. But this is itself a proposition of the second order. He is thus not asserting any proposition of the first order. What he says is, thus, simply false, and the argument that it is also true collapses. Exactly the same argument applies to any proposition of higher order.

It will be found that in all the logical paradoxes there is a kind of reflexive self-reference which is to be condemned on the same ground: viz. that it includes, as a member of a totality, something referring to that totality which can only have a definite meaning if the totality is already fixed.

I must confess that this doctrine has not won wide acceptance, but I have seen no argument against it which seemed to me cogent.

The theory of descriptions, mentioned above, was first set forth in my article 'On Denoting' in *Mind*, 1905. This doctrine struck the then editor as so preposterous that he begged me to reconsider it and not to demand its publication as it stood. I, however, was persuaded of its soundness and refused to give way. It was afterwards generally accepted, and came to be thought my most important contribution to logic. It is true that there is now a reaction against it on the part of those who do not believe in the distinction between names and other words. But I think that this reaction exists only among those who have never attempted mathematical logic. At any rate, I have been unable to see any validity in their criticisms. I will admit, however, that perhaps the doctrine of names is a little more difficult than I thought at one time. For the moment, however, I will ignore these difficulties and deal with ordinary language as commonly employed.

I took for my argument the contrast between the name, 'Scott', and the description, 'the author of *Waverley*'. The statement 'Scott is the author of *Waverley*' expresses an identity and not a tautology. George IV wished to know whether Scott was the author of *Waverley*, but he did not wish to know whether Scott was Scott. Although this is perfectly intelligible to everybody who has not studied logic, it presents a puzzle to the logician. Logicians think (or used to think) that, if two phrases denote the same object, a proposition containing the one may always be replaced by a proposition containing the other without ceasing to be true, if it was true, or false, if it was false. But, as we have just seen, you may turn a true proposition into a false one by substituting 'Scott' for 'the author of *Waverley*'. This shows that it is necessary to distinguish between a name and a description: 'Scott' is a name, but 'the author of *Waverley*' is a description.

Another important distinction between names and descriptions is that a name cannot occur significantly in a proposition unless there is something that it names, whereas a description is not subject to this limitation. Meinong, for whose work I had had a great respect, had failed to note this difference. He pointed out that one can make statements in which the logical subject is 'the golden mountain' although no golden mountain exists. He argued, if you say that the golden mountain does not exist, it is obvious that there is something that you are saying does not exist – namely, the golden mountain; therefore the golden mountain must subsist in some shadowy Platonic world of being, for otherwise your statement that the golden mountain does not exist would have no meaning. I confess that, until I hit upon the theory of descriptions, this argument seemed to me convincing. The essential point of the theory was that, although 'the golden mountain' may be grammatically the subject of a significant proposition, such a proposition when rightly analysed no longer has such a subject. The proposition 'the golden mountain does not exist' becomes 'the propositional function "x is golden and a mountain" is false for all values of x.' The statement 'Scott is the author of *Waverley*' becomes 'for all values of x, "x wrote *Waverley*" is equivalent to "x is Scott"'. Here, the phrase 'the author of *Waverley*' no longer occurs.

The theory also threw light upon what is meant by 'existence'. 'The author of *Waverley* exists' means 'there is a value of c for which the propositional function "x wrote *Waverley*" is always equivalent to "x is c" is true.' Existence in this sense can only be asserted of a description and, when analysed, is found to be a case of a propositional function being true of at least one value of the variable. We can say 'the author of *Waverley* exists' and we can say 'Scott is the author of *Waverley*', but 'Scott exists' is bad grammar. It can, at best, be interpreted as meaning, 'the person named "Scott" exists', but 'the person named "Scott"' is a description, not a name. Whenever a name is properly used as a name it is bad grammar to say 'that exists'.

The central point of the theory of descriptions was that a phrase may contribute to the meaning of a sentence without having any meaning at all in isolation. Of this, in the case of descriptions, there is precise proof: If 'the author of *Waverley*' meant anything other than 'Scott', 'Scott is the author of *Waverley*' would be false, which it is not. If 'the author of *Waverley*' meant 'Scott', 'Scott is the author of *Waverley*' would be a tautology, which it is not. Therefore, 'the author of *Waverley*' means neither 'Scott' nor anything else – i.e. 'the author of *Waverley*' means nothing, Q.E.D.

Chapter 8

Principia Mathematica: Mathematical Aspects

Both Whitehead and I were disappointed that *Principia Mathematica* was only viewed from a philosophical standpoint. People were interested in what was said about the contradictions and in the question whether ordinary mathematics had been validly deduced from purely logical premisses, but they were not interested in the mathematical techniques developed in the course of the work. I used to know of only six people who had read the later parts of the book. Three of these were Poles, subsequently (I believe) liquidated by Hitler. The other three were Texans, subsequently successfully assimilated. Even those who were working on exactly the same subjects did not think it worth while to find out what *Principia Mathematica* had to say on them. I will give two illustrations: *Mathematische Annalen* published about ten years after the publication of *Principia* a long article giving some of the results which (unknown to the author) we had worked out in Part IV of our book. This article fell into certain inaccuracies which we had avoided, but contained nothing valid which we had not already published. The author was obviously totally unaware that he had been anticipated. The second example occurred when I was a colleague of Reichenbach at the University of California. He told me that he had invented an extension of mathematical induction which he called 'transfinite induction'. I told him that this subject was fully treated in the third volume of the *Principia*. When I saw him a week later, he told me that he had verified this. I wish in the present chapter to explain, as far as I can without undue technicality, what seemed to me the important aspects of the *Principia* from a mathematical as opposed to a philosophical point of view.

I will begin with a matter which concerns philosophy and mathematics in equal measure, namely, the importance of relations. In my book on Leibniz I had emphasised the importance of relational facts and propositions as opposed to facts consisting of substance-and-attribute and propositions consisting of subject-and-predicate. I found that the prejudice against relations had had bad consequence in mathematics as well as in philosophy. Boole's mathematical logic, like Leibniz's abortive attempts, was concerned with class-inclusion and was merely a development of the syllogism. Pierce had developed a logic of relations, but had treated a relation as a class of couples. This is technically possible, but does not direct attention naturally towards what is important. What is important in the logic of relations is what is different from the logic of classes, and my philosophical opinion on relations helped to make me emphasise what turned out to be most useful.

I thought of relations, in those days, almost exclusively as *intensions*. I thought of sentences such as, 'x precedes y', 'x is greater than y', 'x is north of y'. It seemed to me – as, indeed, it still seems – that, although from the point of view of a formal calculus one can regard a relation as a set of ordered couples, it is the intension alone which gives unity to the set. The same thing applies, of course, also to classes. What gives unity to a class is solely the intension which is common and peculiar to its members. This is obvious whenever we are dealing with a class whose members we cannot enumerate. In the case of infinite classes, the impossibility of enumeration is obvious; but it is equally true of most finite classes. Who, for example, can enumerate all the members of the class of earwigs? Nevertheless, we can make statements (true or false) about all earwigs, and we do this in virtue of the intension by which the class is defined. Exactly similar considerations apply in the case of relations. We can say many things about order in time because we understand the word 'precede', although we cannot enumerate all the couples x, y such that x precedes y. There is, however, a further argument against the view of relations as classes of couples: the couples have to be *ordered* couples, that is to say, we must be able to distinguish the couple x, y from the couple y, x. This cannot be done except by means of some relation in intension. So long as we confine ourselves to classes and predicates, it remains impossible to interpret order or to distinguish an ordered couple from a class of two terms without order.

All this was the philosophical background of the calculus of relations which we developed in the *Principia*. We were led to symbolise various concepts which mathematical logicians had not previously made prominent. Among these, the most important were: (1) the class of terms having relations R to a given term y; (2) the class of terms to which a given term x has the relation R; (3) the 'domain' of a relation, which consists of the class of all those terms that have the relation R to something or other; (4) the 'converse domain' of R, which is the class of all those terms to which something or other has the relation R; (5) the 'field' of R, which consists of the 'domain' together with the 'converse domain'; (6) the 'converse' of a relation R, which is the relation that holds between y and x whenever R holds between x and y; (7) the 'relative product' of two relations R and S, which holds between x and z when there is an intermediate term y such that x has the relation R to y and y has the relation S to z; (8) plurals, defined as follows: given some class a we form the class of all the terms that have the relation R to some member of a. We can illustrate these various concepts by considering human relationships. Suppose, for example, that R is the relation of parent and child. Then (1) is the parent of y; (2) is the children of x; (3) is the class of all those people who have children; (4) is the class of all those people who have parents – i.e. everybody except Adam and Eve; (5) the field of the relation 'parent' will consist of everybody who is either somebody's parent or somebody's child; (6) the converse of the relation 'parent of' is the relation 'child of'; (7) 'grandparent' is the relative product of parent and parent, 'brother or sister' is the relative product of 'child' and 'parent', 'first-cousin or brother or sister' is the relative product of grandchild and grandparent, and so on; (8) 'parents of Etonians' is a plural in this sense.

Different sorts of relations have different sorts of uses. We may begin with the sort of relation that gives rise to what I call 'descriptive functions'. This is the sort of relation which only one term at most can have to a given term. It gives rise to phrases using the word 'the' in the singular, such as, 'the father of x', 'the double of x', 'the sine of x', and all the usual functions of mathematics. Such functions can only be generated by the sort of relation which I call 'one-many' – i.e. the sort of relation which not more than one term can have to any other. For example, if you are speaking of a Christian country, you can speak of 'the wife of x', but this phrase becomes ambiguous if applied to a country where polygamy exists. In mathematics you may speak of 'the square of x', but not of 'the square-root of x', as x has two square-roots. In the above list 'domain', 'converse domain', and 'field' all give rise to descriptive functions.

A second sort of relation which is very important is the sort which establishes a correlation between two classes. This is the sort of relation which I call 'one-one'. This is the sort of relation where not only is there at most one x having the relation R to a given y, but also there is at most one y to which a given x has the relation R. An example is: marriage where polygamy is forbidden. Where such a correlation exists between two classes, they have the same number of terms. For example: we know without enumeration that the number of wives is the same as the number of husbands, and the number of men's noses is the same as the number of men. There is a special form of correlation which is also of very great importance. This arises when two classes are given as the fields of two relations P and Q and there is a correlation between them such that, whenever two terms have the relation P, their correlates have the relation Q, and vice versa. Take, for example, precedence among married officials and precedence among their wives. Unless the wives are related to the peerage or the officials are bishops, the order of precedence among wives is the same as among husbands. Such a correlator is called an 'ordinal correlator' because whatever order there may be among the members of the field of P is preserved among their correlates in the field of Q.

The third important type of relation is that which gives rise to series. The word 'series' is old and familiar, but I think I was the first person to give it an exact meaning. A series is a set of terms having an order derived from a relation having three properties: (a) it must be asymmetrical – that is to say, if x has the relation to y, then y does not have it to x; (b) it must be transitive – that is to say, if x has the relation to y and y has it to z, then x has it to z; (c) it must be connected – that is to say, if x and y are any two different terms in its field, then either x has the relation to y or y has it to x. If a relation has these three properties, it arranges the terms of its field in a series.

All these properties are easily illustrated by human relationships. Thus the relation *husband* is asymmetrical, because if A is the husband of B, B is not the husband of A. *Spouse*, on the contrary is symmetrical. *Ancestor* is transitive, because an ancestor of an ancestor of A is an ancestor of A; but *father* is intransitive. *Ancestor* has two of the three properties required of a serial relation, but not the third, that of being connected, because it is not the case that of any two different people, one must be an ancestor of the other. On the other hand, if one considers, for example, succession in a royal family in which sons always succeed to fathers, the relation ancestor confined to this royal line is connected, and therefore the kings concerned form a series.

Relations of the above three kinds are those that are of most importance in the transitional region between logic and ordinary mathematics.

I will now proceed to a sketch of some of the developments for which the above logical apparatus was useful, but I will preface this by a few general observations.

When I was young, I was told that mathematics is the science of number and quantity, or, alternatively, of number and measure. This definition is far too narrow. First: the many different kinds of number that are dealt with in conventional mathematics make only a small part of the region to which mathematical methods are applicable, and a great deal of the reasoning required for establishing the foundations of arithmetic has no very close connection with number. Second: in dealing with arithmetic and its prolegomena we had to bear in mind that wherever possible propositions which are true equally of finite and of infinite classes or numbers should not be proved only for the former. More generally, we considered it a waste of time to prove proposition in some particular class of cases when they can just as well be proved much more generally. Third: we considered it as part of the goal at which we were aiming to establish the traditional formal laws of arithmetic, i.e.: the associative law,

$$(a+b)+c = a+(b+c)$$

the commutative law,

$$a+b = b+a$$

with analogous laws for multiplication
and the distributive law

$$a\times(b+c) = (a\times b)+(a\times c)$$

Beginners in mathematics are always informed of these laws without being given proofs of them, or, if proofs are offered, they use mathematical induction and are therefore only valid for finite numbers. The ordinary definitions of addition and multiplication assume that the number of sumands or factors is finite. This is among the limitations which we set ourselves to remove.

The extension of multiplication to an infinite number of factors is effected by means of what are called 'selections'. The notion of a selection can most readily be made familiar by the example of electing Members of Parliament. Assuming that, in the country concerned, every elected representative must be a member of his constituency, the total Parliament constitutes what is called a selection from the constituencies. The general conception is as follows: given a class of classes none of which is null, a selection is a relation which picks out one member of each class as the 'representative' of that class. The number of ways in which this can be done (provided no two classes have any common members) is the product of the number of the several classes. For example, suppose we have three classes, the first consisting of x_1, x_2, x_3, the second of y_1, y_2, y_3, and third of z_1, z_2, z_3, then any class containing one x, one y, and one z is a selection from the class of three classes, and any reader can easily satisfy himself there are twenty-seven ways of making this selection.

After we had adopted this definition of multiplication, we were faced by an unexpected difficulty. It appeared that, when the number of classes is infinite, one cannot be sure that any selections are possible. When the number of classes concerned is finite, we can pick out a representative arbitrarily from each of them, as is done in a General Election; but, when the number of classes concerned is infinite, we cannot make an infinite number of arbitrary acts of choice, and we cannot be sure that a selection is possible unless there is some intension which secures the desired result. I will give an illustration: there was once a millionaire who bought an infinite number of pairs of shoes and, whenever he bought a pair of shoes, he also bought a pair of socks. We can make a selection choosing one out of each pair of shoes, because we can choose always the right shoe or always the left shoe. Thus, so far as the shoes are concerned, selections exist. But, as regards the socks, where there is no distinction of right and left, we cannot use this rule of selection. If we are to be able to make a selection out of the socks, we shall have to adopt some much more elaborate method. We could, for example, find a point such that, in each pair of socks, one of the pair is nearer to this point than to the other. We should then obtain a selection by choosing from each pair the one nearer the point in question. I once put this puzzle to a German mathematician to whom I happened to sit next at the High Table at Trinity, but his only comment was: 'Why a millionaire?'

Some people consider it self-evident that, if none of the classes concerned is null, it must be possible to make a selection of one from each. Some others think otherwise. On this point, the best that can be said was said by Peano: 'Is this principle true or false? Our opinion has no value.' We defined what we called 'the multiplicative axiom': the assumption that it is always possible to make a selection of one representative from each of a set of classes none of which is null. We found no arguments either for or against this axiom, and we therefore included it explicitly in the hypothesis of any proposition which used it. At the same time that we came upon this problem, Zermelo set up what he called 'the principle of selection', which is a slightly different but logically equivalent assumption. He was among those who regarded it as a self-evident truth. Since we did not adopt this view, we sought as many devices as possible for dealing with multiplication without assuming the axiom.

The logical theory of selection does not depend at any point upon the concept 'number', and we developed it in the *Principia* before defining 'number'. The same thing applies to another very important concept, namely, that expressed in ordinary language by the words 'and so on'.

Suppose you wish to define the concept 'ancestor' in terms of the concept 'parent'. You may say that A is an ancestor of Z if A is a parent of B, B is a parent of C, and so on and, after a finite number of steps, you reach some person Y who is a parent of Z. This would be all very well but for the fact that it contains the word 'finite' and that this word has to be defined. The definition of the word 'finite' is only possible by means of a particular application of a completely general notion, namely, that of the ancestral relation derived from any given relation. This notion of the ancestral relation was first developed by Frege as long ago as 1897, but his work remained quite unnoticed until Whitehead and I developed it. The notion that we wished to define may be explained in a preliminary way as follows: if x has the relation R to y let us call the step from x to y an R-step. You may then be able to make another R-step from y to z. We shall define as the 'posterity' of x with respect to R everything that you can reach by R-steps starting from x. We cannot say everything that you can reach be a 'finite number of R-steps' because we have not yet defined the word 'finite', and we can only define it by means of the conception of 'posterity'. The posterity of x with respect to R is defined as follows. We will first define a 'hereditary' class with respect to R. This is a class which has the property that anything reached by an R-step from one of its members is, again, a member of it. For example, the property of being called 'Smith' is hereditary in the relation of father to son, and the property of being human is hereditary in the relation of parent to child. I now define 'y belongs to the posterity of x with respect to R, if y belongs to every hereditary class with respect to R to which x belongs'. Now let us apply this to ordinary whole numbers, putting in the place of R the relation of a number to its immediate successor. If we now consider the posterity of 0 with respect to this number, it is obvious that 1 belongs to this posterity, since $1 = 0 + 1$; and, since 1 belongs to the posterity of 0, so does 2; and, since 2 does, so does 3. Proceeding in this way, we get a whole set of numbers all belonging to the posterity of 0. To all these numbers, we can apply proofs using what is called 'mathematical induction'. Mathematical induction is the principle that, if a property belongs to 0 and to the immediate successor of any number which has this property, then it belongs to all finite numbers. Defining 'finite' numbers as the posterity of 0, this is an immediate result of the definition. It used to be thought that mathematical induction is a principle, since it was thought that all numbers must be finite. This was a mistake. Mathematical induction is not a principle but a definition. It is true of some numbers and not of others. Those of which it is true are defined as the finite numbers. For example, a finite number is increased by adding 1 to it; an infinite number is not.

The whole theory of ancestral relations is very important not only in connection with numbers. For this reason we developed the theory before introducing the definition of number.

I come now to what I call 'relation-arithmetic' which occupied the second half of the second volume of *Principia*. From the mathematical point of view this was my most important contribution to the work. What I called 'relation-numbers' were numbers of an entirely new sort of which ordinal numbers were a very specialised example. I found that all the formal laws which are true of ordinal numbers are true of this far more general kind. I found, also, that relation-numbers are essential to the understanding of structure. 'Structure' is one of those phrases, like 'and so on' or 'series', which are familiarly employed in spite of the fact that no precise significance is attached to them. By means of relation-arithmetic the concept 'structure' can be precisely defined.

The fundamental definition in this subject is that of 'ordinal similarity' or 'likeness', which was mentioned above. Where relations are concerned, this plays the same part as similarity played between classes. Similarity between classes is defined as the existence of a one-

one relation coupling each term of either class to a correlate in the other. Ordinal similarity between two relations P and Q is defined as meaning that there is a correlator of the field of P to the field of Q which is such that whenever two terms have the relation P their correlates have the relation Q, and vice versa. Let us take an illustration: suppose P is the relation of precedence among married government officials, and Q is the relation of precedence among their wives, then the relation of wife to husband so correlates the fields of P and Q that, whenever the wives have the relation Q, their husbands have the relation P, and vice versa. When two relations P and Q are ordinally similar, if S is the correlating relation, Q is the relative product of S and P and the converse of S. In the above illustration, for example, if x and y are two wives and x has the relation Q to y, and if S is the relation of wife to husband, then x is the wife of a man who has the relation P to the husband of y, that is to say, Q is the same relation as the relative product of S and P and the converse of S; the converse of S being the relation of husband to wife. Whenever P and Q are serial relations, their likeness consists in the fact that their terms can be correlated without change of order, but the conception of likeness is applicable to all relations that have fields – i.e. to all relations where the domain and converse domain are of the same type.

We now define the relation-number of a relation P as the class of those relations that are ordinally similar to P. This is exactly analogous to cardinal arithmetic with ordinal similarity substituted for class similarity and relations substituted for classes. The definitions of addition, multiplication and exponentiation are more or less analogous to those in cardinal arithmetic. Both addition and multiplication obey the associative law, and the distributive law holds in one form but, in general, not in another. The commutative law does not hold except when the fields of the relations concerned are finite. For example, take a series which is like the series of natural numbers and add two terms to it. If you add the two terms at the beginning, the new series is like the old one; but, if you add them at the end, it is not. The sum of two relations P and Q is defined as the relation which holds between x and y whenever x has the relation P to y, or x has the relation Q to y, or x belongs to the field of P and y belongs to the field of Q. With this definition the sum of P and Q is not, in general, like the sum of Q and P. This is true not only of relation-numbers in general, but also of ordinal numbers when one or both of these are infinite.

Ordinal numbers are a sub-class of relation-numbers, namely, those that apply to 'well-ordered' series, 'well-ordered' series being those series in which any sub-class that has members has a first term. Transfinite ordinal numbers were studied by Cantor, but relation-numbers in general were, so far as I know, first defined and studied in the *Principia*.

One or two illustrations may be useful. Suppose for example, that you have a series of couples and you wish to form a series of selections from these couples in the sense explained above in connection with the axiom of selection. The procedure is much akin to that in cardinal arithmetic except that we are now concerned to put the selections in an order, whereas before we were only concerned with them as a class. Suppose, again, as we did in considering class-selections, we have three sets, (x_1, x_2, x_3) (y_1, y_2, y_3) and (z_1, z_2, z_3), and we wish to make a series out of selections of these. There are various ways in which this can be done. Perhaps the simplest is as follows: any selection containing x_1 comes before any selection which does not contain it. Among selections of which both or neither contain x_1, those containing y_1 come before those which do not. Among selections of which both or neither contain x_1 and y_1 those containing z_1 come before those which do not. We make similar rules for the suffix 2 and the suffix 3. In this way we get all the possible selections arranged in a series which begins with (x_1, y_1, z_1) and ends with (x_3, y_3, z_3). It is obvious that the series will have twenty-seven terms, but here the number twenty-seven is no longer a cardinal number, as in our earlier example, but an ordinal number – i.e. a particular kind of relation-number. It differs from a cardinal number by establishing an order among the selections, which a cardinal number does not. So long as we confine ourselves to finite numbers, there are no important formal differences between ordinal and cardinal numbers; but, when we allow infinite numbers, the differences become important, owing to the failure of the commutative law.

In proving the formal laws of relation-arithmetic we often have occasion to deal with series of series of series. These can be visualised by the following illustration: suppose you have to make a stack of a number of bricks and, to make the matter more interesting, let us assume that they are gold bricks and you are employed at Fort Knox. I shall assume that you first make a row of bricks, putting each brick due East of the previous one; you then make another row, touching your first row but due North of it; and so on, until you have made as many rows as seems appropriate. You then make a second layer on top of the first layer; and a third on top of the second; and so on, until all the bricks are stacked. Then each row is a series, each layer is a series of series, and the whole stack is a series of series of series. We can symbolise this process as follows: let P be the relation of above to below among the layers; the field of P will consist of the layers; and each layer is a series of rows. Let Q_1 be the relation South to North among the rows of the top layer, Q_2 the relation among the rows of the second layer, and so on. The field of Q_1 is a series of rows. Let us call R_{11} the relation of East to West in the most Southern row of the top layer; R_{12} the relation of East to West in the second row of the top layer; and so on, ending with R_{mn} if m is the number of layers and n is the number of rows in each layer. In this illustration, I have assumed that the number of layers and rows is finite, but this is a quite unnecessary restriction made only to make the illustration simpler. In ordinary language all this is complicated and lengthy, but in symbols it becomes short and easy. Let F be the relation of x to P consisting in x being a member of the field of P. Then F^3 is the relative product of F and F and F. The separate bricks, for example, are the terms having the relation F^3 to P – that is to say, each brick is a member of the field of a member of the field of a member of the field of P. We need such series of series of series in proving the associative law for addition and multiplication.

When two relation-numbers are ordinally similar, we can say that they generate the same 'structure', but structure is a somewhat more general conception than this since it is not confined to dyadic relations – i.e. relations between two terms. Relations between three or between four terms are important in geometry, and Whitehead was to have dealt with them in the fourth volume of the *Principia*, but, after he had done a lot of the preliminary work, his interest flagged and he abandoned the enterprise for philosophy. It is, however, fairly easy to see how the conception of structure can be generalised. Suppose that P and Q are no longer dyadic but triadic relations. There are many familiar examples of such relations, for example, *between* and *jealousy*. We shall say of P and Q that they have the same structure if their fields can be correlated so that whenever $x\ y\ z$, in that order, have the relation P, their correlates, in the same order, have the relation Q, and vice versa. Structure is important for empirical reasons, but there are also purely logical reasons for its importance. When two relations have the same structure, their logical properties are identical, except such as depend upon the membership of their fields. I mean by 'logical properties', properties such as can be *expressed* in logical terms, not only such as can be *proved* by logic. Take, for example, the three characteristics by which serial relations are defined – viz. that they are asymmetrical, transitive and connected. These characteristics can be expressed in logical terms; and if a relation has any one of them, so has every relation which is ordinally similar to it. Each relation-number, whether finite or infinite, is a logical property of any relation which has this number. Broadly speaking, anything that you can say about a relation, without mentioning the terms between which it holds and without bringing in any property that cannot be expressed in logical terms, will be equally true of any relation similar to the one with which you start. The distinction between logical and other properties is important. For example, if P is a relation among colours – such, for example, as their order in the rainbow – the property of being a relation between colours will not belong to all relations ordinally similar to P; but the property of being serial, will. To take a more complex illustration: a gramophone record and the music that it plays are indistinguishable as regards their logical properties although the empirical material of which they are composed is very different in the two cases.

Another illustration may help to elucidate the notion of structure. Let us suppose that in a certain language you know the rules of syntax but none of the words except those belonging to logic, and suppose you are offered a sentence in this language: what are the different meanings that it may have? and what have they all in common? You may give to the separate words any meaning that makes the whole sentence significant – i.e. not logically nonsense. There will thus be a very great many, probably an infinite number, of possible meanings for your sentence, but all of them will have the same logical structure. If your language fulfils certain logical requirements, there will be a corresponding identity of structure among the facts that make some of your sentences true.

I think relation-arithmetic important, not only as an interesting generalisation, but because it supplies a symbolic technique required for dealing with structure. It has seemed to me that those who are not familiar with mathematical logic find great difficulty in understanding what is meant by 'structure', and, owing to this difficulty, are apt to go astray in attempting to understand the empirical world. For this reason, if for no other, I am sorry that the theory of relation-arithmetic has been largely unnoticed.

That it was not wholly unnoticed I learnt, to my surprise, through a letter, received in 1956, from Professor Jürgen Schmidt of the Humboldt University in Berlin. Some parts of the theory, as he informed me, were used in what is called the 'lexicographical problem', which consists in defining alphabetical order among words in a language of which the alphabet is infinite.

Chapter 9

The External World

Shortly after the writing of *Principia Mathematica* was finished, and while the book was still printing, I was invited by Gilbert Murray to write a little book for The Home University Library setting out in popular terms a general outline of my philosophy. This invitation came at a fortunate moment. I was glad to escape from the rigours of symbolic deductive reasoning, and my opinions at that moment had a clear-cut definiteness which they did not have earlier or later and which made them easy to expound in a simple manner. The book had a great success and still sells widely. I think that most philosophers still regard it as an adequate exposition of my opinions.

I find, on re-reading, that there is a great deal in it which I still believe in. I still agree that 'knowledge' is not a precise conception, but merges into 'probable opinion'. I still agree that self-evidence has degrees and that it is possible to know a general proposition without knowing any single instance of its truth – e.g. 'all the pairs of numbers that have never been multiplied together have products greater than 1,000'. But there are other matters on which my views have undergone important changes. I no longer think that the laws of logic are laws of things; on the contrary, I now regard them as purely linguistic. I no longer think of points, instants, and particles as part of the raw material of the world. What I said about induction in this little book now seems to me very crude. I spoke about universals and our knowledge of them with a confident assurance which I no longer feel, though I have not any new opinions on the subject which I feel prepared to advocate with equal confidence.

As regards points, instants, and particles, I was awakened from my 'dogmatic slumbers' by Whitehead. Whitehead invented a method of constructing points, instants, and particles as sets of events, each of finite extent. This made it possible to use Occam's razor in physics in the same sort of way in which we had used it in arithmetic. I was delighted with this fresh application of the methods of mathematical logic. It seemed to suggest that all the smoothness of the concepts used in theoretical physics could be attributed to the ingenuity of mathematicians rather than to the nature of the world. It seemed, also, to open an entirely new vista on the problems of perception. Having been invited to deliver the Lowell Lectures in Boston in the spring of

1914, I chose as my subject 'Our Knowledge of the External World' and, in connection with this problem, I set to work to utilise White-head's novel apparatus.

The problem of perception as the source of our physical knowledge seemed to me very perplexing. When two people look at a given object there are differences between what they see owing to perspective and the way the light falls. There is no reason to single out one per-cipient as seeing the thing as it is. We cannot, therefore, suppose that the physical thing is what anybody sees. To the physicist this is a commonplace: we do not see atoms and molecules, which, the physicist assures us, are the constituents of physical objects. The physiologist is equally discouraging. He makes it clear that there is an elaborate causal chain from the eye to the brain and that what you see depends upon what happens in the brain. If the same state of brain can be produced by other than the usual causes, you may have a visual sensation not connected in the usual way with a physical object. This sort of thing is not specially concerned with the sense of sight. It is illustrated by the familiar example of the man who feels pain in his great toe although his leg has been amputated. Such arguments make it clear that what we directly experience cannot be the external object with which physics deals, and yet it is only what we directly experience that gives us reason to believe in the world of physics.

There are various ways in which we may attempt to tackle this problem. The simplest is that of solipsism. I am thinking of solipsism as a hypothesis and not a dogma. That is to say, I am considering the doctrine that there is no valid reason either to assert or to deny any-thing except my own experiences. I do not think this theory can be refuted, but I also do not think that anybody can sincerely believe it.

There are some who hold that it is reasonable to accept experiences, whether one's own or other people's, but that it is not reasonable to believe in events which no one experiences. This theory accepts testimony from other people but refuses to believe in lifeless matter.

Lastly, there is the full-fledged theory in which the naïve realist and the physicist are agreed, according to which some things are alive and are sets of experiences and others are lifeless.

The second and third of these theories demand inferences from what I experience to something which I do not experience. Such inferences cannot be logically demonstrative and can only be validated by accept-ing principles which lie outside deductive logic. In the *Problems of Philosophy* and in all my previous thinking, I had accepted matter as it appears in physics. But this left an uncomfortable gulf between physics and perception, or, in other language, between mind and matter. In my first enthusiasm on abandoning the 'matter' of the physicist, I hoped to be able to exhibit the hypothetical entities that a given percipient does not perceive as structures composed entirely of elements that he does perceive. This was suggested as a possibility in my first exposition of the theory that I advanced in the Lowell Lectures. This first exposition was in a paper called 'The Relation of Sense-Data to Physics', published in *Scientia* in 1914. In this paper I said: 'If physics is to be verifiable we are faced with the following problem: Physics exhibits sense-data as functions of physical objects, but verification is only possible if physical objects can be exhibited as functions of sense-data. We have therefore to solve the equations giving sense-data in terms of physical objects, so as to make them instead give physical objects in terms of sense-data.' I soon, however, became persuaded that this is an impossible programme and that physical objects cannot be interpreted as structures composed of elements actually experienced. In this same paper, in a later passage, I explain that I allow myself two sorts of inferences: (*a*) the sense-data of other people and, (*b*), what I call 'sensibilia', which I suppose to be the appearances that things present in places where there are no minds to perceive them. I go on to say that I should like to be able to dispense with these two kinds of inferences 'and thus establish physics upon a solipsistic basis; but those – and I fear they are the majority – in whom the human affections are stronger than the desire for logical economy, will, no doubt, not share my desire to render solipsism scientifically satisfactory'. Accordingly, I gave up the attempt to construct 'matter' out of experienced data alone, and contented myself with a picture of the world which fitted physics and perception harmoniously into a single whole.

There were several novelties in the theory as to our knowledge of the external world which burst upon me on New Year's Day, 1914. The most important of these was the theory that space has six dimensions and not only three. I came to the conclusion that what, in the space of physics, counts as a point, or, more exactly, as a 'minimal region', is really a three-dimensional complex of which the total of one man's percepts is an instance. Various considerations led me to this view. Perhaps the most cogent is that instruments can be constructed which, at places where there are no living percipients, will make records of the sort of things that a man might perceive if he were at those places. A photographic plate can produce a picture of any selected portion of the starry heavens. A dictaphone can take down what people say in its neighbourhood. There is no theoretical limit to what can be done in this way to make mechanical records analogous to what a person would perceive if he were similarly situated. The case of photographing the starry heavens is perhaps the best for illustrating what is involved. Any star can be photographed at any place from which it would be visible if a human eye were there. It follows that, at the place where a photographic plate is put, things are happening which are connected with all the different stars that can be photographed there. It follows that in one tiny region of physical space there is at every moment a vast multiplicity of occurrences corresponding to all the things that could be seen there by a person or recorded by an instrument. These things, moreover, have spatial relations to each other which correspond more or less accurately with the correlated objects in physical space. The whole complex world that appears in a photograph of stars is at the place where the photograph is taken and, likewise, the whole complex world of my percepts is where I am – speaking, in each case, from the standpoint of physics. According to this theory, when I see a star, three places are involved: two in physical space and one in my private space. There is the place where the star is in physical space; there is the place where I am in physical space; and there is the place where my percept of the star is among my other percepts.

There are, in this theory, two ways of collecting events into bundles. On the one hand, you may make a bundle of all the events which can be considered as appearances of one 'thing'. Suppose, for example, that the thing concerned is the sun. You have, to begin with, all the visual percepts of the people who are seeing the sun. Next, you have all the photographs of the sun that are being taken by astronomers. And lastly, you have all those occurrences at various places in virtue of which it would be possible to see or photograph the sun at those places. The whole of this bundle of events is causally connected with the sun of physics. The events proceed outward with the velocity of light from the place in physical space where the sun is. As they proceed outward from the sun, their character changes in two ways. There is first what may be called a 'regular' way, which consists of a diminution of size and intensity in accordance with the inverse square law. To a fairly close degree of approximation, this kind of change is alone operative in empty space. But the aspects presented by the sun in places where there is matter change in ways which depend upon the nature of the matter. Mist will make the sun look red, thin clouds will make it look dim, completely opaque matter will make it cease to present any appearance at all. (When I speak of 'appearance', I am not thinking only of what people see, but also of occurrences connected with the sun in places where there is no percipient.) When the intervening medium contains an eye and an optic nerve, the resulting appearance of the sun is what somebody actually sees.

The appearances of a given object from different places, so long as they are 'regular', are connected by the laws of perspective when they are visual and by not wholly dissimilar laws when they are such as would be revealed by other senses.

There is, as I remarked above, another way of collecting events into bundles. In this way, instead of collecting all the events which are appearances of one thing, we collect all the events which are appearances at one physical place. The whole of the events at one physical place, I call a 'perspective'. The total of my percepts at a given time constitutes one perspective. So does the total of all the events that instruments could record at a given place. In our previous way of making bundles, we had a bundle consisting of many appearances of the sun. But, in this second way, one bundle contains only one appearance of the sun associated with one appearance of each 'thing' that is perceptible from that place. It is this second way of making bundles that is especially appropriate in psychology. One perspective, when it happens to be in a brain, will consist of all the momentary percepts of the man whose brain is concerned. All these, from the standpoint of physics, are in one place, but, within the perspective concerned, there are spatial relations in virtue of which what was for physics one place becomes a three-dimensional complex.

All the puzzles about the differences between different people's perceptions of one thing, and about the causal relation between a physical thing and its appearances at different places, and, finally (perhaps most important of all), between mind and matter, are cleared away by this theory. The puzzles have all been caused by failure to distinguish the three places associated with any given percept which are (I repeat): (1) the place in physical space where the 'thing' is; (2) the place in physical space where I am; (3) the place in my perspective which my percept occupies in relation to other percepts.

I did not offer the above theory as the only theory which would explain the facts, or as necessarily true. I offered it as a theory which is consistent with all the known facts and as, so far, the only theory of which this can be said. In this respect it is on the same level as, for example, Einstein's General Theory of Relativity. All such theories go beyond what the facts prove and are acceptable, at least *pro tem.*, if they solve puzzles and are not at any point incompatible with known facts. This is what I claim for the above theory, and it is as much as any general scientific theory ought to claim.

Whitehead's method of constructing points as classes of events was a great help to me in arriving at the above theory. I think, however, that it is doubtful whether events do, in fact, lend themselves to the construction of anything having quite the characteristics that we expect of a geometrical point. Whitehead assumed that every event is of finite extent, but that there is no minimum to the extent of an event. I found a way of constructing a point out of classes of events none of which is smaller than an assigned minimum; but both his method and mine will only work on certain assumptions. Without these assumptions, although one can arrive at very small regions, one may be unable to arrive at points. It is for this reason that in the above account I have spoken of 'minimal regions' rather than points. I do not think that this makes any important difference.

Chapter 10

The Impact of Wittgenstein

Principia Mathematica had at first a somewhat unfavourable reception. Mathematical philosophy on the Continent was divided between two schools, the Formalists and the Intuitionists, both of whom rejected totally the derivation of mathematics from logic and took advantage of the contradictions to justify their rejection.

The Formalists, led by Hilbert, maintain that arithmetical symbols are merely marks on paper, devoid of meaning, and that arithmetic consists of certain arbitrary rules, like the rules of chess, by which these marks can be manipulated. This theory had the advantage of avoiding all philosophical controversy, but it had the disadvantage of failing to explain the application of numbers in counting. All the rules of manipulation given by the Formalists are verified if the symbol o is taken to mean one hundred or one thousand or any other finite number. The theory is unable to explain what is meant by simple statements such as 'there are three men in this room' or 'there were twelve apostles'. The theory is perfectly adequate for doing sums, but not for the applications of number. Since it is the applications of number that make it important, the Formalists' theory must be regarded as an unsatisfactory evasion.

The Intuitionists' theory, led by Brouwer, demands more serious discussion. The nerve of this theory is the denial of the law of excluded middle. It holds that a proposition can only be accounted true or false when there is some method of ascertaining which of these it is. One of the stock examples is the proposition 'there are three successsive sevens in the decimal determination of π'. So far as the value of π has been worked out there are not three successive sevens, but there is no reason to suppose that these might not occur at a later point. If it should hereafter appear that there is a point where three successive sevens occur, that would decide the matter, but, if no such point is reached, that does not prove that there may not be such a point later on. Therefore, although we might succeed in proving that there *are* three successive sevens, we can never prove that there are not. The matter has great importance in connection with analysis. Decimals which do not terminate sometimes proceed according to a law which enables us to calculate as many terms as we choose. But sometimes (so we must suppose) they do not proceed according to any law. On the generally accepted principles, this latter case is infinitely commoner than the former, and, unless such 'lawless' decimals are admitted, the whole theory of real numbers collapses and, with it, the infinitesimal calculus and almost the whole of higher mathematics. Brouwer faced this disaster unflinchingly, but most mathematicians found it unbearable.

The issue is much more general than it appears in the above mathematical examples. The issue is: 'Is there any sense in saying that a proposition is either true or false when there is no way of deciding the alternative?' or, to put the matter in a different form, 'Should "true" be identified with "verifiable"?' I do not think we can make such an identification unless we commit ourselves to gross and gratuitous paradoxes. Take such a proposition as the following: 'It snowed on Manhattan Island on the 1st January in the year 1 A.D.'. There is no conceivable method by which we can discover whether this proposition is true or false, but it seems preposterous to maintain that it is neither. I will not now pursue this matter further, as I discussed it in detail in Chapters XX and XXI of the *Inquiry into Meaning and Truth* to which I shall return in a later chapter. Meantime, I shall assume that the Intuitionists' theory is to be rejected.

Both the Intuitionists and the Formalists attacked the doctrines of *Principia Mathematica* from without, and it did not seem very difficult to repel their attacks. It was another matter with the criticisms of Wittgenstein and his school, which were attacks from within and deserving of all respect.

Wittgenstein's doctrines influenced me profoundly. I have come to think that on many points I went too far in agreeing with him, but I must first explain what were the points at issue.

Wittgenstein's impact upon me came in two waves: the first of these was before the First World War; the second was immediately after the War when he sent me the manuscript of his *Tractatus*. His later doctrines, as they appear in his *Philosophical Investigations*, have not influenced me at all.

At the beginning of 1914, Wittgenstein gave me a short typescript consisting of notes on various logical points. This, together with a large number of conversations, affected my thinking during the war years while he was in the Austrian army and I was, therefore, cut off from all contact with him. What I knew of his doctrines at this time was derived entirely from unpublished sources. I do not feel sure that, either then or later, the views which I believed myself to have derived from him were in fact his views. He always vehemently repudiated expositions of his doctrines by others, even when those others were ardent disciples. The only exception that I know of was F. P. Ramsey, whom I will consider presently.

At the beginning of 1918, I gave a course of lectures in London which were subsequently printed in *The Monist* (1918 and 1919). I prefaced these lectures by the following acknowledgement of my indebtedness to Wittgenstein: 'The following articles are the first two lectures of a course of eight lectures delivered in London in the first months of 1918, and are very largely concerned with explaining certain ideas which I learnt from my friend and former pupil Ludwig Wittgenstein. I have had no opportunity of knowing his views since August 1914, and I do not even know whether he is alive or dead. He has therefore no responsibility for what is said in these lectures beyond that of having originally supplied many of the theories contained in them. The six other lectures will appear in the three following numbers of *The Monist*.'

It was in these lectures that I first adopted the name 'Logical Atomism' to describe my philosophy. But it is not worth while to linger upon this phase, since Wittgenstein's doctrines in 1914 were in an immature stage. What was important was the *Tractatus*, of which Wittgenstein sent me the typescript very soon after the Armistice, while he was still a prisoner at Monte Cassino. I shall consider the doctrines of the *Tractatus*, first as they affected me at the time, and then as I have since come to think of them.

Perhaps the basic doctrine in the philosophy of the *Tractatus* is that a proposition is a picture of the facts which it asserts. A map clearly conveys information, correct or incorrect; and when the information is correct, this is because there is a similarity of structure between the map and the region concerned. Wittgenstein held that the same is true of the linguistic assertions of a fact. He said, for example, that, if you use the symbol '*aRb*' to represent the fact that *a* has the relation R to *b*, your symbol is able to do so because it establishes a relation between '*a*' and '*b*' which represents the relation between *a* and *b*. This doctrine went with an emphasis upon the importance of structure. He says, for example, 'The gramophone record, the musical thought, the score, the waves of sound, all stand to one another in that pictorial internal relation, which holds between language and the world. To all of them the logical structure is common.'

'(Like the two youths, their two horses and their lilies in the story. They are all in a certain sense one.)' (*Tractatus* 4.014.)

In emphasising the importance of structure, I still think he was right, but as to the doctrine that a true proposition must reproduce the structure of the facts concerned, I now feel very doubtful, although at the time I accepted it. In any case, I do not think that, even if it be in some sense true, it has any great importance. For Wittgenstein, however, it was fundamental. He made it the basis of a curious kind of logical mysticism. He maintained that the *form* which a true proposition shares with the corresponding fact can only be shown, not said, since it is not another word in the language but an arrangement of words or corresponding things: 'Propositions can represent the whole reality, but they cannot represent what they must have in common with reality in order to be able to represent it – the logical form.

'To be able to represent the logical form, we should have to be able to put ourselves with the propositions outside logic, that is outside the world.' (*Tractatus*, 4.12.) This raises the only point on which, at the time when I most nearly agreed with Wittgenstein, I still remained unconvinced. In my introduction to the *Tractatus*, I suggested that, although in any given language there are things which that language cannot express, it is yet always possible to construct a language of higher order in which these things can be said. There will, in the new language, still be things which it cannot say, but which can be said in the next language, and so on *ad infinitum*. This suggestion, which was then new, has now become an accepted commonplace of logic. It disposes of Wittgenstein's mysticism and, I think, also of the newer puzzles presented by Gödel.

I come next to what Wittgenstein had to say about identity, which has an importance that may not be obvious at once. To explain this theory, I must first say something about the definition of identity in *Principia Mathematica*. Among the properties that an object may have, Whitehead and I distinguished some as what we called 'predicative'. These were properties which did not refer to any totality of properties. You may say, for instance, 'Napoleon was Corsican' or 'Napoleon was fat', and, in saying such things, you do not refer to any assemblage of properties. But if you say 'Napoleon had all the qualities of a great general' or 'Queen Elizabeth I had all the virtues of her father and grandfather and the vices of neither' you are referring to a totality of qualities. Properties that in this way refer to a totality we distinguished from predicative functions in order to avoid certain contradictions. We defined 'x is identical with y' as meaning 'y has all the predicative properties of x', and, in our system, it followed that y had any property that x had, whether predicative or not. To this, Wittgenstein objected as follows: 'Russell's definition of " $=$ " won't do; because according to it one cannot say that two objects have all their properties in common. (Even if this proposition is never true, it is nevertheless *significant*.)

'Roughly speaking: to say of *two* things that they are identical is nonsense, and to say of *one* thing that it is identical with itself is to say nothing' (*Tractatus*, 5.5302 and 5.5303). At one time I accepted this criticism, but I soon came to the conclusion that it made mathematical logic impossible and, in fact, that Wittgenstein's criticism is invalid. This appears especially if we consider counting: if a and b have all their properties in common, you can never mention a without mentioning *b* or count *a* without at the same time counting *b*, not as a separate item but in the same act of counting. You could, therefore, never conceivably discover that *a* and *b* were two. Wittgenstein's position assumes that diversity is an indefinable relation, although I do not think that he knew he was making this assumption. But if he is not making it, I do not see on what grounds he can say, as he does, that it is significant, to say that two objects have all their properties in common. If, however, diversity is admitted, then, if *a* and *b* are two, *a* has a property which *b* has not, namely, that of being diverse from *b*. I think, therefore, that Wittgenstein's contention as to identity is mistaken. And, if so, it invalidates a large part of his system.

Take, for example, the definition of the number 2. We say that a class has two members if it has members *x* and *y* and *x* is not identical with *y*, and, if *z* is a member of the class, then *z* is identical with either *x* or *y*. It is very difficult to adapt this definition to Wittgenstein's convention which requires that we should never use an expression of the form '$x = y$' or '$x \neq y$', but that we should use different letters to represent different things and never use two different letters to represent the same thing. Apart from such technical difficulties, it is obvious, for the reason mentioned above, that, if two things have all their properties in common, they cannot be *counted* as two, since this involves distinguishing them and thereby conferring different properties upon them.

There is a further consequence, namely, that we cannot manufacture an intension which shall be common and peculiar to a given set of enumerated objects. Suppose, for example, we have three objects, *a*, *b*, *c*, then the property of being identical with *a* or identical with *b* or identical with *c* is one which is common and peculiar to these three objects. But, in Wittgenstein's system, this method is not available.

There is another point of very considerable importance, and that is that Wittgenstein will not permit any statement about all the things in the world. In *Principia Mathematica*, the totality of things is defined as the class of all those *x*'s which are such that $x = x$, and we can assign a number to this class just as to any other class, although of course we do not know what is the right number to assign. Wittgenstein will not admit this. He says that such a proposition as 'there are more than three things in the world' is meaningless. When I was discussing the *Tractatus* with him at The Hague in 1919, I had before me a sheet of white paper and I made on it three blobs of ink. I besought him to admit that, since there were these three blobs, there must be at least three things in the world; but he refused, resolutely. He would admit that there were three blobs on the page, because that was a finite assertion, but he would not admit that anything at all could be said about the world as a whole. This was connected with his mysticism, but was justified by his refusal to admit identity.

Another respect in which the same kind of question was relevant was as to what I had called 'the axiom of infinity'. In a world containing only a finite number of things, that number would be the greatest possible for a collection of things. In such a world, all higher mathematics would collapse. It seemed to me to be a purely empirical question how many things there are in the world, and I did not think that the logician, as such, ought to permit himself an opinion on the subject. I therefore treated all those parts of mathematics which require an infinite number of things as hypothetical. All this outraged Wittgenstein. According to him, you could ask 'How many people are there in London ?' or 'How many molecules are there in the sun ?' but to infer that there are at least that number of things in the world was, according to him, meaningless. This part of his doctrine is to my mind definitely mistaken.

Wittgenstein announced two general principles which, if true, are very important. They are the principle of extensionality and the principle of atomicity.

The principle of extensionality says that the truth or falsehood of any statement about a proposition p depends only upon the truth or falsehood of p and that the truth or falsehood of any statement involving a propositional function depends only upon the extension of the function – that is to say, upon the range of values for which the propositional function is true. On the face of it, there are obvious arguments against this thesis. Take, for instance. 'A believes p'. It is obvious that a man may believe some true propositions but not others, so that the truth of 'A believes p' does not depend only upon the truth or falsehood of p. Wittgenstein has a very cryptic passage on this subject. He says, 'In the general propositional form, propositions occur in a proposition only as bases of the truth-operations.

'At first sight it appears as if there were also a different way in which one proposition could occur in another.

'Especially in certain propositional forms of psychology, like "A thinks, that p is the case", or "A thinks p", etc.

'Here it appears superficially as if the proposition p stood to the object A in a kind of relation.

'[And in modern epistemology (Russell, Moore, etc.) those propositions have been conceived in this way.]

'But it is clear that "A believes that p", "A thinks p", "A says p", are of the form "'p' says p"; and here we have no co-ordination of a fact and an object, but a co-ordination of facts by means of a co-ordination of their objects.

'This shows that there is no such thing as the soul – the subject, etc. – as it is conceived in contemporary superficial psychology' (*Tractatus*, 5.54ff.).

Wittgenstein's argument is that 'A believes p' is not a function of

p, but of the words in which A expresses the proposition p or the bodily state, whatever it be, which constitutes his believing. He, himself, as usual, is oracular and emits his opinion as if it were a Czar's ukase, but humbler folk can hardly content themselves with this procedure. I have examined the problem at length in *An Inquiry into Meaning and Truth* (pages 267ff.), but the conclusion at which I arrived is somewhat hesitant.

The principle of atomicity is stated by Wittgenstein in the following terms: 'Every statement about complexes can be analysed into a statement about their constituent parts, and into those propositions which completely describe the complexes' (*Tractatus*, 2.0201). This principle may be taken as embodying the belief in analysis. At the time when Wittgenstein wrote the *Tractatus* he believed (what, I understand, he came later to disbelieve) that the world consists of a number of simples with various properties and relations. The simple properties and simple relations of simples are 'atomic facts' and the assertions of them are 'atomic propositions'. The gist of the principle is that, if you knew all atomic facts and also knew that they were all, you would be in a position to infer all other true propositions by logic alone. The most important difficulties that arise in connection with this principle are, again, concerned with such propositions as 'A believes p', for here p is complex and enters *as* a complex. Such propositions are characterised by the fact that they contain two verbs, one principal and the other subordinate. Let us take a very simple example, say: 'A believes that B is hot.' Here 'believes' is the principal verb and 'is' is the subordinate verb. The principle of atomicity would require us to find a way of expressing the fact without introducing the subordinate complex 'B is hot'. This principle, also, I discussed at length in the *Inquiry* (pages 262ff.).

The conclusion that I reached in regard to both principles was as follows: '(1) that the principle of extensionality is not shown to be false, when strictly interpreted, by the analysis of such sentences as "A believes p"; (2) that this same analysis does not prove the principle of atomicity to be false, but does not suffice to prove it true' (*Inquiry*, page 273).

The more usual criticism of both Wittgenstein's principles is that there is no reason to believe in simples or in atomic facts. I understand that he himself came to think so later on. But to discuss this question would take us too far from the *Tractatus*. I shall return to it in a later chapter.

Wittgenstein maintains that logic consists wholly of tautologies. I think he is right in this, although I did not think so until I read what he had to say on the subject. There is another point connected with this which is very important, and that is that all atomic propositions are mutually independent. It used to be thought that one fact could be logically dependent upon another. This can only be the case if one of the facts is really two facts put together. From 'A and B are men' it follows logically that A is a man, but that is because 'A and B are men' is really two propositions put together. The consequence of the principle we are considering is that any selection of the atomic facts which are true in the actual world, might be the total of atomic facts so far as logic can show, but, as is obvious, the principle of atomicity is essential in this connection, and, if it is not true, we cannot be sure that the simplest obtainable facts may not be sometimes logically connected.

In the second edition of *Principia Mathematica* (1925), I took account of some of Wittgenstein's doctrines. I adopted the principle of extensionality in a new Introduction and considered the obvious objections to it in Appendix C, deciding, on the whole, that they are invalid. My chief purpose in this new edition was to minimise the uses of the 'axiom of reducibility'. This axiom, which I shall explain in a moment, seemed necessary if we are, on the one hand, to avoid contradictions and, on the other hand, to preserve all of mathematics that is usually considered indisputable. But it was an objectionable axiom because its truth might be doubted and because (what is more important) its truth, if it is true, seems to be empirical and not logical. Whitehead and I recognised that the axiom was a blot upon our system, but I at least thought of it on the analogy of the axiom of parallels, which had been considered a blot upon Euclid's geometry. I thought that some way of dispensing with the axiom would be found sooner or later, and that meantime it was a good thing to have the difficulties concentrated in one single point. In the second edition of the *Principia*, I succeeded in dispensing with the axiom in a number of cases in which it had formerly seemed indispensable, and, more particularly, in all uses of mathematical induction.

I must now try to explain what the axiom asserts and why it seemed necessary. I have explained earlier the difference between properties which refer to some totality of properties and properties which do not. Properties which refer to a totality of properties are apt to be a source of trouble. Suppose, for example, you were to suggest the definition, 'a typical Englishman is one who possesses all the properties possessed by a majority of Englishmen'. You will easily realise that most Englishmen do not possess *all* the properties that most Englishmen possess, and therefore a typical Englishman, according to your own definition, would be untypical. The trouble has arisen through the fact that the word 'typical' has been defined by a reference to all properties and has then been treated as itself a property. It seemed therefore that, if it is to be legitimate to speak of 'all properties', you must not really mean 'all properties', but only 'all properties that do not refer to a totality of properties'. Such properties, as I explained earlier, we defined as 'predicative'. The axiom of reducibility asserted that a property which is not predicative is always formally equivalent to some predicative property. (Two properties are formally equivalent when they belong to the same set of objects, or, to state the matter more exactly, when their truth-values are the same for every argument.)

In the first edition of the *Principia* we set out the reasons for accepting the axiom as follows: 'That the axiom of reducibility is self-evident is a proposition which can hardly be maintained. But in fact self-evidence is never more than a part of the reason for accepting an axiom, and is never indispensable. The reason for accepting an axiom, as for accepting any other proposition, is always largely inductive, namely that many propositions which are nearly indubitable can be deduced from it, and that no equally plausible way is known by which these propositions could be true if the axiom were false, and nothing which is probably false can be deduced from it. If the axiom is apparently self-evident, that only means, practically, that it is nearly indubitable; for things have been thought to be self-evident and have yet turned out to be false. And if the axiom itself is nearly undubitable, that merely adds to the inductive evidence derived from the fact that its consequences are nearly indubitable; it does not provide new evidence of a radically different kind. Infallibility is never attainable, and therefore some element of doubt should always attach to every axiom and to all its consequences. In formal logic, the element of doubt is less than in most sciences, but it is not absent, as appears from the fact that the paradoxes followed from premisses which were not previously known to require limitations. In the case of the axiom of reducibility, the inductive evidence in its favour is very strong, since the reasonings which it permits and the results to which it leads are all such as appear valid. But although it seems very improbable that the axiom should turn out to be false, it is by no means improbable that it should be found to be deducible from some other more fundamental and more evident axiom. It is possible that the use of the vicious-circle principle, as embodied in the above hierarchy of types, is more drastic than it need be, and that by a less drastic use the necessity for the axiom might be avoided. Such changes, however, would not render anything false which had been asserted on the basis of the principles explained above: they would merely provide easier proofs of the same theorems. There would seem, therefore, to be but the slenderest ground for fearing that the use of the axiom of reducibility may lead us into error' (Introduction, Chapter II, Section VII).

In the second edition, we say: 'One point in regard to which improvement is obviously desirable is the axiom of reducibility. This axiom has a purely pragmatic justification: it leads to the desired results, and to no others. But clearly it is not the sort of axiom with which we can rest content. On this subject, however, it cannot be said that a satisfactory solution is as yet obtainable. Dr Leon Chwistek took the heroic course of dispensing with the axiom without adopting any substitute; from his work it is clear that this course compels us to sacrifice a great deal of ordinary mathematics. There is another course, recommended by Wittgenstein for philosophical reasons. This is to assume that functions of propositions are always truth-functions, and that a function can only occur in a proposition through its values. There are difficulties in the way of this view, but perhaps they are not insurmountable. It involves the consequence that all functions of functions are extensional. It requires us to maintain that "A believes p" is not a function of p. How this is possible is shown in *Tractatus Logico-Philosophicus* (*loc. cit.* and pages 19–21). We are not prepared to assert that this theory is certainly right, but it has seemed worth while to work out its consequences in the following pages. It appears that everything in Vol. I remains true (though often new proofs are required); the theory of inductive cardinals and ordinals survives; but it seems that the theory of infinite Dedekindian and well-ordered series largely collapses, so that irrationals, and real numbers generally, can no longer be adequately dealt with. Also Cantor's proof that $2^n > n$ breaks down unless n is finite. Perhaps some further axiom, less objectionable than the axiom of reducibility, might give these results, but we have not succeeded in finding such an axiom' (Introduction, page XIV).

Shortly after the second edition of the *Principia* was published, the problem of the axiom of reducibility was taken up by F. P. Ramsey in two very important papers: *The Foundations of Mathematics*, published in 1925, and *Mathematical Logic*, published in 1926. Ramsey's early death, unfortunately, prevented a full and complete development of his views, but what he had achieved was very important and deserves most serious consideration. His main thesis was that mathematics must be rendered purely extensional and that the troubles of the *Principia* arose from an illegitimate intrusion of an intensional point of view. Whitehead and I had held that a class can only be defined by means of a propositional function and that this applies even to classes that seem to be defined by enumeration. For example, the class consisting of the three individuals a, b, and c is defined by the propositional function '$x = a$ or $x = b$ or $x = c$'. Wittgenstein's rejection of identity (which Ramsey accepted) made this method impossible, but, on the other hand, Ramsey considered that there is no *logical* objection to the definition of an infinite class by enumeration. *We* cannot define an infinite class in this way because we are mortal, but our mortality is an empirical fact which logicians should ignore. On this ground, he held, the multiplicative axiom is a tautology. To revert, for example, to the millionaire who had an infinite number of pairs of socks, Ramsey held that it was not necessary to have a *rule* by which to pick one sock out of each pair. He thought that so far as logic is concerned an infinite number of arbitrary choices is just as allowable as a finite number.

He applied a similar point of view in changing the conception of a propositional function. Whitehead and I thought of a propositional function as an expression containing an undetermined variable and becoming an ordinary sentence as soon as a value is assigned to the variable: '*x* is human', for example, becomes an ordinary sentence as soon as we substitute a proper name for '*x*'. In this view of propositional functions, they are constituted by intensions except as regards the variable or variables. The words 'is human' form part of a number of ordinary sentences, and the propositional function is a method of making a bundle of such sentences. The values of the function are determinate for the several values of the variable in virtue of the intrinsic character of the phrase. Ramsey conceived of propositional functions quite differently. He thought of them as merely a means of correlating propositions with values of variables. He says, 'in addition to the previously defined concept of a predicative function, which we shall still require for certain purposes, we define, or rather explain, for in our system it must be taken as indefinable, the new concept of a propositional function in extension. Such a function of one individual results from any one-many relation in extension between propositions and individuals; that is to say, a correlation, practicable or impracticable, which to every individual associates a unique proposition, the individual being the argument to the function, the proposition its value.

Thus ϕ (Socrates) may be Queen Anne is dead,

ϕ (Plato) may be Einstein is a great man;

$\phi\hat{x}$ being simply an arbitrary association of propositions ϕx to individuals x'' (*Foundations of Mathematics*, page 52).

By using this new explanation of the concept 'propositional function', he is able to dispense with the axiom of reducibility and is also able to define '$x = y$' in what is symbolically indistinguishable from the definition in the *Principia*, though it now has a new interpretation. In this way he succeeds in preserving the symbolic parts of *Principia Mathematica* almost unchanged. He says concerning this symbolic part, 'Formally it is almost unaltered; but its meaning has been considerably changed. And in thus preserving the form while modifying the interpretation, I am following the great school of mathematical logicians who, in virtue of a series of startling definitions, have saved mathematics from the sceptics, and provided a rigid demonstration of its propositions. Only so can we preserve it from the Bolshevik menace of Brouwer and Weyl' (*Foundations of Mathematics*, page 56).

I find it very difficult to make up my mind as to the validity of Ramsey's new interpretation of the concept 'propositional function'. I feel that a correlation of entities to propositions which is wholly arbitrary is unsatisfactory. Take, for example, the inference from 'fx is true for all values of *x*' to '*fa*'. With Ramsey's explanation of the concept '*fx*' we cannot tell what '*fa*' may be. On the contrary, before we can know what '*fx*' means, we have to know '*fa*' and '*fb*' and '*fc*' and so on, throughout the whole universe. General propositions thus lose their *raison d'être* since what they assert can only be set forth by enumeration of all the separate cases. Whatever may be thought of this objection, Ramsey's suggestion is certainly ingenious, and, if not a complete solution of the difficulties, is probably on the right lines. Ramsey himself had doubts. He said, 'Although my attempted reconstruction of the view of Whitehead and Russell overcomes, I think, many of the difficulties, it is impossible to regard it as altogether satisfactory' (*Mathematical Logic*, page 81).

There is another matter on which Ramsey's work should, I think, be accepted as definitely right. I had enumerated various contradictions, one class of which is exemplified by the man who says 'I am lying', while the other class is illustrated by the problem as to whether there is a greatest cardinal number. Ramsey showed that the former class has to do with the relation of a word or phrase to its meaning and results from a confusion of these two. When this confusion is avoided, contradictions of this class disappear. The other class of contradictions, Ramsey holds, can only be solved by means of the doctrine of types. In the *Principia* there were two different kinds of hierarchies of types. There was the extensional hierarchy: individuals, classes of individuals, classes of classes of individuals, and so on. This hierarchy Ramsey retains. But there was also another hierarchy, and it was this other that necessitated the axiom of reducibility. This was the hierarchy of functions of a given argument or properties of a given object. There were first predicative functions, which did not refer to any totality of functions; next, there were functions referring to the totality of predicative functions such as, 'Napoleon had all the qualities of a great general'. These we might call 'first order functions'. Then there were functions referring to the totality of first order functions, and so on, *ad infinitum*. Ramsey abolishes this hierarchy by means of his new interpretation of the concept 'propositional function', and is thus left with only the extensional hierarchy. I hope his theories are valid.

Although he writes as a disciple of Wittgenstein and follows him in everything except mysticism, the way in which he approaches problems is extraordinarily different. Wittgenstein announces aphorisms and leaves the reader to estimate their profundity as best he may. Some of his aphorisms, taken literally, are scarcely compatible with the existence of symbolic logic. Ramsey, on the contrary, is careful, even when he follows Wittgenstein most closely, to show how whatever doctrine is concerned can be fitted into the corpus of mathematical logic.

There is a large and very abstruse literature on the foundations of mathematical logic. I have done no definitely logical work since the second edition of the *Principia* in 1925, except the discussion of the principles of extensionality and atomicity and excluded middle in the *Inquiry into Meaning and Truth*. Consequently, the later work on this subject has not affected my philosophical development and therefore lies outside the scope of the present volume.

Chapter 11

Theory of Knowledge

From August 1914 until the end of 1917 I was wholly occupied with matters arising out of my opposition to the war, but by the beginning of 1918 I had become persuaded that there was no further pacifist work that I could usefully do. I wrote as quickly as I could a book, which I had contracted to produce, called *Roads to Freedom*, but when that was out of the way I began again to work at philosophical subjects. I have dealt in the preceding chapter with the lectures on Logical Atomism which I finished just before going to prison. In prison, I wrote first a polemical criticism of Dewey and then the *Introduction to Mathematical Philosophy*. After this I found my thoughts turning to theory of knowledge and to those parts of psychology and of linguistics which seemed relevant to that subject. This was a more or less permanent change in my philosophical interests. The outcome, so far as my own thinking was concerned, is embodied in three books: *The Analysis of Mind* (1921); *An Inquiry into Meaning and Truth* (1940); *Human Knowledge: Its Scope and Limits* (1948).

At the beginning of this work I had no fixed convictions, but only a certain store of maxims and prejudices. I read widely and found, in the end, as I had with the reading that preceded the *Principles of Mathematics*, that a great part of what I had read was irrelevant to my purposes.

Among the prejudices with which I had started, I should enumerate six as specially important:

First. It seemed to me desirable to emphasise the continuity between animal and human minds. I found it common to protest against intellectualist interpretations of animal behaviour, and with these protests I was in broad agreement, but I thought that the methods adopted in interpreting animal behaviour have much more scope than is usually admitted in interpreting what in human beings would be regarded as 'thought' or 'knowledge' or 'inference'. This preconception led me to read a great deal of animal psychology. I found, somewhat to my amusement, that there were two schools in this field, of whom the the most important representatives were Thorndike, in America and Köhler in Germany. It seemed that animals always behave in a manner showing the rightness of the philosophy entertained by the man who observes them. This devastating discovery holds over a wider field. In

the seventeenth century, animals were ferocious, but under the influence of Rousseau they began to exemplify the cult of the Noble
Savage which Peacock makes fun of in Sir Oran Haut-ton. Throughout
the reign of Queen Victoria all apes were virtuous monogamists, but
during the dissolute 'twenties their morals underwent a disastrous
deterioration. This aspect of animal behaviour, however, did not
concern me. What concerned me were the observations on how
animals learn. Animals observed by Americans rush about frantically
until they hit upon the solution by chance. Animals observed by Ger-
mans sit still and scratch their heads until they evolve the solution
out of their inner consciousness. I believe both sets of observations to
be entirely reliable, and that what an animal will do depends upon the
kind of problem that you set before it. The net result of my reading in
this subject was to make me very wary of extending any theory
beyond the region within which observation had confirmed it.

There was one region where there was a very considerable body of
precise experimental knowledge. It was the region of Pavlov's observations on conditioned reflexes in dogs. These experiments led to a
philosophy called Behaviourism which had a considerable vogue.
The gist of this philosophy is that in psychology we are to rely wholly
upon external observations and never to accept data for which the
evidence is entirely derived from introspection. As a philosophy, I
never felt any inclination to accept this view, but, as a method to be
pursued as far as possible, I thought it valuable. I determined in advance that I would push it as far as possible while remaining persuaded
that it had very definite limits.

Second. Along with the prejudice in favour of behaviourist methods
there went another prejudice in favour of explanations in terms of
physics wherever possible. I have always been deeply persuaded that,
from a cosmic point of view, life and experience are causally of little
importance. The world of astronomy dominates my imagination and I
am very conscious of the minuteness of our planet in comparison with
the systems of galaxies. I found in Ramsey's *Foundations of Mathematics* a passage expressing what I do *not* feel:

'Where I seem to differ from some of my friends is in attaching little
importance to physical size. I don't feel the least humble before the
vastness of the heavens. The stars may be large, but they cannot
think or love; and these are qualities which impress me far more than
size does. I take no credit for weighing nearly seventeen stone.

'My picture of the world is drawn in perspective, and not like a
model to scale. The foreground is occupied by human beings and the
stars are all as small as threepenny bits. I don't really believe in astronomy, except as a complicated description of part of the course of
human and possibly animal sensation. I apply my perspective not
merely to space but also to time. In time the world will cool and every-

thing will die; but that is a long time off still, and its present value at compound discount is almost nothing. Nor is the present less valuable because the future will be blank. Humanity, which fills the foreground of my picture, I find interesting and on the whole admirable.'

There is no arguing about feelings, and I do not pretend for a moment that my way of feeling is better than Ramsey's, but it is vastly different. I find little satisfaction in contemplating the human race and its follies. I am happier thinking about the nebula in Andromeda than thinking about Genghis Khan. I cannot, like Kant, put the moral law on the same plane as the starry heavens. The attempt to humanise the cosmos, which underlies the philosophy that calls itself 'Idealism', is displeasing to me quite independently of the question whether it is true or false. I have no wish to think that the world results from the lucubrations of Hegel or even of his Celestial Prototype. In any empirical subject-matter I expect, though without complete confidence, that a thorough understanding will reduce the more important causal laws to those of physics, but where the matter is very complex, I doubt the practical feasibility of the reduction.

Third. I feel that the concept of 'experience' has been very much over-emphasised, especially in the Idealist philosophy, but also in many forms of empiricism. I found, when I began to think about theory of knowledge, that none of the philosophers who emphasise 'experience' tells us what they mean by the word. They seem willing to accept it as an indefinable of which the significance should be obvious. They tend to think that only what is experienced can be known to exist and that it is meaningless to assert that some things exist although we do not know them to exist. I think that this sort of view gives much too much importance to knowledge, or at any rate to something analogous to knowledge. I think also that those who profess such views have not realised all their implications. Few philosophers seem to understand that one may know a proposition of the form 'All A is B' or 'There are A's' without knowing any single A individually. If you are on a pebbly beach you may be quite sure that there are pebbles on the beach that you have not seen or touched. Everybody, in fact, accepts innumerable propositions about things not experienced, but when people begin to philosophise they seem to think it necessary to make themselves artificially stupid. I will admit at once that there are difficulties in explaining how we acquire knowledge that transcends experience, but I think the view that we have no such knowledge is utterly untenable.

Fourth. I had, and have, another prejudice which works in the opposite direction from the one we have just been considering. I think that all knowledge as to what there is in the world, if it does not directly report facts known through perception or memory, must be inferred from premisses of which one, at least, is known by perception or memory. I do not think that there is any wholly *a priori* method of proving the existence of anything, but I do think that there are forms of probable inference which must be accepted although they cannot be *proved* by experience.

Fifth. One of the things that I realised in 1918 was that I had not paid enough attention to 'meaning' and to linguistic problems generally. It was then that I began to be aware of the many problems concerned with the relation between words and things. There is first the classification of single words: proper names, adjectives, relation words, conjunctions and such words as 'all' and 'some'. Then there is the question of the significance of sentences and how it comes about that they have the duality of truth and falsehood. I found that, just as there are formalists in arithmetic, who are content to lay down rules for doing sums without reflecting that numbers have to be used in counting, so there are formalists in the wider field of language in general who think that truth is a matter of following certain rules and not of correspondence with fact. Many philosophers speak critically of the 'correspondence theory' of truth, but it always seemed to me that, except in logic and mathematics, no other theory had any chance of being right.

I thought, also, as a consequence of my desire to preserve continuity with animal intelligence, that the importance of language, great as it is, has been over-emphasised. It seemed to me that belief and knowledge have pre-verbal forms, and that they cannot be rightly analysed if this is not realised.

When I first became interested in linguistic problems, I did not at all apprehend their difficulty and complexity. I had only the feeling that they were important, without at first knowing quite what they were. I do not pretend to have arrived at any completeness of knowledge in this sphere, but at any rate my thinking has gradually become more articulated, more definite, and more conscious of the problems involved.

Sixth. This brings me to the last of my initial prejudices, which has been perhaps the most important in all my thinking. This is concerned with method. My method invariably is to start from something vague but puzzling, something which seems indubitable but which I cannot express with any precision. I go through a process which is like that of first seeing something with the naked eye and then examining it through a microscope. I find that by fixity of attention divisions and distinctions appear where none at first was visible, just as through a microscope you can see the bacilli in impure water which without the microscope are not discernible. There are many who decry analysis, but it has seemed to me evident, as in the case of the impure water, that analysis gives new knowledge without destroying any of the previously existing knowledge. This applies not only to the structure of physical things, but quite as much to concepts. 'Knowledge', for example, as commonly used is a very imprecise term covering a number of different things and a number of stages from certainty to slight probability.

It seems to me that philosophical investigation, as far as I have experience of it, starts from that curious and unsatisfactory state of mind in which one feels complete certainty without being able to say what one is certain of. The process that results from prolonged attention is just like that of watching an object approaching through a thick fog: at first it is only a vague darkness, but as it approaches articulations appear and one discovers that it is a man or a woman, or a horse or a cow or what not. It seems to me that those who object to analysis would wish us to be content with the initial dark blur. Belief in the above process is my strongest and most unshakable prejudice as regards the methods of philosophical investigation.

Chapter 12

Consciousness and Experience

During 1918 my view as to mental events underwent a very important change. I had originally accepted Brentano's view that in sensation there are three elements: act, content and object. I had come to think that the distinction of content and object is unnecessary, but I still thought that sensation is a fundamentally relational occurrence in which a subject is 'aware' of an object. I had used the concept 'awareness' or 'acquaintance' to express this relation of subject and object, and had regarded it as fundamental in the theory of empirical knowledge, but I became gradually more doubtful as to this relational character of mental occurrences. In my lectures on logical Atomism I expressed this doubt, but soon after I gave these lectures I became convinced that William James had been right in denying the relational character of sensations. In a long paper 'On the Nature of Acquaintance' published in *The Monist* in 1914, I criticised James's view and rejected it. The argument is reprinted in *Logic and Knowledge*, edited by Robert C. Marsh, page 139ff. The contrary view which I came to adopt was first published in 1919 in a paper read before the Aristotleian Society called 'On Propositions: What they are and how they mean'. This article is also reprinted in Mr Marsh's collection, and the relevant passage occurs on page 305ff. James's view was first set forth in an essay called 'Does "Consciousness" Exist ?' In this essay he contended that the supposed subject is 'the name of a nonentity'. He goes on to say: 'Those who still cling to it are clinging to a mere echo, the faint rumour left behind by the disappearing "soul" upon the air of philosophy.' This essay was published in 1904, but it was not until fourteen years later that I became persuaded of its rightness.

The issue was more important than might at first be apparent. It is obvious that we learn by experience and it at least seemed obvious to me that learning does not consist merely in acquiring certain ways of behaving but also in the generation of something that may be called 'knowledge'. So long as I adhered to the relational theory of sensation, this offered little difficulty. Every sensation, according to this view, was itself a cognition which consisted in awareness of what I called the 'sense-datum'. In the *Analysis of Mind* (1921) I explicitly abandoned 'sense-data'. I said: 'Sensations are obviously the source of our knowledge of the world, including our own body. It might seem natural to regard a sensation as itself a cognition, and until lately I did so regard it. When, say, I see a person I know coming towards me in the street, it *seems* as though the mere seeing were knowledge. It is of course undeniable that knowledge comes *through* the seeing, but I think it is a mistake to regard the mere seeing itself as knowledge. If we are so to regard it, we must distinguish the seeing from what is seen: we must say that, when we see a patch of colour of a certain shape, the patch of colour is one thing and our seeing of it is another. This view, however, demands the admission of the subject, or act, in the sense discussed in our first lecture. If there is a subject, it can have a relation to the patch of colour, namely, the sort of relation which we might call awareness. In that case the sensation, as a mental event, will consist of awareness of the colour, while the colour itself will remain wholly physical, and may be called the sense-datum, to distinguish it from the sensation. The subject, however, appears to be a logical fiction, like mathematical points and instants. It is introduced, not because observation reveals it, but because it is linguistically convenient and apparently demanded by grammar. Nominal entities of this sort may or may not exist, but there is no good ground for assuming that they do. The functions that they appear to perform can always be performed by classes or series or other logical constructions, consisting of less dubious entities. If we are to avoid a perfectly gratuitous assumption, we must dispense with the subject as one of the actual ingredients of the world. But when we do this, the possibility of distinguishing the sensation from the sense-datum vanishes; at least I see no way of preserving the distinction. Accordingly the sensation that we have when we see a patch of colour simply *is* that patch of colour, an actual constituent of the physical world, and part of what physics is concerned with. A patch of colour is certainly not knowledge, and therefore we cannot say that pure sensation is cognitive. Through its psychological effects, it is the cause of cognitions, partly by being itself a sign of things that are correlated with it, as e.g. sensations of sight and touch are correlated, and partly by giving rise to images and memories after the sensation is faded. But in itself the pure sensation is not cognitive' (pages 141–2).

But new problems, of which at first I was not fully conscious, arose as a consequence of the abandonment of 'sense-data'. Such words as 'awareness', 'acquaintance', and 'experience' had to be re-defined, and this was by no means an easy task. At the beginning of *An Inquiry into Meaning and Truth*, I stated the problem as follows: 'If you say to a person untrained in philosophy, "How do you know I have two eyes?" he or she will reply, "What a silly question! I can see you have". It is not to be supposed that, when our inquiry is finished, we shall have arrived at anything radically different from this unphilosophical position. What will have happened will be that we shall have come to see a complicated structure where we thought everything was simple, that we shall have become aware of the penumbra of uncertainty surrounding the situations which inspire no doubt, that we shall find doubt more frequently justified than we supposed, and that even the most plausible premisses will have shown themselves capable of yielding unplausible conclusions. The net result is to substitute articulate hesitation for inarticulate certainty. Whether this result has any value is a question which I shall not consider' (page 11).

But at the time when I wrote the *Analysis of Mind* I was not fully aware of the need for re-interpreting what common sense calls 'the evidence of the senses'.

A part of the problem can be dealt with by behaviourist methods. One of the differences between dead matter and a living body is that the response of the living body to a frequently applied stimulus changes with repetitions of the stimulus, whereas the response of dead matter in general shows no such change. This is embodied in the proverb, 'a burnt child dreads the fire'. An automatic machine, however often it has responded to the insertion of a penny, never learns to respond to the mere sight of a penny. Habit, which is one of the most fundamental characteristics of living matter, and especially of the higher forms of life, consists essentially in the 'conditioned reflex'. The essence of the 'conditioned reflex' is this: Given that an animal responds to a stimulus A by a certain action and that the stimulus A is frequently presented to it along with another stimulus B, the animal tends in time to react to B as it formerly reacted to A. Pavlov carried out a large number of experiments on dogs showing how they learnt to view one thing as a 'sign' of another and to behave in a manner which showed that in one sense of the word they had 'knowledge'. For instance, there were two doors, on one of which an ellipse was painted and on the other a circle. If the dog chose the door that had a circle, it got a good dinner, but if it chose the door that had an ellipse it got an electric shock. After a certain number of trials, the dog invariably chose the circle. The dog, however, was inferior to Kepler in the capacity of distinguishing ellipses from circles. Pavlov made the ellipse gradually more nearly circular until at last the dog was unable to make the distinction and suffered a nervous breakdown. Much the same thing happens to schoolboys when they are asked. 'What is six times nine?' or 'What is seven times eight?' They soon get to know that the answer is either fifty-four or fifty-six, but it may be a long time before they can choose between these two numbers. Such experiments with dogs and schoolboys can be conducted in a purely behaviourist manner – that is to say, we are investigating a bodily response to a bodily stimulus, and we do not have to ask ourselves whether the dog or the schoolboy 'thinks'.

Response to stimulus is not, in itself, a characteristic of living matter. A galvanometer responds to an electric current and a thermometer responds to temperature. What is characteristic of animals, and especially of the higher animals, is what may be called 'learning', which consists in changing the response to a given stimulus as the result of the acquisition of a habit. There is a great difference between higher and lower animals in the capacity of acquiring habits that are useful. A fly will continue indefinitely to try to get through a pane of glass, whereas a cat or a dog very soon learns that this is impossible. A large part of the superiority of human beings to other animals consists in their greater capacity for acquiring numerous and complex habits.

Will this principle cover the whole of what is meant by 'knowledge derived from experience'? I have never myself thought that it will, but I think it may cover more of the ground than one might naturally suppose. If, when you see a dog you say 'dog', and when you see a cat you say 'cat', that will be taken as evidence that you 'know' the difference between a cat and a dog. But it is clear that you could make a machine that would do this, and if you said that the machine 'knew' anything you would be thought to be speaking metaphorically. Everybody who is not a philosopher addicted to Behaviourism is persuaded that things happen in us which do not happen in any machine. If you have a toothache, you know that you are feeling pain. You could make a machine which would groan and even say, 'This is unendurable', but you would still not believe that the machine was undergoing what you undergo when you feel toothache.

One of the most important issues affected by the question whether sensation is essentially relational is as to the theory which is called 'Neutral Monism'. So long as the 'subject' was retained there was a 'mental' entity to which there was nothing analogous in the material world, but, if sensations are occurrences which are not essentially relational, there is not the same need to regard mental and physical occurrences as fundamentally different. It becomes possible to regard both a mind and a piece of matter as logical constructions formed out of materials not differing vitally and sometimes actually identical. It became possible to think that what the physiologist regards as matter in the brain is actually composed of thoughts and feelings, and that the difference between mind and matter is merely one of arrangement. I illustrated this by the analogy of the Post Office Directory, which classifies people in two ways, alphabetical and geographical. In the first arrangement, a man's neighbours are those who come near him in the alphabet; in the other, they are those who live next door. In like manner, a sensation may be grouped with a number of other occurrences by a memory-chain, in which case it becomes part of a mind; or it may be grouped with its causal antecedents, in which case it appears as part of the physical world. This view affords an immense simplification. I was glad when I realised that abandonment of the 'subject' made it possible to accept this simplification and to regard the traditional problem of the relation of mind and matter as definitively solved.

There were, however, other respects in which the consequences of the new view were less convenient. There is a duality which is essential in any form of knowledge except that which is shown in mere bodily behaviour. We are aware *of* something, we have a recollection *of* something, and, generally, knowing is distinct from that which is known. This duality, after it has been banished from sensation, has to be somehow re-introduced. The first form in which the problem arises is as to 'perception'. In this respect there is a difference between different sensations. Smells and tastes and bodily feelings such as headache or stomach-ache do not suggest this duality as forcibly as sight and touch and hearing. Before we begin to reflect, we think of the things that we see and hear and touch as external to ourselves, and it is only by an effort that we can turn our attention to seeing as opposed to what is seen. When a dog sees a rabbit, we can hardly suppose that it says to itself, 'I am having a visual sensation which probably has an external cause'. But if the view of James and Mach is right, what occurs in the dog when it 'sees a rabbit' has only an indirect and causal relation to the rabbit. This view strikes one as odd, and it is on account of the oddity that I was so slow in adopting it. I think, however, that the whole theory as to the causes of sensation, which are partly physical and partly physiological, makes it unavoidable that we should regard 'perception' as something much less direct than it seems to be.

From the point of view of theory of knowledge, this raises very difficult questions as to what is meant by 'empirical evidence'. In the *Inquiry into Meaning and Truth*, which is largely concerned with this problem, I replaced 'acquaintance' by 'noticing', which I accepted as an undefined term. A quotation will make this point clear:

'Suppose you are out walking on a wet day, and you see a puddle and avoid it. You are not likely to say to yourself: "there is a puddle; it will be advisable not to step into it". But if somebody said "why did you suddenly step aside?" you would answer "because I didn't wish to step into that puddle". You know, retrospectively, that you had a visual perception, to which you reacted appropriately; and in the case supposed, you express this knowledge in words. But what would you have known, and in what sense, if your attention had not been called to the matter by your questioner?

'When you were questioned, the incident was over, and you answered by memory. Can one remember what one never knew? That depends upon the meaning of the word "know".

'The word "know" is highly ambiguous. In most senses of the word, "knowing" an event is a different occurrence from the event which is known; but there is a sense of "knowing" in which, when you have an experience, there is no difference between the experience and knowing that you have it. It might be maintained that we always know our present experiences; but this cannot be the case if the knowing is something different from the experience. For, if an experience is one thing and knowing it is another, the supposition that we always know an experience when it is happening involves an infinite multiplication of every event. I feel hot; this is one event. I know that I feel hot; this is a second event. I know that I know that I feel hot; this is a third event. And so on *ad infinitum*, which is absurd. We must therefore say either that my present experience is indistinguishable from my knowing it while it is present, or that, as a rule, we do not know our present experiences. On the whole, I prefer to use the word "know" in a sense, which implies that the knowing is different from what is known, and to accept the consequence that, as a rule, we do not know our present experiences.

'We are to say, then, that it is one thing to see a puddle, and another to know that I see a puddle. "Knowing" *may* be defined as "acting appropriately"; this is the sense in which we say that a dog knows his name, or that a carrier pigeon knows the way home. In this sense, my knowing of the puddle consisted of my stepping aside. But this is vague, both because other things might have made me step aside, and because "appropriate" can only be defined in terms of my desires. I might have wished to get wet, because I had just insured my life for a large sum, and thought death from pneumonia would be convenient; in that case, my stepping aside would be evidence that I did *not* see the puddle. Moreover, if desire is excluded, appropriate reaction to certain stimuli is shown by scientific instruments, but no one would say that the thermometer "knows" when it is cold.

'What must be done with an experience in order that we may know it ? Various things are possible. We may use words describing it, we may remember it either in words or in images, or we may merely "notice" it. But "noticing" is a matter of degree, and very hard to define; it seems to consist mainly in isolating from the sensible environment. You may, for instance, in listening to a piece of music, deliberately notice only the part of the cello. You hear the rest, as is said, "unconsciously" – but this is a word to which it would be hopeless to attempt to attach any definite meaning. In one sense, it may be said that you "know" a present experience if it rouses in you any emotion, however faint – if it pleases or displeases you, or interests or bores you, or surprises you or is just what you were expecting.

'There is an important sense in which you *can* know anything that is in your present sensible field. If somebody says to you "are you now seeing yellow ?" or "do you hear a noise ?" you can answer with perfect confidence, even if, until you were asked, you were not noticing the yellow or the noise. And often you can be sure that it was already there before your attention was called to it.

'It seems, then, that the most immediate knowing of which we have experience involves sensible presence *plus* something more, but that any very exact definition of the more that is needed is likely to mislead by its very exactness, since the matter is essentially vague and one of degree. What is wanted may be called "attention"; this is partly a sharpening of the appropriate sense-organs, partly an emotional reaction. A sudden loud noise is almost sure to command attention, but so does a very faint sound that has emotional significance.

'Every empirical proposition is based upon one or more sensible occurrences that were noticed when they occurred, or immediately after, while they still formed part of the specious present. Such occurrences, we shall say, are "known" when they are noticed. The word "know" has many meanings, and this is only one of them; but for the purposes of our inquiry it is fundamental' (pages 49–51).

'Perception' as opposed to 'sensation' involves habit based upon past experience. We may distinguish sensation as that part of our total experience which is due to the stimulus alone, independently of past history. This is a theoretical core in the total occurrence. The total occurrence is always an interpretation in which the sensational core has accretions embodying habits. When you see a dog, the sensational core is a patch of colour stripped of all the adjuncts involved in recognising it as a dog. You expect the patch of colour to move in the way that is characteristic of dogs, you expect that if it makes a noise it will bark or growl, and not crow like a cock. You are convinced that it could be touched and that it will not vanish into thin air, but has a future and a past. I do not mean that all this is 'conscious', but its presence is shown by the astonishment that you would feel if things worked out otherwise. It is these accretions that turn a sensation into a perception, and it is these, also, that make perception possibly misleading. Walt Disney might lead you to suppose that you were seeing a 'real' dog, and it might astonish you by crowing or vanishing. Since, however, your expectations are the result of experience, it is clear that they must represent what usually happens – always assuming that the laws of nature are constant.

Another form of duality arises in imagination and memory. If I remember now what happened on some past occasion, it is obvious that what is happening in me now is not identical with the events remembered, since one is in the present and one is in the past. There is, therefore, in memory something that may be called a relation of subject and object. And this will require careful interpretation. I do not think the interpretation is possible without introducing 'belief'. When I remember, I believe that something happened in the past, and the something that happened is in some sense 'represented' by what is happening in me now. The essential problem here is the relation of an image to its sensational prototype. I can visualise my room, and then go into my room and find that it 'agrees' with my visual image. Such experiences lead us to give a certain credence to memory images, but not that absolute credence that we give to sensations which we notice, because memories are found sometimes to be misleading.

There are two words which have been very frequently employed by philosophers. They are the words 'consciousness' and 'experience'. Both will need to be re-defined – or, rather, to be defined, for in general they are employed as if their meaning were obvious.

What can we mean when we say that a man or an animal is 'conscious' but a stone is not ? There are two different things that may be meant, of which the first, but not the second, is open to external observation. The first is that the man or the animal behaves in future in a way in which he would not behave if the event in question had not happened. This might perhaps be better taken as the definition of 'experience'. The second definition of 'consciousness' will be derived from the relation of 'noticing'. When anything happens to me, I may or may not notice it. If I notice it, I may be said to be 'conscious' of it. According to this definition, 'consciousness' consists in the knowledge that something is happening to me or has happened to me. What is meant by 'knowledge' in this definition remains to be investigated.

Under the influence of Idealist philosophers the importance of 'experience' has, it seems to me, been enormously exaggerated. It has even come to be thought that there can be nothing which is not experienced or experience. I cannot see that there is any ground whatever for this opinion, nor even for the view that we cannot know that there are things we do not know. I do not think that the opinion which I am combating could have flourished if people had taken the trouble to find out what the word 'experience' is capable of meaning.

Chapter 13

Language

It was in 1918, as I remarked before, that I first became interested in the definition of 'meaning' and in the relation of language to fact. Until then I had regarded language as 'transparent' and had never examined what makes its relation to the non-linguistic world. The first result of my thinking on this subject appeared in Lecture X of *The Analysis of Mind*.

The first thing that struck me was exceedingly obvious but seemed to have been unduly ignored by all previous writers on the subject. This was that a word is a universal of which the instances are the occasions on which an instance of the word is spoken or heard or written or read. Those who philosophised about universals realised that DOG is a universal because there are many dogs, but they failed to notice that the word 'dog' is a universal in exactly the same sense. Those who denied universals always spoke as though there were one word which applied to all the instances. This is quite contrary to the fact. There are innumerable dogs and innumerable instances of the word 'dog'. Each of the instances of the word has a certain relation to each of the instances of the quadruped. But the word itself has only that metaphysical status (whatever this may be) that belongs to the Platonic DOG laid up in heaven. This fact is important since it makes words much less different than they had been thought to be from the objects that they 'mean'. It also becomes obvious that 'meaning' must be a relation between an individual instance of a word and an individual instance of what the word means. That is to say, if you want to explain the meaning of the word 'dog' you have to examine particular utterances of this word and consider how they are related to particular members of the canine species.

In seeking the definition of 'meaning', I pursued, as elsewhere, the plan of proceeding as far as possible on behaviourist principles while expecting these principles to prove ultimately inadequate. It is obvious that a child acquires the habit of using the word 'dog' on appropriate occasions exactly as he acquires any other habit. He frequently hears the word 'dog' uttered while his attention is fixed upon a dog. By the ordinary process of telescoping, a dog comes in time to give him an impulse to say 'dog', and hearing the word 'dog' makes him expect or look for a dog. When these two habits have been acquired the child may be said to know the meaning of the word 'dog'. This does not mean that the child has a state of mind consisting in a definition of the word 'dog'; it means only that he has two modes of behaviour, one leading from a dog to an instance of the word 'dog', and the other, from an instance of the word to an instance of the canine species. When he has acquired these two habits, he can speak correctly. So far as the word 'dog' is concerned, he needs nothing more until he becomes a lexicographer.

In regard to what may be called 'object-words', nothing more is needed for the definition of 'meaning'. To say that the word 'dog' means DOG is only to say that these two habits have been acquired. The two habits may be called, respectively, active and passive understanding of the word. Active understanding consists of uttering the word in the presence of a dog, and passive understanding consists of expecting or looking for a dog when you hear the word 'dog'. Passive understanding comes earlier than active understanding and is not confined to human beings. Dogs and horses learn the passive understanding of a certain number of words. Parrots, on the other hand, can utter words, but show no sign of knowing what they mean.

I gave the following definition of what is meant by using a word 'correctly' (*loc. cit.*, page 198):

'A word is used "correctly" when the average hearer will be affected by it in the way intended. This is a psychological, not a literary, definition of "correctness". The literary definition would substitute, for the average hearer, a person of high education living a long time ago; the purpose of this definition is to make it difficult to speak or write correctly.

'The relation of a word to its meaning is of the nature of a causal law governing our use of the word and our actions when we hear it used. There is no more reason why a person who uses a word correctly should be able to tell what it means than there is why a planet which is moving correctly should know Kepler's laws.'

The essential thing in the understanding of an object-word is that the word shares some of the properties of what the word means. If you are waked in the middle of the night by a cry of 'Fire!' you will behave in much the same way as you would if you smelt burning. There are, of course, differences between a word and what it means. The word 'fire' cannot make you hot or cause you to die, but it is the causal similarities, not the causal differences, that are involved in defining meaning.

The above definition of 'meaning', though I think it correct so far as it goes, in no degree exhausts the subject of meaning. For one thing, it is only applicable to object-words. You can take a child to the zoo and say 'tiger' while he is looking at this beast, but there is no zoo where you can show him the meaning of the word 'than'. There is another limitation to the above theory, which is that it is only adequate in regard to the indicative or exclamatory use of words. It does not explain, until it is supplemented, the use of words in narrative or imagination or desire or command. In theory of knowledge it is especially the indicative use of language that is relevant, but its other uses are equally important in other spheres. In this connection, I will quote from *Human Knowledge* (page 85):

'I think the elementary uses of a word may be distinguished as indicative, imperative, and interrogative. When a child sees his mother coming, he may say "mother"; this is the indicative use. When he wants her, he calls "mother!"; this is the imperative use. When she dresses up as a witch and he begins to pierce the disguise, he may say "mother?"; this is the interrogative use. The indicative use must come first in the acquisition of language, since the association of word and object signified can only be created by the simultaneous presence of both. But the imperative use very quickly follows. This is relevant in considering what we mean by "thinking of" an object. It is obvious that the child who has just learnt to call his mother has found verbal expression for a state in which he had often been previously, that the state was associated with his mother, and that it has now become associated with the word "mother". Before language, his state was only partially communicable; an adult, hearing him cry, would know that he wanted something, but had to guess what it was. But the fact that the word "mother!" expresses his state shows that, even before the acquisition of language, his state had a relation to his mother, namely the relation called "thinking of". This relation is not created by language, but ante-dates it. What language does is to make it communicable.'

Philosophers and bookish people generally tend to live a life dominated by words, and even to forget that it is the essential function of words to have a connection of one sort or another with facts, which are in general non-linguistic. Some modern philosophers have gone so far as to say that words should never be confronted with facts but should live in a pure, autonomous world where they are compared only with other words. When you say, 'the cat is a carnivorous animal', you do not mean that actual cats eat actual meat, but only that in zoology books the cat is classified among carnivora. These authors tell us that the attempt to confront language with fact is 'metaphysics' and is on this ground to be condemned. This is one of those views which are so absurd that only very learned men could possibly adopt them. What makes it peculiarly absurd is its blindness to the position of language in the world of fact. Language consists of sensible phenomena just as much as eating or walking, and if we can know nothing about facts we cannot know what other people say or even what we are saying ourselves. Language, like other acquired ways of behaving, consists of useful habits and has none of the mystery with which it is often surrounded. There is nothing new in the superstitious view of language, which has come down to us from pre-historic ages:

'Words from the earliest times of which we have historical records, have been objects of superstitious awe. The man who knew his enemy's name could, by means of it, acquire magic powers over him. We still use such phrases as "in the name of the Law". It is easy to assent to the statement "in the beginning was the Word". This view underlies the philosophies of Plato and Carnap and of most of the intermediate metaphysicians' (*An Inquiry into Meaning and Truth*, page 23).

In *The Analysis of Mind* I argued the thesis that the 'stuff' of mental occurrences consists entirely of sensations and images. I do not know whether this thesis was sound, but I am still quite convinced that many uses of language are inexplicable except by introducing images. Behaviourists refuse to admit images because they cannot be observed from without, but this causes them difficulties when they attempt to explain either memory or imagination. I thought when I wrote *The Analysis of Mind* that it was possible to give a behaviouristic account of desire, but as to this I now feel very doubtful. I still, however, adhere to all that I said in that book about the necessity of images for explaining the use of words in regard to things not sensibly present.

I summed up what constitutes the understanding of an object-word under six heads: (1) Using the word properly in suitable circumstances on suitable occasions; (2) Acting appropriately when you hear it; (3) associating the word with another word (say, in a different language) which has the appropriate effect on behaviour; (4) in learning the word, associating it with an object or objects which is or are what it 'means'; (5) using the word to describe or recall a memory-image; (6) using the word to describe or create an imagination-image. I stated these six points as if they applied to words in general, but, in fact, they do not apply without modification to words which are not object-words.

New problems, however, arise as soon as we pass to the consideration of sentences and of words which can only be used significantly as parts of sentences. You can use such words as 'fire' or 'fox' in an exclamatory manner without the need of putting them into sentences, but there are a great many words which cannot be thus used in isolation. Take such a sentence as 'the earth is greater than the moon'. 'The', 'is', and 'than' only acquire significance when they are parts of sentences. One might have doubts about the word 'greater'. If you had been looking at horses and suddenly saw an elephant, you *might* exclaim 'Greater!' But I think everyone would recognise this as an ellipsis. The fact that some words presuppose sentences makes it impossible to carry the analysis of meaning any further without first considering sentences or at any rate what mental occurrences are expressed by means of sentences.

I began to be puzzled about sentences when I was writing *The Principles of Mathematics*, and it was at that time particularly the function of verbs that interested me. What struck me as important then was that the verb confers unity upon the sentence. The sentence 'A is greater than B' is complex since it contains several words, and it seemed plain to me, as it still does, that there must be a corresponding complexity in the fact which makes the sentence true, if it is true. In addition to this kind of complex unity, a sentence has another property which is the duality of truth and falsehood. For these two reasons, the problems involved in explaining the significance of sentences are both more difficult and more important than those involved in defining the meaning of object-words. In *The Analysis of Mind* I did not deal at all fully with these problems, but in *An Inquiry into Meaning and Truth* I endeavoured to offer adequate explanations in this region.

I do not think it is possible to construct a tenable theory of truth and falsehood without certain presuppositions which many modern philosophers consider unduly metaphysical. I think one must say that there are *facts* and that 'truth' consists in one sort of relation to facts while 'falsehood' consists in another sort of relation. I think the kind of modest agnosticism which pretends that we never know facts is absurd. To pretend that I do not know when I am feeling pain, or when I hear a noise, or see the sun, is the kind of thing that is only possible for those in whom theory has killed all sense of reality. Moreover, even the most passionate adherents of the view that I am rejecting will admit that sentences consist of words, and cannot well deny that uttering or hearing a sentence is a fact of just the kind that they regard as unknowable. Language is a form of bodily behaviour like walking or eating or drinking, and whatever we cannot know about walking or eating or drinking we also cannot know about language.

Many things in the world can be seen to be complex. There may be things which are not complex, but it is unnecessary to have an opinion on this point. When things are complex, they consist of parts with relations between them. A table consists of legs and a flat top. A knife consists of a handle and a blade. Facts, as I am using the word, consist always of relations between parts of a whole or qualities of single things. Facts, in a word, are whatever there is except what (if anything) is completely simple. When two things are interrelated they form together a complex which may be regarded as one thing. It is convenient to use the word 'fact' to express the analysed connection of the parts rather than the complex whole that they compose. Sentences express such relations when the sentences are true, and fail to express them when the sentences are false. All sentences that consist of more than one word used explosively embody some analysis of a complex. If a number of complexes all have a common constituent, this may be shown by the fact that the sentences analysing them all contain a common word. Take, for example, the following sentences: 'Socrates was wise'; 'Socrates was Athenian'; 'Socrates loved Plato'; 'Socrates drank the hemlock'. All these sentences contain the word 'Socrates', and all the facts that make them true contain the man Socrates as a constituent. This is what we mean when we say that the sentences are 'about' Socrates. Socrates enters into the facts that make these sentences true as an unanalysed whole. But Socrates was, of course, himself complex, and we can make other sentences in which this complexity is asserted, as, for example, 'Socrates was snub-nosed' or 'Socrates had two legs'. Such sentences analyse a given whole. How far the analysis can be carried at any one time depends upon the state of science at that time. The manner in which the parts of a whole are interrelated constitutes the 'structure' of the whole. As to this, I will quote the following passage from *Human Knowledge* (pages 267–9):

'To exhibit the structure of an object is to mention its parts and the ways in which they are interrelated. If you were learning anatomy, you might first learn the names and shapes of the various bones, and then be taught where each bone belongs in the skeleton. You would then know the structure of the skeleton in so far as anatomy has anything to say about it. But you would not have come to an end of what can be said about structure in relation to the skeleton. Bones are composed of cells, and cells of molecules, and each molecule has an atomic structure which it is the business of chemistry to study. Atoms, in turn, have a structure which is studied in physics. At this point orthodox science ceases its analysis, but there is no reason to suppose that further analysis is impossible. We shall have occasion to suggest the analysis of physical entities into structures of events, and even events, as I shall try to show, may be regarded with advantage as having a structure.

'Let us consider next a somewhat different example of structure, namely sentences. A sentence is a series of words, arranged in order by the relation of earlier and later if the sentence is spoken, and of left to right if it is written. But these relations are not really between words; they are between *instances* of words. A word is a class of similar noises, all having the same meaning or nearly the same meaning. (For simplicity I shall confine myself to speech as opposed to writing.) A sentence also is a class of noises, since many people can utter the same sentence. We must say, then, not that a sentence is a temporal series of words, but that a sentence is a class of noises, each consisting of a series of noises in quick temporal succession, each of these latter noises being an instance of a word. (This is a necessary but not a sufficient characteristic of a sentence; it is not sufficient because some series of words are not significant.) I will not linger on the distinction between different parts of speech, but will go on to the next stage in analysis, which belongs no longer to syntax, but to phonetics. Each instance of a word is a complex sound, the parts being the separate letters (assuming a phonetic alphabet). Behind the phonetic analysis there is a further stage: the analysis of the complex physiological process of uttering or hearing a single letter. Behind the physiological analysis is the analysis of physics, and from this point onward analysis proceeds as in the case of the bones. . . .

'There is nothing erroneous in an account of structure which starts from units that are afterwards found to be themselves complex. For example, points may be defined as classes of events, but that does not falsify anything in traditional geometry, which treated points as simples. Every account of structure is relative to certain units which are, for the time being, treated as if they were devoid of structure, but it must never be assumed that these units will not, in another context, have a structure which it is important to recognise.'

A sentence in the indicative may be uttered because the speaker believes it, or because he hopes that it will arouse some action or emotion in the hearer. As I pointed out, when an actor says, 'This is I, Hamlet the Dane', nobody believes him, but nobody thinks he is lying. This makes it clear that truth and falsehood belong only to sentences expressing belief or intended to cause belief. In regard to truth and falsehood, a sentence, is only important as a vehicle of belief. It is clear that beliefs, if they are not complicated, can exist without the use of words. We are thus taken outside the linguistic sphere and are compelled to consider, first, unverbalised beliefs, and then the relation of such beliefs to the sentences in which they can be expressed.

Belief is not a precise concept, because of the continuity between the lowest animals and man. Animals show ways of behaviour which might be interpreted as involving this or that belief. But, while this should be borne in mind, it is especially human beliefs as we know them in our own experience with which we are concerned. It is only the simpler kinds of belief that are possible without the use of words. We all believe that the ratio of the circumference of the circle to the diameter is approximately 3·14159, but I do not see how this belief could exist in the absence of language. Many beliefs, however, clearly ante-date language. When you see a dog, you may say 'dog' and thus give verbal expression to your belief. A cat, seeing a dog, expresses its belief differently: its hairs stand on end, it arches its back, and hisses. This is an expression of belief, just as much as your use of the word 'dog'. The same sort of thing applies to memory. If you have just heard a loud clap of thunder, you are in a state which, if you used words, would be expressed in the sentence, 'there has just been a loud clap of thunder'. But you are believing what this sentence expresses even if no words come into your mind. 'A belief, as I understand the term, is a certain state of body or mind or both. To avoid verbiage, I shall call it a state of an organism, and ignore the distinction of bodily and mental factors' (*Human Knowledge*, page 161). I go on to say, 'Any state of an organism which consists in believing something can, theoretically, be fully described without mentioning the something. When you believe "a car is coming" your belief consists in a certain state of the muscles' sense-organs, and emotions, together perhaps with certain visual images. All this, and whatever else may go to make up your belief, could, in theory, be fully described by a psychologist and physiologist working together, without their ever having to mention anything outside your mind and body.' The utterance of an appropriate sentence is only one of the states of mind and body which constitute the belief. The verbal expression derives its importance through being communicable and through being capable of more precision than any non-verbal state embodying the same belief.

Chapter 14

Universals and Particulars and Names

The problems connected with universals and particulars and with the closely related matter of proper names have occupied a great deal of my thought ever since I abandoned the monistic logic. The problems are old, in fact at least as old as Aristotle. They occupied much of the speculation of the mediaeval Schoolmen, whose work in this connection still deserves serious consideration. In the seventeenth and eighteenth centuries, differences as to the psychological and metaphysical status of universals were among the most important points of controversy between Continental philosophers and British empiricists. I set forth some of these traditional views in *Polemic* in the form of a fable (No. 2, 1946, pages 24–5):

'There was once a company of philosophers of various schools travelling in an out-of-the-way region on the Continent. They found an unpretentious inn and ordered dinner; the innkeeper promised them a joint of beef. But the joint, when it came, was unappetising. One of the philosophers, a disciple of Hume and an experienced traveller, summoned mine host and said: "This is not beef, it is horse." He did not know that the innkeeper had seen better days, but had neglected his affairs and come down in the world through devotion to philosophy; he was therefore amazed when the innkeeper replied: "Sir, I am surprised to hear you saying something which you believe to be devoid of meaning. 'Beef' and 'horse', according to you, are only words, and do not denote anything in the non-linguistic world. The dispute is therefore only about words. If you prefer the word 'horse', well and good; but I find the word 'beef' more profitable."

'This reply set all the philosophers talking at once. "The innkeeper is right," said a disciple of Roscelin, "'beef' and 'horse' are only sounds uttered by human breath, and neither can denote this abominable piece of very tough meat." "Nonsense," retorted a Platonist, "this joint comes from an animal which, when alive, was a copy of the eternal horse in heaven, and not of the eternal ox." An Augustinian remarked:

"'Beef' and 'horse' are ideas in the mind of God, and I am sure the divine idea of beef is something very different from this." There was only one point on which they were all agreed, and that was, that any person who sold such nasty stuff under the name of "beef" deserved to be prosecuted for fraud. At this the innkeeper, who knew the local magistrate to be no philosopher, became frightened, and produced another joint, which gave universal satisfaction.

'The sole point of this parable is that the question of "universals" is not merely one of words, but one which arises through the attempt to state facts.'

For my part, I was led in two directions: on the one hand, by the study of Leibniz; and, on the other hand, by the fact that many of the fundamental concepts of mathematics demand asymmetrical relations, which cannot be reduced to predicates of the related terms or of the whole which the terms compose. Having become firmly convinced of the 'reality' of relations, I could not accept either the subject-predicate logic or the empiricist view that there are only particulars.

Throughout my philosophical development since abandoning monism, I have retained, in spite of changes, certain fundamental beliefs, which I do not know how to demonstrate, but which I cannot bring myself to doubt. The first of these, which seems so obvious that I should blush to mention it but for the circumstance that the contrary opinion has been maintained, is that 'truth' depends upon some kind of relation to 'fact'. The second is that the world consists of many inter-related things. The third is that syntax – i.e. the structure of sentences – must have some relation to the structure of facts, at any rate in those aspects of syntax which are unavoidable and not peculiar to this or that language. Lastly, there is a principle of which I feel less certain, but which I wish to adhere to except where very powerful considerations compel me to depart from it. This is the principle that what can be said about a complex can be said without mentioning it by setting forth its parts and their mutual relations.

These assumptions were implicit in the symbolism of *Principia Mathematica*. This symbolism assumed that there are 'things' which have properties and have, also, relations to other 'things'. I employed, at first, two fundamental kinds of syntactical symbolism, the first stating that a 'thing' is a member of a class, the second stating that one 'thing' has such and such a relation to another 'thing'. I employed small Latin letters for 'things', small Greek letters for classes, and capital Latin letters for relations. Classes, however, were gradually more and more replaced by properties, and in the end disappeared except as a symbolic convenience.

My first attempt to state the metaphysical beliefs involved in my logical symbolism was set forth in Chapter IV of the *Principles of*

Mathematics, entitled 'Proper Names, Adjectives and Verbs'. Roughly speaking, what I thought then had to do with the values that could be assigned to variables. The variables for which I used small Latin letters were to have as their possible values entities which have properties or relations. A Greek letter was to denote a property or the class of things having that property. Capital Latin letters were to denote relations. I thought, at that time, that the assigning of a value to a small Latin letter consisted in substituting a proper name for the variable – for example, if we know that whatever x may be, if x is a man x is mortal, we can substitute the name 'Socrates' for 'x'. Similarly, for a Greek letter, we can substitute a property; and, for a capital Latin letter, we can substitute a relation. This substitution of a constant for a variable is the process of applying logic. It is a process which lies outside logic, for the logician, as such, does not know of the existence of Socrates or of anything else.

My views at that time had a kind of morning innocence which they lost in the labour and heat of the day. I imagined that, if a word contributes to the meaning of a sentence, there must be something that the word means. In this connection I will quote §47 of *The Principles of Mathematics*:

'Philosophy is familiar with a certain set of distinctions, all more or less equivalent: I mean, the distinction of subject and predicate, substance and adjective, *this* and *what*. I wish now to point out briefly what appears to me to be the truth concerning these cognate distinctions. The subject is important, since the issues between monism and monadism, between idealism and empiricism, and between those who maintain and those who deny that all truth is concerned with what exists, all depend, in whole or in part, upon the theory we adopt in regard to the present question. But the subject is treated here only because it is essential to any doctrine of number or of the nature of the variable. Its bearings on general philosophy, important as they are, will be left wholly out of account.

'Whatever may be an object of thought, or may occur in any true or false proposition, or can be counted as *one*, I call a *term*. This, then, is the widest word in the philosophical vocabulary. I shall use as synonymous with it the words unit, individual, and entity. The first two emphasise the fact that every term is *one*, while the third is derived from the fact that every term has being, i.e. *is* in some sense. A man, a moment, a number, a class, a relation, a chimaera, or anything else that can be mentioned, is sure to be a term: and to deny that such and such a thing is a term must always be false.

'It might perhaps be thought that a word of such extreme generality could not be of any great use. Such a view, however, owing to certain widespread philosophical doctrines, would be erroneous. A term is, in fact, possessed of all the properties commonly assigned to substances or substantives. Every term, to begin with, is a logical subject: it is, for example, the subject of the proposition that itself is one. Again every term is immutable and indestructible. What a term is, it is, and no change can be conceived in it which would not destroy its identity and make it another term. Another mark which belongs to terms is numerical identity with themselves and numerical diversity from all other terms. Numerical identity and diversity are the source of unity and plurality; and thus the admission of many terms destroys monism. And it seems undeniable that every constituent of every proposition can be counted as one, and that no proposition contains less than two constituents. *Term* is, therefore, a useful word, since it marks dissent from various philosophies, as well as because, in many statements, we wish to speak of *any* term or *some* term.'

There is much in this paragraph that I came later to think erroneous. I was led to alter my views by the theory of descriptions and the doctrine of types. The theory of descriptions persuaded me that a word may contribute to the significance of a sentence without having any meaning in isolation. I had thought that the word 'the', for example, denotes some curious kind of object which the virtuous logician may hope to meet in the Platonic heaven. Such hopes the theory of descriptions caused me to abandon. The doctrine of types caused me another departure from the naïve simplicity of *The Principles of Mathematics*. It appeared that some words cannot be substituted for others without producing nonsense. I had been impressed by the fact that a verbal noun has the same meaning as a verb, but can be the subject of a sentence as, for example, in the statement: 'killing no murder'. I came to think that such statements, when not nonsensical, are abbreviations of sentences in which the verb appears as a verb and not as a noun. 'Killing no murder', for example, would have to be expanded into 'If A kills B, it does not follow that A murders B'. When such a translation is impossible, the sentence is nonsense. 'Socrates and killing are two' would be an illegitimate sentence according to the doctrine of types; and so would 'Socrates and killing are one'.

There was another class of difficulty which was connected with the well-established objections to the notion of substance. It seemed as if the particulars which I had denoted by small Latin letters would have to be substances in a syntactical sense, though they would not need to have the property of indestructibility which substances were traditionally supposed to possess. If the statement that x has such and such a property is always significant, and never analytic, it seems to follow that x is something different from the sum of all its properties, and that it must differ from another particular, y, purely numerically, so that it should be logically possible for the two particulars, x and y, to share all their properties and yet be two. We could not, of course, know that they were two, for that would involve knowing that x differs from y, which y does not do: x, in fact, would become a mere unknowable substratum, or an invisible peg from which properties would hang like hams from the beams of a farmhouse. Such considerations make the concept of 'particulars' difficult, and invite a search for some way of escape.

My first attempt to deal with the above difficulties as to particulars was a paper read before the Aristotelian Society in 1911, 'On the Relations of Universals and Particulars'. The occasion was dignified by the presence of Bergson, who remarked, with surprise, that I seemed to think it was the existence of particulars, not of universals, that needed proving. In this paper I examined, but rejected, a hypothesis which I have since adopted. According to this hypothesis, there is no need of particulars as subjects in which qualities inhere. Bundles of qualities, according to this hypothesis, can take the place of particulars. What led me to reject this view at that time was the problem of numerical diversity and its connection with space and time. I believed, at that time, that mental phenomena consist in relations between subjects and objects, and that the subjects have the character of pin-point particulars. After arguing from the relativity of spatio-temporal position to the need of particulars in the sensible world, I went on to a closely similar argument as regards the difference between two persons. I said:

'The argument as to numerical diversity which we have derived from perceived space may be reinforced by a similar argument as regards the contents of different minds. If two people are both believing that two and two are four, it is at least theoretically possible that the meanings they attach to the words *two* and *and* and *are* and *four* are the same, and that therefore, so far as the objects of their beliefs are concerned, there is nothing to distinguish the one from the other. Nevertheless, it seems plain that there are two entities, one the belief of the one man and the other the belief of the other. A particular belief is a complex of which something which we may call a subject is a constituent; in our case, it is the diversity of the subjects that produces the diversity of the beliefs. But these subjects cannot be mere bundles of general qualities. Suppose one of our men is characterised by benevolence, stupidity, and love of puns. It would not be correct to say: "Benevolence, stupidity, and love of puns believe that two and two are four." Nor would this become correct by the addition of a larger number of general qualities. Moreover, however many qualities we add, it remains possible that the other subject may also have them; hence qualities cannot be what constitutes the diversity of the subjects. The

only respect in which two different subjects *must* differ is in their relations to particulars: for example, each will have to the other relations
which he does not have to himself. But it is not logically impossible
that everything concerning one of the subjects and otherwise only
concerning universals might be true of the other subject. Hence, even
when differences in regard to such propositions occur, it is not these
differences that constitute the diversity of the two subjects. The
subjects, therefore, must be regarded as particulars, and as radically
different from any collection of those general qualities which may be
predicated of them.'

I came later to think these arguments invalid. As regards the sensible
world, it is clear on reflection that position in experienced space is not
relative, like position in the space of physics. In my momentary visual
field, position is defined by qualities. What is in the centre of the field
of vision has a quality that we may call 'centrality'. Everything else
that I am seeing at the moment has various degrees of two qualities:
up-and-down and right-and-left. This, however, is not the most
serious point on which I have abandoned the views in the paper we are
considering. The most serious point has to do with the logical properties of spatio-temporal relations. Such relations are conceived as
generating series. For the sake of simplicity we may confine ourselves
to time, and even to time in one person's experience. We think that if
A is before B, A and B are necessarily different. We think that, if A is
before B and B is before C, then A is before C. If these characteristics
of temporal relations are called in question, it becomes difficult to see
how the time series can be constructed. It seemed to me, in 1911, that
the time series and the space of geometry could not be constructed
without the use of materials that had unique spatio-temporal position,
and that such materials could not be found if particulars were rejected.

The question of the construction of point-instants, which was
shortly afterwards taken up by Whitehead and developed in my book
on *Our Knowledge of the External World*, was already very much in my
mind in 1911. It already seemed clear that the particulars (if any) used
in constructing space-time should not themselves be punctual but
should have a finite extension. The punctual quality which physics
seems to require would only belong to bundles of particulars of which
each separate one had a finite extent. But it did not, at that time, seem
to be doubtful that, if there are two patches of red in two different
places, there are two particular reds. The necessity of thinking them
two was bound up with the relativity of position: the two patches, I
thought, differ only in position, and since position is not a quality
(or so I thought), it presupposes diversity and cannot constitute it.
With the recognition that position in sensible space is absolute, the
situation changed. A red patch on my right can be a complex of the two

qualities redness and rightness; and a red patch on my left can be a complex of the two qualities redness and leftness. Right and left, as well as up and down, have, in all their various degrees, the logical characteristics that are required for geometry, and it is their union with some one quality, such as redness, which gives plurality to two patches of redness seen simultaneously. I applied similar considerations to order in time. Suppose that some quality occurs twice over in one man's experience, as, for example, when a clock is striking the hour. What is it that makes you recognise two strokes as two, and not as one thing repeated? I came to the conclusion that this recognition depends upon a quality which we may call 'subjective pastness'. The contents of my mind, in so far as they are concerned with experienced occurrences, can be arranged in a series beginning with sensation, going on to akoluthic sensation, thence to immediate memory, and thence to memories having a quality of more or less distance from present sensation. In this way a subjective time series is generated consisting of items which, from an objective point of view, are all *now*. When you hear the striking clock repeating closely similar noises, the noises that you have already heard have varying degrees of what we may call 'fading', and it is the complex of noise plus fading that is plural, not the actual quality which is the noise. This theory, which I developed in *Human Knowledge*, still seems to me satisfactory, and I prefer it because it gets rid of the need for assuming the unrecognisable and unknowable entities which particulars would otherwise be.

There is, however, still a difficulty, and it is one which, in 1911, I thought insuperable. It cannot be thought logically impossible for two states of mind to be exactly similar. One might argue that this cannot occur in one person's experience owing to the difference between the accompanying memories on the two occasions. But such complete similarity might, so far as logic can show, occur between the experiences of two different people, A and B. If this were to occur, my present theory would compel me to say that the state of mind of A is numerically identical with the state of mind of B. At first sight this seems preposterous. We feel that it must be possible to find or construct things having the property that, if one is before the other, then the two are numerically different. I think, however, that this view results from undue excursion of experience into the field of logic. So far as experience goes, we never find such complete recurrence. The total contents of a mind at one time are never, so far as we can discover empirically, exactly similar to the contents of that mind at any other time, or of any other mind at any time.

For those who do not like *a priori* intuitions in an extra-logical realm, this theory has the advantage of disposing of certain instances of *a priori* synthetic knowledge. The statement, 'if A is before B, and B is before C, then A is before C', is certainly synthetic, and *feels* as if it were *a priori*. According to my theory, while it remains synthetic, it ceases to be *a priori* and is a generalisation from our experience that the total complex making up the momentary content of a mind never exactly recurs. From the point of view of an empiricist, this is a definite advantage.

I come now to a subject closely connected with that of universals and particulars, namely, the question of proper names. But, before embarking upon this question, I should wish to say something on the very controversial question of a logical language. A logical language, as I conceived it, would be one in which everything that we might wish to say in the way of propositions that are intelligible to us, could be said, and in which, further, structure would always be made explicit. We should need in such a language, words expressing structure, but we should also need words denoting the terms that have the structure. These latter terms, so I maintained, would be denoted by proper names. I thought that the construction of such a language would be a great help to clear thinking, though I never thought that such a language would be suitable for the purposes of daily life. At one time, Wittgenstein agreed with me in thinking that a logical language would be useful in philosophy, and I attributed this view to him in the introduction which I wrote to his *Tractatus Logico-Philosophicus*. Unfortunately, by this time, he had not only abandoned the view, but had apparently forgotten that he ever held it. What I said about it therefore appeared to him as a misrepresentation. His followers ever since have vehemently rejected the suggestion that a logical language could possibly be useful.

On one important point, I am prepared to concede that their criticisms are just. I believed, originally, with Leibniz, that everything complex is composed of simples, and that it is important in considering analysis to regard simples as our goal. I have come to think, however, that, although many things can be known to be complex, nothing can be *known* to be simple, and, moreover, that statements in which complexes are named can be completely accurate, in spite of the fact that the complexes are not recognised as complex. Many scientific advances consist in the recognition that what has been thought simple is complex: for example, molecules are composed of atoms, and atoms have a structure which has been becoming known in recent years. But, so long as we abstain from asserting that the thing we are considering is simple, nothing that we say about it need be falsified by the subsequent discovery of complexity. It follows that the whole question whether there are simples to be reached by analysis is unnecessary.

This has a bearing on the question of proper names. I thought, originally, that, if we were omniscient, we should have a proper name for each simple, but no proper names for complexes, since these could be defined by mentioning their simple constituents and their structure.

This view I now reject; but its rejection still leaves many problems as regards the functions of proper names.

Traditionally, there were two sorts of names: proper names and common names. 'Socrates' was a proper name; 'man' was a common name. Common names, however, are unnecessary. The statement 'Socrates is a man' has the same meaning as the statement 'Socrates is human', so that the common name 'man' is unnecessary and can be replaced by the predicate 'human'. It is necessary to distinguish between a predicate and a property. The latter is a wider conception which includes the former. A predicate will be something that can occur in a proposition containing nothing else except a name – e.g. 'Socrates is human'. A property will be what is left of any proposition in which a name occurs when that name is omitted or replaced by a variable. You may say, for example, 'If Socrates had been more conciliatory, he need not have drunk the hemlock'. This may be considered as asserting a property of Socrates, but not as assigning a predicate to him.

Traditionally, proper names were distinguished from common names by the fact that common names can have *instances*, whereas proper names denote some unique object. But the conception of instances is bound up with that of classes, and is not logically fundamental. What logic requires is propositional functions – that is to say, expressions in which there are one or more variables and which are such that, when values are assigned to the variables, the result is a proposition. Instances then become the values of the variable for which the propositional function in question is true. The variable may represent a variable 'thing' or a variable predicate or a variable property or a variable relation. The constant values that may be assigned to it will differ according to the sort of variable that it is. If a value of the wrong sort is assigned, the result is nonsense. Take, say, the proposition 'Socrates is human': your proposition is still significant, whether true of false, if you substitute for 'Socrates' the name of any other man or animal; and it is still significant if you substitute for 'human' any other predicate. If you start with a relational proposition, such as 'Socrates loves Plato', you can substitute for the word 'loves' any other word denoting a relation without causing your proposition to become nonsensical, but you cannot substitute for it any word not denoting a relation.

The above considerations suggest a syntactical definition of proper names. We may say that a proper name is a word not denoting a predicate or relation, which can occur in a proposition containing no variable. (The presence of a variable is indicated, in common language, by the presence of some such word as *a, the, some, all,* etc.) So far as syntax is concerned, I do not think that much more can be said about proper names.

But there are also epistemological considerations which must be taken into account. A proper name, if it is to fulfil its function completely, should not need to be defined in terms of other words: it should denote something of which we are immediately aware. This aspect of proper names, however, raises difficulties. If somebody mentions Socrates and you have never previously heard of him, you can look him up in the encyclopaedia and you may take what you find there as the definition of the word 'Socrates'. In that case 'Socrates' is not, for you, strictly a name, but a substitute for a description. It is obvious that, since words can only be defined by means of other words, there must be words which we understand otherwise than by means of definitions. A child learns the names of the members of his family by hearing the names pronounced when the members in question are present; even if his parents occur in the encyclopaedia, it is not from its pages that the child learns who they are and what they are called. This is the primitive use of proper names, and their use as abbreviated descriptions is derivative. There was a time when, if you had lived at Athens and had said, 'Who is Socrates?' the man of whom you asked the question might have pointed and said, 'That is Socrates'. It is because of this now distant connection with the experience of people long since dead that propositions about Socrates are part of history and not of fable, like propositions about Hamlet. 'Hamlet' pretends to be a name, but is not; and all statements about Hamlet are false. They only become true when, for Hamlet, we substitute 'Hamlet'. This illustrates one of the peculiarities of proper names: that, unlike descriptions, they are meaningless unless there is an object which they designate. Although France is now a Republic, I can make statements about the present King of France which, though false, are not meaningless. But if I pretend that he is called Louis XIX, any statement in which 'Louis XIX' is used as a name will be meaningless, not false.

I do not suggest that in ordinary language or in grammar we should refuse to regard 'Socrates' (say) as a name, but, from an epistemological point of view, our knowledge about him is very different from our knowledge of things with which we are acquainted. In fact, everything that we know about Socrates can only be stated fully by substituting some description of him in the place of his name, since, for us, it is only from the description that we understand what the word 'Socrates' means.

I have maintained a principle, which still seems to me completely valid, to the effect that, if we can understand what a sentence means, it must be composed entirely of words denoting things with which we are acquainted or definable in terms of such words. It is perhaps necessary to place some limitation upon this principle as regards logical words – e.g. *or*, *not*, *some*, *all*. We can eliminate the need of this limitation by confining our principle to sentences containing no variables and containing no parts that are sentences. In that case, we may say that, if our sentence attributes a predicate to a subject or asserts a relation between two or more terms, the words for the subject or for the terms of the relation must be proper names in the narrowest sense.

If we adopt this view, we are faced with the problem of deciding whether ordinary language contains any words that are proper names in the above sense. The question of particulars and universals is connected with our present question, but not in a very simple way. We have to ask ourselves: What are the words that we can understand otherwise than by means of a verbal definition? Again omitting logical words, the words that we can understand without a verbal definition must denote things that can, in some sense, be pointed out. 'Red' and 'blue', for example, are words for certain kinds of experience, and we get to know what these words mean by hearing them pronounced when we are noticing red things or blue things. There is a little more difficulty about psychological words, such as 'remembering', but the principle is the same. If you can see that a child is remembering something, and you then say to him, 'Do you remember that?' he comes in time to know what you mean by the word. It is only by some such process that words acquire their relation to facts.

Names in this restricted sense can only be given to something experienced, whether in sense or in thought. The question whether what is experienced is simple or complex is irrelevant, but it is not irrelevant that we never experience the kind of pin-point particular which our discussion earlier in this chapter rejected as unnecessary. The subject in psychology, and the particle of matter in physics, if they are to be intelligible, must both be regarded either as bundles of experienced qualities and relations or as related to such bundles by relations known to experience. The fundamental apparatus out of which ordinary proper names are manufactured must, according to the above theory, be composed of what would ordinarily be regarded as qualities rather than substances – e.g. red and blue and hard and soft and pleasant and unpleasant. This requires some syntactical rearrangement. Instead of saying, 'This is red', we shall have to say, 'Redness is compresent with centrality'; if the red thing concerned is in the centre of our field of vision. If it is not, we shall have to substitute for centrality the appropriate degree of rightness or leftness and of up or down.

I repeat that I am not suggesting the abandonment of ordinary language in favour of these odd ways of speaking. Perhaps the matter may be made clearer by introducing what I have called 'minimum vocabularies'. These are defined as follows: given any body of sentences which we can understand, what is the smallest number of words in terms of which all the other words of the sentences in question can be defined? In general, there is not a unique answer to this question, but the different possible answers will, as a rule, contain some words common to them all. These words represent the hard core of experience by which our sentences are attached to the non-linguistic world. I do not believe that, among such words, there are any having the kind of uniqueness habitually supposed to belong to particulars. We may perhaps define the 'stuff' of the world as what is designated by words which, when correctly used, occur as subjects of predicates or terms of relations. In that sense, I should say that the stuff of the world consists of things like whiteness, rather than of objects having the property of being white. This is the main conclusion of the above long discussion. The importance of the conclusion lies in the fact that it involves the rejection of minds and bits of matter as the stuff out of which the world is built.

The problem of the status of universals acquires a somewhat new form if the above theory as to qualities is accepted. Traditionally, qualities, such as white or hard or sweet, counted as universals, but if the above theory is valid, they are syntactically more akin to substances. They differ from substances, as traditionally conceived, by not having the spatio-temporal continuity which common sense ascribes to persons and things. There are complexes composed of compresent qualities. I give the name of a 'complete complex of compresence' to a complex whose members are all compresent with each other, but not all compresent with anything outside the complex. Such complete complexes take the place of particulars, and in place of such a statement as 'this is white', we have 'whiteness is a constituent of a complex of compresence consisting of my present mental content'.

But, although the above theory covers many of the traditional universals, it does not dispose of the need for universals. There are still universals denoted by predicates, such as colour, sound, taste, etc. It is obvious that all colours have something in common. This is illustrated by the fact that you can pass from any one colour to any other by imperceptible gradations. The same thing is true of sound. But there is no way of passing gradually from a colour to a sound. For such reasons, I should regard 'red is a colour' as a genuine subject-predicate proposition, assigning to the 'substance' *red* the quality *colour*.

But much more important than such subject-predicate propositions are propositions asserting relations. A language cannot express all that we know about the world unless it has means of saying such things as, 'A is before B', 'A is to the right of B', 'A is more like B than like C'. Such words as 'before' and 'like', or synonyms for them, are a necessary part of language. Perhaps these actual words may not be necessary. It is possible, by various artificial devices, to substitute the word 'similar' for many, if not for all, relation-words. But 'similar' is still a relation-word, and there is no obvious gain in eliminating other relation-words if this one has to be retained. It is relation-words that are the most stubborn of words of which the meaning is in some sense universal.

There is a point which has been overlooked in practically all theorising about universals and particulars. Those who dislike universals have thought that they could be merely words. The trouble with this view is that a word itself is a universal. The word 'cat' has many instances. The spoken word is a set of similar noises and the written word is a set of similar shapes. If universals are denied as vigorously as some nominalists deny them, there is no such thing as the word 'cat', but only instances of the word. This consideration brings us to the more difficult aspect of the problem of universals, namely, the question of their metaphysical status.

When we pass from the sentences asserting facts to the facts which they assert, we have to ask ourselves what characteristics of the sentences, if any, must belong to the facts asserted. It is quite clear that there are relational facts. The sentences, 'Philip was the father of Alexander' and 'Alexander preceded Caesar' clearly assert facts about the world. Idealists used to say that relations are the work of the mind; and Kant imagined that real things are not in space or time, but that spatio-temporal order is created by our subjective apparatus. But this whole view about relations was based upon a faulty logic and could only be accepted by those who failed to see its implications. For my part, I think it as certain as anything can be that there are relational facts such as 'A is earlier than B'. But does it follow that there is an object of which the name is 'earlier'? It is very difficult to make out what can be meant by such a question, and still more difficult to see how an answer can be found. There certainly are complex wholes which have a structure, and we cannot describe the structure without relation-words. But if we try to descry some entity denoted by these relation-words and capable of some shadowy kind of subsistence outside the complex in which it is embodied, it is not at all clear that we can succeed. What I think is clear is a fact about language, namely, as was suggested earlier, that relation-words ought only to be employed as actually relating and that sentences in which such words appear as subjects are only significant when they can be translated into sentences in which the relation-words perform their proper function of denoting a relation between terms. Or, as it may be put in other words: verbs are necessary, but verbal nouns are not. This does not answer the metaphysical question, but it comes as near to giving an answer as I know how to come.

This whole subject is discussed in the last chapter of my *Inquiry into Meaning and Truth*. I have nothing to add to what I said there, and I will therefore quote the last two paragraphs of the book:

'Some propositions containing the word "similarity" can be replaced by equivalent propositions containing the word "similar", while others cannot. These latter need not be admitted. Suppose, for example, I say "similarity exists". If "exists" means what it does when I say "the President of the United States exists", my statement is nonsense. What I can mean may, to begin with, be expressed in the statement: "there are occurrences which require for their verbal descriptions sentences of the form '*a* is similar to *b*'." But this linguistic fact seems to imply a fact about the occurrences described, namely the sort of fact that is asserted when I say "*a* is similar to *b*". When I say "similarity exists", it is this fact about the world, not a fact about language, that I mean to assert. The word "yellow" is necessary because there are yellow things; the word "similar" is necessary because there are pairs of similar things. And the similarity of two things is as truly a non-linguistic fact as the yellowness of one thing.

'We have arrived, in this chapter, at a result which has been, in a sense, the goal of all our discussions. The result I have in mind is this: that complete metaphysical agnosticism is not compatible with the maintenance of linguistic propositions. Some modern philosophers hold that we know much about language, but nothing about anything else. This view forgets that language is an empirical phenomenon like another, and that a man who is metaphysically agnostic must deny that he knows when he uses a word. For my part, I believe that, partly by means of the study of syntax, we can arrive at considerable knowledge concerning the structure of the world.'

Chapter 15

The Definition of 'Truth'

The question of the definition of 'truth' is one which I wrote about at two different periods. Four essays on this topic, written in the years 1906–9, were reprinted in *Philosophical Essays* (1910). I took up the subject again in the late 'thirties, and what I had to say as a result of this second investigation appeared in *An Inquiry into Meaning and Truth* (1940) and, slightly modified, in *Human Knowledge* (1948).

From the moment when I abandoned monism, I had no doubt that truth is to be defined by some kind of relation to fact, but exactly what this relation is to be must depend upon the character of the truth concerned. I began by controverting two theories from which I radically dissented: first, that of monism: and then, that of pragmatism. The monistic theory was set forth in Harold Joachim's book, *The Nature of Truth* (Oxford, 1906). I have dealt in an earlier chapter with this book in so far as it advocates monism in general, but I wish now to consider more specially what monism has to say as regards truth.

Monism defines 'truth' by means of coherence. It maintains that no one truth is independent of any other, but each, stated in all its fullness and without illegitimate abstraction, turns out to be the whole truth about the whole universe. Falsehood, according to this theory, consists in abstraction and in treating parts as if they were independent wholes. As Joachim says, 'The erring subject's confident belief in the truth of his knowledge distinctively characterises error, and converts a partial apprehension of the truth into falsity'. As regards this definition I said:

'Now this view has one great merit, namely, that it makes error consist wholly and solely in rejection of the monistic theory of truth. As long as this theory is accepted, no judgement is an error; as soon as it is rejected, every judgement is an error. But there are some objections to be urged against this comfortable conclusion. If I affirm, with a "confident belief in the truth of my knowledge", that Bishop Stubbs used to wear episcopal gaiters, that is an error; if a monistic philosopher, remembering that all finite truth is only partially true, affirms that Bishop Stubbs was hanged for murder, that is not an error. Thus it seems plain that Mr Joachim's criterion does not distinguish between right and wrong judgements as ordinarily understood, and that its inability to make such a distinction is a mark of defect' (*Phil. Es.*, page 155).

I concluded that:

'There is a sense in which such a proposition as "A murdered B" is true or false; and that in this sense the proposition in question does not depend, for its truth or falsehood, upon whether it is regarded as a partial truth or not. And this sense, it seems to me, is presupposed in constructing the whole of truth; for the whole of truth is composed of propositions which are true in this sense, since it is impossible to believe that the proposition "Bishop Stubbs was hanged for murder" is part of the whole of truth' (*Phil. Es.*, pages 155-6).

The monistic theory of truth is now no longer very widely advocated, but the pragmatist theory, which I criticised at the same time, still has vigorous advocates. I wrote two articles on this subject, of which the first was a review of William James's *Pragmatism: A New Name for Some Old Ways of Thinking*, while the second, which was published in the *Edinburgh Review*, April 1909, dealt with pragmatism in general. The essential point on which I differ from pragmatism is this: pragmatism holds that a belief is to be judged true if it has certain kinds of *effects*, whereas I hold that an empirical belief is to be judged true if it has certain kinds of *causes*. Some quotations will make James's position clear. He says, 'Ideas . . . become true just in so far as they help us to get into satisfactory relations with other parts of our experience'. Again, he says, 'Truth is one species of good, and not, as is usually supposed, a category distinct from good, and co-ordinate with it. The truth is the name of whatever proves itself to be good in the way of belief, and good, too, for definite assignable reasons'. There are two more quotations from James which are even more emphatic. They are as follows:

' *"The true", to put it very briefly, is only the expedient in the way of our thinking, just as "the right" is only the expedient in the way of our behaving.* Expedient in almost any fashion; and expedient in the long run and on the whole of course' (*Pragmatism*, page 222).
'Our account of truth is an account of truths in the plural, of processes of leading, realised *in rebus*, and having only this quality in common, that they *pay*' (*Ibid.*, page 218).

I paraphrased this last definition as the assertion that 'a truth is anything which it pays to believe'. Pragmatists have urged vehemently that this is a gross misrepresentation of James's words, but I have never been able to understand what other meaning his words can have.
Apart from more general objections to the view that a belief is

rendered true by the excellence of its effects, there is what I should have thought a quite insuperable difficulty. It is this: that we are supposed to know, before we know whether any belief is true or false, (*a*) what are the effects of the belief and (*b*) whether these effects are good or bad. I presume that we must apply the pragmatist criterion to (*a*) and (*b*): as to what are in fact the effects of a given belief, we shall adopt the view which 'pays', and, as to whether these effects are good or bad, we shall similarly adopt the view that 'pays'. It is obvious that this lands us in an endless regress. As I said in criticism of James:

'The notion that it is quite easy to know when the consequences of a belief are good, so easy, in fact, that a theory of knowledge need take no account of anything so simple – this notion, I must say, seems to me one of the strangest assumptions for a theory of knowledge to make. Let us take another illustration. Many of the men of the French Revolution were disciples of Rousseau, and their belief in his doctrines had far-reaching effects, which make Europe at this day, a different place from what it would have been without that belief. If, on the whole, the effects of their belief have been good, we shall have to say that their belief was true; if bad, that it was false. But how are we to strike the balance? It is almost impossible to disentangle what the effects have been; and even if we could ascertain them, our judgement as to whether they have been good or bad would depend upon our political opinions. It is surely far easier to discover by direct investigation that the *Contrat Social* is a myth than to decide whether belief in it has done harm or good on the whole (*Phil. Es.*, pages 135–6).'

Apart from such purely theoretic criticisms of the pragmatist definition of 'truth', there are others of a more practical sort which are, perhaps, better designed to appeal to the pragmatic temper of mind. The question as to what sort of beliefs will have good consequences in the life of an individual is one which often depends upon the Government and the police. Beliefs which pay in America are disastrous in Russia, and vice versa. The beliefs of the Nazis failed to satisfy the pragmatist criterion of truth because Germany was defeated in the Second World War; but, if Germany had been victorious, pragmatists would have had to hail the Nazi creed as pragmatically 'true'. Pragmatists reject such arguments by alluding to James's proviso, 'in the long run and on the whole of course'. I do not think that this proviso really improves matters. Mohammedans believe that, if they die in battle for the defence of the True Faith, they will go to Paradise. This belief, so far as I can see, has paid 'in the long run and on the whole'. Are we, on this account, to suppose it true even if, in fact, the dead

Mohammedan experiences no such bliss as he has been expecting? If he does, in fact, experience such bliss, what are we to say of the contrary belief formerly held by Christians, that when a disciple of the Prophet dies he goes straight to Hell? This belief was useful to the Christians, but it is impossible that the beliefs of both parties can have been in accordance with the facts.

Apart from theoretical objections to pragmatism, I thought, fifty years ago, before the era of the World Wars, what subsequent history has confirmed, that, in addition to being theoretically mistaken, pragmatism as a philosophy is socially disastrous. I concluded my criticism of pragmatism at that time as follows:

'The hopes of international peace, like the achievement of internal peace, depend upon the creation of an effective force of public opinion formed upon an estimate of the rights and wrongs of disputes. Thus it would be misleading to say that the dispute is decided by force, without adding that force is dependent upon justice. But the possibility of such a public opinion depends upon the possibility of a standard of justice which is a cause, not an effect, of the wishes of the community; and such a standard of justice seems incompatible with the pragmatist philosophy. This philosophy, therefore, although it begins with liberty and toleration, develops, by inherent necessity, into the appeal to force and the arbitrament of the big battalions. By this development it becomes equally adapted to democracy at home and to imperialism abroad. Thus here, again, it is more delicately adjusted to the requirements of the time than any other philosophy which has hitherto been invented.

'To sum up: Pragmatism appeals to the temper of mind which finds on the surface of this planet the whole of its imaginative material; which feels confident of progress, and unaware of non-human limitations to human power; which loves battle, with all the attendant risks, because it has no real doubt that it will achieve victory; which desires religion, as it desires railways and electric light, as a comfort and a help in the affairs of this world, not as providing non-human objects to satisfy the hunger for perfection and for something to be worshipped without reserve. But for those who feel that life on this planet would be a life in prison if it were not for the windows into a greater world beyond; for those to whom a belief in man's omnipotence seems arrogant, who desire rather the Stoic freedom that comes of mastery over the passions that the Napoleonic domination that sees the kingdoms of this world at its feet – in a word, to men who do not find Man an adequate object of their worship, the pragmatist's world will seem narrow and petty, robbing life of all that gives it value, and making Man himself smaller by depriving the universe which he contemplates of all its splendour' (*Phil. Es.*, pages 125–6).

William James replied to my criticisms in an article called 'Two English Critics' published in *The Meaning of Truth* (1909). He accused me, as other pragmatists have done, of misrepresentation; and his ground for this accusation, like that of other pragmatists, was that I supposed he meant what he said. In this article he admits that it is easier to decide whether Popes have always been infallible than whether the effects of thinking them so have been good, and he continues, 'We affirm nothing as silly as Mr Russell supposes'. When, however, he explains what he does mean, it seems to me even sillier than what I had thought he meant. He says that what he means is not that the consequences of the belief *are* good, but that the believer thinks they will be. It follows – and he admits the consequences – that if A believes one thing and B believes the opposite, A and B may both be believing truly. He says: 'I may hold it true that Shakespeare wrote the plays that bear his name, and may express my opinion to a critic. If the critic be both a pragmatist and a Baconian, he will in his capacity of pragmatist see plainly that the working of my opinion, I being what I am, makes it perfectly true for me, while in his capacity of Baconian he still believes that Shakespeare never wrote the plays in question.' I confess I find this position unintelligible. It seems to me that if 'Shakespeare wrote *Hamlet*' is true, there was a time when Shakespeare sat with a pen in his hand and wrote down certain words; but, if Bacon wrote *Hamlet*, it was Bacon who wrote down these words. Whether one of these happened, or the other, is a question of fact, totally independent of what anybody now living may think. And if I say the statement about Shakespeare is true, and the statement about Bacon is false, my statement is true if there was one sort of fact and false if there was another. For James, however, the question what was happening when *Hamlet* was being written is wholly irrelevant; the only thing relevant is the feelings of present-day critics.

I had pointed out what still seems to me to follow from James's doctrine, that the statement that 'A exists' may be true in the pragmatist sense even if A does not exist. After James's death, I was sent his copy of my article with his comments. His comment on this statement was the one word 'silly!' In print, he somewhat expanded this word. He says, 'Mr Russell next joins the army of those who inform their readers that according to the pragmatist definition of the word "truth" the belief that A exists may be "true" even when A does *not* exist. This is the usual slander, repeated to satiety by our critics.' I am quite unable to see that this is a slander. I will go further and add what pragmatists may consider a worse slander. James was anxious to find some way of asserting that the statement 'God exists' is true without involving himself in metaphysics, and his interests were so exclusively terrestrial that he was only interested in the terrestrial consequences of this statement. The question whether there is, in fact, an omnipotent Being, outside space and time, who wisely orders the cosmos, did not interest him, and so he thought that in finding an argument to prove that the statement 'God exists' is 'true' he had done all that the religious consciousness should demand. I confess that on this point my feelings are with the Pope, who condemned pragmatism as an unsatisfactory way of defending religious belief.

I wrote a later criticism of pragmatism in 1939 which was printed in *The Library of Living Philosophers*, edited by Dr Schilpp, in the volume dealing with Dewey. Dewey replied in the same volume. I do not think that what either he or I said added much to the earlier discussion.

My own definition of 'truth', at that earlier time, was published as the last chapter of *Philosophical Essays*. I had, later, to abandon this theory because it depended upon the view that sensation is an essentially relational occurrence – a view which, as explained in an earlier chapter, I abandoned under the influence of William James. The view which I held at that time can be best set forth by an example. Take such a proposition as 'Socrates loves Plato': if you can understand this proposition, you must understand its three constituent words; and I thought that understanding the words consisted in relations to what the words mean. Accordingly, when I believe 'Socrates loves Plato', there is a four-term relation between me and Socrates and love and Plato. When, in fact, Socrates loves Plato there is a two-term relation of Socrates and Plato. In my belief, the unity of the complex depends upon the relation *believing*, where *love* does not enter as a relating relation, but as one of the terms between which the relation of believing holds. When the belief is true, there is a complex consisting of Socrates and Plato related by the relation *love*. It is the existence of this complex – so I maintained – that confers truth upon the complex in which believing is the relating relation. I abandoned this theory, both because I ceased to believe in the 'subject', and because I no longer thought that a relation can occur significantly as a term, except when a paraphrase is possible in which it does not so occur. For these reasons, while I adhered to my criticisms of the monistic and pragmatist theories of truth, I had to find a new theory to allow for the rejection of the 'subject'.

I set forth this theory in *An Inquiry into Meaning and Truth*. A large part of this book is occupied with the meaning of words, and it is only after dealing with this topic that I come to the significance of sentences. In going backward towards what is primitive, there are various stages. There is first the sentence; then that which is in common between sentences in different languages which all say the same thing. This something I call the 'proposition'. Thus, 'Caesar is dead' and 'César est mort' assert the same proposition, although the sentences are different. Behind the proposition, there is belief. People who can speak are apt to express their beliefs in sentences, though sentences have other uses besides the expression of belief. They may be used mendaciously with a view to creating in someone else a belief which we do not hold. They may also be used to express a command or a desire or a question. But from the point of view of theory of knowledge and of the definition of 'truth', it is sentences expressing belief that are important. Truth and falsehood both belong primarily to beliefs and only derivatively to propositions and sentences. Beliefs, if they are sufficiently simple, can exist without words, and there is every reason to suppose that they exist in the higher animals. A belief is 'true' when it has an appropriate relation to one or more facts, and is false when it does not have such a relation. The problem of defining 'truth', therefore, consists of two parts: first, the analysis of what is meant by 'belief'; and then, the investigation of the relation between belief and fact which makes the belief true.

A belief, as I understand the term, is a state of an organism involving no very direct relation to the fact or facts which make the belief true or false. In a person who knows language, all except the simplest beliefs will be expressed in words, but the use of words is only one of the states of an organism by which a belief can be expressed. The most obvious case of the kind of thing that I have in mind is expectation of a notable event in the near future. For example, if you see a door being blown to by the wind and expect a bang, while you are expecting it you are in a certain state which, if you put it into words, would be expressed by the sentence 'There is about to be a bang'. But it is obvious that you can have the expectation without using words about it. I think it may be said generally that the state of an organism, which is believing something other than its present actual condition, could always, in theory, be described without mentioning the verifier of the belief. This is concealed by the fact that when we mention words we are apt to think that we are mentioning what the words mean. The essential character of a belief is most easily seen in such a case as the one I mentioned a moment ago, when you are expecting something in the immediate future. In this case, you have in the immediate future a feeling which might be expressed by the words 'Quite so!' or by the words 'How surprising!', according as your feeling is true or false. I think it may be said, broadly, that surprise is a criterion of error, but it is not always possible to apply this criterion.

In this investigation, I tried to proceed from what is most simple and primitive and unquestionable towards the more difficult complex and doubtful cases. I should have thought this procedure the obvious one to adopt on general methodological grounds, but I found that most of the writers who concern themselves with the definition of 'truth' proceed in a quite different manner. They start with what is complex or questionable, such as the law of gravitation or the existence of God or quantum theory. They do not trouble their heads with plain matters of fact, such as 'I feel hot'. This criticism applies not only to pragmatists, but equally to logical positivists. Philosophers of almost every school fail to investigate our knowledge of particular facts, and prefer to start their investigation with our knowledge of general laws. I think this is a fundamental error which vitiates most of their thinking.

For my part, I try to start, as I said a moment ago, with what is simplest and most nearly immediate and least removed from the animal. If I say 'I feel hot', and in saying so, am expressing a belief, the belief consists in a certain bodily state which can exist without the use of words, but which, in those who possess language, suggests certain words as 'expressing' it. Experience has established in me a causal connection between a certain bodily state and the word 'hot'. It is on account of this connection that the words 'I feel hot' become an 'expression' of my state. But I can quite easily feel hot, and know that I feel hot, without using words at all. Words, moreover, are only the most efficient and convenient of a number of ways in which I can 'express' my state. I may pant, I may wipe my sweating forehead, I may cast aside half my clothing. Such actions, like the action of saying 'I feel hot', indicate my condition. In such a case, there seems almost no possibility of error. I might, of course, be just getting warm after having been cold, and there might then be a transitional period during which I should not be sure whether I felt hot. But it is quite clear that we are sometimes sure on such a point. This applies generally to vivid sensations that we notice. If I see a flash of lightning or hear a loud noise or smell an intolerable stink, I am pretty certain to notice the occurrence, and there can be no reasonable doubt that it has taken place.

My abandonment of the relational character of sensation led me to substitute 'noticing' for 'acquaintance'. Most of the occurrences in our sensational life are not noticed; and when they are not noticed they are not data for empirical knowledge. If we use words about them, that is clear proof that we have noticed them; but we habitually notice many things that we do not mention in words.

I distinguish, in a belief, what it 'expresses' and what it 'indicates'. What it expresses in a state of myself; what it indicates need not be. But, in the simplest cases, such as 'I feel hot', what is expressed and what is indicated are identical. That is why the risk of error is here at a minimum. In this simplest case, if we use language, the utterance of the words is caused by what the words mean: when I say 'hot', my utterance is caused by my feeling hot. This is the bed-rock upon which all empirical knowledge is based.

In general, however, there is no such simple relation between an utterance and the fact which makes it true, if it is true. If I say 'Caesar crossed the Rubicon,' my statement is true because of an event which happened long ago. I can do nothing to alter this event now; and, if a law were passed making it a capital offence to say that Caesar crossed the Rubicon, that would have no bearing whatever upon the truth of the statement that he did so. The truth of the statement depends upon a certain kind of relation to a certain fact. I call the fact which makes the statement true its 'verifier'. It is only the simpler sort of statement that has a single verifier; the statement 'all men are mortal' has as many verifiers as there are men. But whether there is one verifier or there are many, it is always a fact, or many facts, that make the statement true or false as the case may be; and the fact or facts concerned, except in a linguistic statement, are independent of language and may be independent of all human experience.

I come now to beliefs which, if expressed in words, involve some such words as *all* or *some* or *a* or *the*. Take such a sentence as 'I met a man on the moor'. If this sentence is true, there was some one definite man whom I met, and my meeting with him is the verifier of my sentence. But I can know the sentence to be true without knowing who it was that I met. What I am knowing in such a case, I explain as follows: there is a state expressed by 'I met A' and another expressed by 'I met B', where A and B are men, and so on throughout the whole catalogue of the human race. All these states have something in common. What they have in common is expressed in the words 'I met a man'. Consequently, if I met my friend Jones, the knowledge that I met a man is an actual part of the knowledge that I met Jones. That is why the inference from 'Jones' to 'a man' is valid.

The importance of this kind of analysis is in regard to the understanding of sentences which go beyond the limits of my personal experience. Take such a sentence as 'there are men whom I have never met'. We all believe this sentence to be true. I have found that even solipsists are surprised by the fact that they have never met any other solipsist. The important point is that in the sentence 'there are men whom I have never met', the men whom I have never met are not mentioned individually. This is already the case with the simpler sentence 'I met a man' if in fact it was Jones whom I met. Although Jones is the verifier of my statement, my statement does not allude to him, and similarly when I say 'there are men whom I have never met'. It is not necessary, either for the understanding of the statement or for the knowledge of its truth, that I should be able to give any instance of a man whom I have never met. Statements about 'there are' or 'some' assert less than the statements that result when some particular person or thing is substituted; and it is for this reason that they can be known when no sentence substituting something definite is known. We are all quite certain that we know, not only that there are people whom we have never met, but that there are people whom we have never heard of and never shall hear of. We cannot give an instance of any such person, but we can, nevertheless, know the general assertion that there are such persons. I find that many empiricists go astray on this point and think it impossible that we should know that there are things of such and such a sort unless we can give at least one instance of such a thing. This opinion, if seriously entertained, leads to quite intolerable paradoxes and can only be held by those who have failed to notice these paradoxes.

It is important to realise that the fact or facts by which a statement is verified need not have a logical form bearing any close relation to the logical form of the statement. The simplest example of this is a disjunction. Suppose I see a volcano and believe 'that is either Etna or Stromboli', and suppose my belief to be true, what verifies my state-ment is the fact that it is Etna or, alternatively, the fact that it is Stromboli. Thus the relation of a disjunction to its verifier is less direct than the relation of the true half of a disjunction to its verifier. The same sort of thing applies to statements containing the word 'some' or the word 'a'. In all such statements, there is a general term such as 'man', and we can understand this term in the sense that we can notice what is in common between the sentences 'I met A', 'I met B', and so on, where A and B and so on are various men. It is by means of this sort of mechanism that we can pass beyond the limits of particulars of which we have had experience, though we must have learnt through experience the meaning of the general terms such as 'man', which are used in general statements of which we cannot give particular instances.

To sum up: It is primarily beliefs and only derivatively sentences that have the property of being true or false, as the case may be. A belief is a fact which has or may have a certain relation to another fact. I can believe that today is Thursday both on Thursday and on other days. If I believe it on a Thursday there is a fact – namely that today is Thursday – to which my belief has a certain distinctive rela-tion. If I believe the same thing on another day of the week, there is no such fact. When a belief is true, I call the fact in virtue of which it is true its 'verifier'. In order to complete this definition we must be able, given the belief, to describe the fact or facts which, if existent, will make the belief true. This is a long business because the kind of rela-tion that can subsist between a belief and its verifier varies according to the character of the belief. The simplest case from this point of view is that of a complex memory-image. Suppose I visualise a familiar room and in my visual image there is a table surrounded by four chairs, and suppose that on going into the room I see the table and the four chairs, what I see is the verifier of what I imaged; the memory-image with the belief had a close and obvious kind of correspondence with the perception that verified it. Putting the matter in the schematically simplest terms: I have (let us say), a visual, not verbal, memory of A to the left of B, and in fact A is to the left of B. The correspondence in this case is quite direct and straightforward. The image of A is like A, the image of B is like B, and the relation 'to the left of' is the same in the image and in the verifier. But as soon as we use words this simplest type of correspondence becomes impossible, because the word for a relation is not a relation. If I say 'A precedes B', my sentence is a relation between *three* words, whereas what I wish to assert is a relation between *two* things. The complexity of the correspondence grows greater with the introduction of logical words such as 'or' and 'not' and 'all' and 'some'. But, although the complexity is increased, the principle remains the same. In *Human Knowledge* I concluded the discussion of truth and falsehood with the following definition: 'Every belief which is not merely an impulse to action is in the nature of a picture, combined with a yes-feeling or a no-feeling; in the case of a yes-feeling it is "true" if there is a fact having to the picture the kind of similarity that a prototype has to an image; in the case of a no-feeling it is "true" if there is no such fact. A belief which is not true is called "false".' (Page 170.)

The definition of 'truth' does not, of itself, afford a definition of 'knowledge'. Knowledge consists of certain true beliefs, but not of all of them. The stock example to the contrary is that of a clock which has stopped but which I believe to be going and which I happen to look at when, by chance, it shows the right time. In that case, I have a true belief as to the time, but not knowledge. The question of what constitutes knowledge is, however, a very large subject which I do not propose to discuss in the present chapter.

The theory of truth developed in *An Inquiry into Meaning and Truth* is fundamentally a correspondence theory – that is to say, that when a sentence or belief is 'true', it is so in virtue of some relation to one or more facts; but the relation is not always simple, and varies both according to the structure of the sentence concerned and according to the relation of what is asserted to experience. Although this variation introduces unavoidable complexities, the theory aims at as close an adherence to common sense as is in any way compatible with the avoidance of demonstrable error.

Chapter 16

Non-Demonstrative Inference

I returned to England in June 1944, after three weeks on the Atlantic. Trinity had awarded me a five-years lectureship and I chose as the subject of my annual course, 'Non-Demonstrative Inference', or N-D.I. for short. I had become increasingly aware of the very limited scope of deductive inference as practised in logic and pure mathematics. I realised that all the inferences used both in common sense and in science are of a different sort from those in deductive logic, and are such that, when the premisses are true and the reasoning correct, the conclusion is only probable. During the first six months after my return from America I had rooms in College and enjoyed a feeling of peacefulness in spite of V1's and V2's. I set to work to investigate probability and the kind of inference which confers probability. I found the subject at first somewhat bewildering as there was a tangle of different problems and each thread had to be separated from every other. The positive outcome appeared in *Human Knowledge*, but I did not, in that book, mention the various perplexities and tentative hypotheses through which I had arrived at my final conclusions. I now think this was a mistake, as it made the conclusions appear more slap-dash and less solid than, in fact, they were.

I found the subject of non-demonstrative inference much larger and much more interesting than I had expected. I found that it had in most discussions been unduly confined to the investigation of induction. I came to the conclusion that inductive arguments, unless they are confined within the limits of common sense, will lead to false conclusions much more often than to true ones. The limitations imposed by common sense are easy to feel but very difficult to formulate. In the end, I came to the conclusion that, although scientific inference needs indemonstrable extra-logical principles, induction is not one of them. It has a part to play, but not as a premiss. I shall return to this subject presently.

Another conclusion which was forced upon me was that not only science, but a great deal that no one sincerely doubts to be knowledge, is impossible if we only know what can be experienced and verified. I felt that much too much emphasis had been laid upon experience, and that, therefore, empiricism as a philosophy must be subjected to important limitations.

I was at first bewildered by the vastness and multiplicity of the problems involved. Seeing that it is of the essence of non-demonstrative inference to confer only probability upon its conclusions, I thought it prudent to begin with an investigation of probability, especially as, on this subject, there existed a body of positive knowledge floating like a raft upon the great ocean of uncertainty. For some months, I studied the calculus of probability and its applications. There are two kinds of probability, of which one is exemplified by statistics, and the other by doubtfulness. Some theorists have thought that they could do with only one of these, and some have thought that they could do with only the other. The mathematical calculus, as usually interpreted, is concerned with the statistical kind of probability. There are fifty-two cards in a pack, and, therefore, if you draw a card at random, the chance that it will be the seven of diamonds is one in fifty-two. It is generally assumed, without conclusive evidence, that, if you drew cards at random a great many times, the seven of diamonds would appear about once in every fifty-two times. The subject of probability owed its origin to the interest of aristocrats in games of chance. They hired mathematicians to work out systems which should make gambling lucrative rather than expensive. The mathematicians produced a lot of interesting work, but it does not appear to have enriched their employers.

The theory which considers that all probability is of this statistical kind is called the 'frequency' theory. What, for example, is the probability that a person chosen at random from the population of England will be called 'Smith'? You find out how many people there are in England and how many of them are called 'Smith'. You then *define* the probability that a person chosen at random will be called 'Smith' as the ratio of the number of Smiths to the number of the total population. This is a perfectly precise mathematical conception, having nothing whatever to do with uncertainty. Uncertainty only comes in when you *apply* the conception as, for example, if you see a stranger across the street and you bet a hundred to one that he is not called 'Smith'. But so long as you do not apply the calculus of probability to empirical material, it is a perfectly straightforward branch of mathematics with all the exactness and certainty characteristic of mathematics.

There is, however, another, quite different, theory which was adopted by Keynes in his *Treatise on Probability*. He held that there can be a relation between two propositions consisting in the fact that one of them makes the other probable in a greater or less degree. He held that this relation is indefinable and capable of varying degrees, the extreme degrees being when the one proposition makes the truth of the other certain, and when it makes its falsehood certain. He did not believe that all probabilities are numerically measurable or reducible, even in theory, to frequencies.

I came to the conclusion that, wherever probability is definite, the frequency theory is applicable, but that there is another conception, misleadingly called by the same name, to which something more like Keynes's theory is applicable. This other conception I called 'degree of credibility', or 'degree of doubtfulness'. It is obvious that we are much more certain about some things than we are about others, and that our uncertainty often has no statistical aspect. It is true that the statistical aspect can sometimes be discovered where it is not obvious at first sight. I read a book about the Saxon invasion of England which led me to think that Hengist was indubitable but Horsa was perhaps a legend. It would perhaps be possible to put the evidence for Horsa alongside of evidence for other historical characters, and discover in what proportion of cases such evidence had been found to lead aright or to lead astray. But, although this sort of thing is sometimes possible, it certainly does not cover the ground, and leaves degrees of doubtfulness as a necessary conception in the investigation of what passes for knowledge.

It seemed to me that, in the problems with which I was concerned, doubtfulness was much more important than mathematical probability. It was not only that, in the inferences with which I was concerned, the premisses, even if true, do not make the conclusion certain. What was much more important was that the premisses themselves are uncertain. This led me to the conclusion that the mathematical aspects of probability have less to do than might be thought with the problems of scientific inference.

I next devoted myself to a collection of instances where we make inferences that we feel to be quite solid although the inferences in question can only be validated by extra-logical principles. In collecting such instances, I accepted whatever would only be doubted by a philosopher in defence of a theory. Broadly speaking, I did not reject common sense, except where there was some very cogent scientific argument against it. Take a very simple example: suppose you are walking out-of-doors on a sunny day; your shadow walks with you; if you wave your arms, your shadow waves its arms; if you jump, your shadow jumps; for such reasons, you unhesitatingly call it *your* shadow and you have no doubt whatever that it has a causal connection with your body. But, although the inference is one which no sane man would question, it is not logically demonstrative. It is not logically impossible that there should be a dark patch going through movements not unlike the movements of your body, but having an independent existence of its own. I attempted, by collecting as many instances as I could think of in which non-demonstrative inferences seem to us unquestionable, to discover by analysis what extra-logical principles must be true if we are not mistaken in such cases. The evidence in favour of the principles is derived from the instances and not vice versa. There seemed to me to be several such principles, but I came to the conclusion that induction is not one of them.

I found that, for lack of analysis, people had admitted blocks of non-demonstrative inference because they had a subjective prejudice in favour of certain kinds of knowledge, and had rejected other blocks on account of a contrary prejudice. It appeared to me that, in any particular case of an inference which seemed unquestionable, one should discover the principle upon which it depended and accept other inferences depending upon the same principle. I found that almost all philosophers had been mistaken as to what can and what cannot be inferred from experience alone. I divided the problem of empirical knowledge into three stages: (1) knowledge about myself; (2) knowledge about other minds – which includes the acceptance of testimony; and (3) knowledge about the physical world. Beginning with knowledge about myself, I found that solipsism as commonly expounded admits a great deal that is incompatible with the caution by which such a system is inspired. I do not remember anything that happened to me before I was two years old, but I do not think it plausible to maintain that I began to exist at the age of two. And in later life, I am quite convinced that many things happened to me which I do not remember. Even what I remember may have never happened. I have sometimes had dreams in which there were dream-memories that were wholly imaginary. I once dreamt that I was in terror of the police because I 'remembered' that, a month ago, Whitehead and I together had murdered Lloyd George. It follows that my recollecting something is not, *per se*, conclusive evidence that the something really happened. The solipsist, therefore, if he is to attain the logical safety of which he is in search, will be confined to what I call 'solipsism of the moment'. He will say not only 'I do not know whether the physical world exists or whether there are minds other than my own', but he will have to go further and say, 'I do not know whether I had a past or shall have a future, for these things are just as doubtful as the existence of other people or of the physical world'. No solipsist has ever gone as far as this, and therefore every solipsist has been inconsistent in accepting inferences about himself which have no better warrant than inferences about other people and things.

A very great deal of what we all unquestioningly accept as knowledge depends upon testimony, and testimony, in turn, depends upon the belief that there are other minds besides our own. To common sense, the existence of other minds does not appear open to doubt, and I do not myself see any reason to disagree with common sense on this point. But, undoubtedly, it is through experiences of my own that I am led to believe in the minds of others; and, undoubtedly, as a matter of pure logic, it would be possible for me to have these experiences even if other minds did not exist. Part of our reason for believing in other minds is derived from analogy, but part is derived from another source which has a wider application. Suppose you compare two copies of the same book and find that they agree word for word, you cannot resist the conclusion that they have a common cause, and you can trace this common cause backward through compositors and publishers to the author. You do not find it credible that the author's body went through the motions of writing the book without his having any thoughts meanwhile. Such grounds for admitting other minds are not demonstrative in the logical sense. You might have experiences in a dream which would be equally convincing while you still slept, but which you would regard as misleading when you woke. Such facts warrant a certain degree of doubtfulness, but usually only a very small degree. In the immense majority of cases, they justify you in accepting testimony if there is no evidence to the contrary.

I come next to purely physical occurrences. Take, for example, our reason for believing in sound-waves. If a loud explosion occurs at some point, the time when different people hear it depends upon their distance from that point. We find it incredible that these different people, at different times, should all experience a loud noise, unless something had been happening in the intervening spaces. A system of events at places where there were ears, combined with a total absence of connected events elsewhere, strikes us as altogether too staccato to be credible. An even simpler example is the persistence of material objects. We cannot believe that Mount Everest ceases to exist when no one is seeing it, or that our room goes out with a pop when we leave it. There is no reason why we should believe such absurdities. The principles which lead us to reject them are essentially the same as those which lead us to believe that things have happened to us which we have now forgotten.

Not only science, but a great deal of common sense, is concerned, not with individual occurrences, but with general laws. Our knowledge of general laws, however, when it is empirical, is inferred, validly or invalidly, from our knowledge of a number of particular occurrences. 'Dogs bark' is a general law, but it could not be known if people had not heard particular dogs barking on particular occasions. I found that our knowledge of such particular occurrences raises problems which some philosophers, notably the logical positivists, have not sufficiently considered. These problems, however, are not those involved in non-demonstrative inference, since the inferences with which we are concerned can only be justifiable in virtue of some general law such as you employ when, hearing a bark, you infer a dog. The laws that science seeks are, for the most part, in some sense causal. And this brings me to the question, 'What do we mean by causal laws, and what evidence is there of their occurrence?'

It used to be the custom among philosophers to think that causal laws can be stated in the form 'A causes B', interpreted as meaning that whenever an event of a certain kind A occurs, it is followed by an event of another specified kind, B. It was held by many that a causal sequence involves something more than invariability and must have some character that can be called 'necessity'. Many empiricists, however, denied this and thought that nothing was involved except invariable sequence. This whole point of view, however, could never have persisted among philosophers if they had had any acquaintance with science. Causal laws must be either not invariable or such as state only tendencies. In classical dynamics they take the form of differential equations, stating acceleration, not actual occurrences. In modern physics the laws have become statistical: they do not state what will happen in any particular case, but only different things, each of which will happen in an assigned proportion of cases. For such reasons, causation is no longer what it used to be in the books of old-fashioned philosophers. Nevertheless, it still retains an essential place. Take, for example, what we mean by a single 'thing' which is more or less persistent. This 'thing' must really consist of a series of sets of occurrences, each set characterising what we may call a momentary state of the 'thing'. The states of the 'thing' at different times are, often, though not always, connected by means of laws which can be stated without mentioning other 'things'. If this were not the case, scientific knowledge could never get a start. Unless we can know something without knowing everything, it is obvious that we can never know something. And this applies, not only to particular events, but also to the laws connecting events. In physics, atoms and molecules persist for a time, and, if they did not, the conception of motion would become meaningless. A human body persists for a time, although the atoms and molecules of which it is composed are not always the same. A photon which travels from a star to a human eye persists throughout its journey, and, if it did not, we could not be able to state what we mean by seeing a star. But all these kinds of persistence are only usual, not invariable, and the causal laws with which science begins must state only an approximation to what usually happens. Whether, in the end, something more exact is attainable, we do not know. What I think we can say is something like this: given any event, there is usually, at any neighbouring time and in some neighbouring place, an event very like the given event; and, as a rule, it is possible to discover some law approximately determining its small difference from the given event. Some such principle is necessary to explain the approximate persistence of many 'things', and also to explain the difference between perceiving

A and perceiving B – for example, if A and B are stars, both of which we are seeing.

I give the name of 'causal line' to a series of events having the property that from any one of them something can be inferred as to neighbouring events in the series. It is the fact that such causal lines exist which has made the conception of 'things' useful to common sense, and the conception of 'matter' useful to physics. It is the fact that such causal lines are approximate, impermanent, and not universal which has caused modern physics to regard the conception of 'matter' as unsatisfactory.

There is another conception which seemed to me of great utility in non-demonstrative inference, namely that of 'structure'. It seems reasonable to suppose that, if you see red in one direction and blue in another, there is some difference between what is happening in the one direction and what is happening in the other. It follows that, though we may be compelled to admit that the external causes for our sensations of colour are not themselves coloured in the same sense in which our sensations are, nevertheless, when you see a pattern of colours, there must be a similar pattern in the causes of your sensations of colour. The conception of space-time structure as something which often remains constant, or approximately constant, throughout a series of causally connected events, is very important and very fruitful. Suppose, to take a very simple example, A reads aloud from a book and B takes down what he hears from dictation, and what A saw in the book is verbally identical with what B has written, it would be quite absurd to deny a causal connection between four sets of events – viz. (1) what is printed in the book, (2) the noises made by A in reading aloud, (3) the noises heard by B, and (4) the words written by B. The same sort of thing applies to the relation between a gramophone record and the music that it produces. Or, again, consider broadcasting, where sounds are transformed into electro-magnetic waves, and the electro-magnetic waves are transformed back into sound. It would be impossible for the spoken sounds and the heard sounds to resemble each other as closely as they do unless the intervening electro-magnetic waves had had a space-time structure very closely similar to that of the words, spoken and heard. There are, in nature, innumerable examples of complex structures transmitted causally throughout changes of intrinsic quality, such as those between sound and electro-magnetic waves in broadcasting. In fact, all visual and auditory perceptions have this character of transmitting structure but not intrinsic quality.

People unaccustomed to modern logic find it difficult to suppose that we can know about a space-time structure without knowing the qualities that compose it. This is part of a larger aspect of knowledge. Unless we are to land ourselves in preposterous paradoxes, we shall find it necessary to admit that we may know such propositions as 'all A is B' or 'some A is B', without being able to give any instances of A – e.g. 'all the numbers that I have never thought of and never shall think of are greater than a thousand'. Although this proposition is undeniable, I should contradict myself if I attempted to give an instance. The same sort of thing applies to space-time structure in the purely physical world, there is no reason to suppose that the qualities composing the structure bear any intrinsic resemblance to the qualities that I know in sensible experience.

The general principles necessary to validate scientific inferences are not susceptible of proof in any ordinary sense. They are distilled out by analysis from particular cases which seem totally obvious, like the one that I gave a moment ago in which A dictates to B. There is a gradual development from what I call 'animal' expectation up to the most refined laws of quantum physics. The whole process starts from experiencing A and expecting B. An animal experiences a certain smell and expects the food to be good to eat. If its expectation were usually mistaken, it would die. Evolution and adaptation to environment cause expectations to be more often right than wrong, although the expectations go beyond anything logically demonstrable. Nature, we may say, has certain habits. The habits of animals must have a certain adaptation to the habits of nature if the animals are to survive.

This would be a poor argument if employed against Cartesian scepticism. But I do not think it is possible to get anywhere if we start from scepticism. We must start from a broad acceptance of whatever seems to be knowledge and is not rejected for some specific reason. Hypothetical scepticism is useful in logical dissection. It enables us to see how far we can get without this or that premiss – as, for example, we can inquire how much of geometry is possible without the axiom of parallels. But it is only for such purposes that hypothetical scepticism is useful.

Before explaining the exact epistemological function of the indemonstrable premisses of non-demonstrative inference something further must be said about induction.

Induction, as I said above, is not among the premisses of non-demonstrative inference. But this is not because it is not used; it is because in the form in which it is used it is not indemonstrable. Keynes, in his *Treatise on Probability*, made an extremely able investigation of the possibility of deriving induction from the mathematical theory of probability. The question that he had to investigate was this: given a number of instances of As which are Bs and no contrary instances, in what circumstances does the probability of the generalisation 'all A is B' approach certainty as a limit when the number of As that are Bs is continually increased? The conclusion that he arrives at is that two conditions must be fulfilled if this is to happen. The first and more important of these conditions is that, before we know any instances of As that are Bs, the generalisation 'all A is B' should have a finite probability on the basis of the remainder of our knowledge. The second condition is that the probability of our observing only favourable instances, if the generalisation is false, should tend to zero as a limit when the number of inferences is sufficiently increased. This condition is found by Keynes to be satisfied if there is some probability short of certainty, say P, such that, given that the generalisation is false and that $n - 1$ As have been found to be Bs, the chance that the nth A will be found to be a B is always less than P provided n is sufficiently great.

The second of these two conditions is less important than the first, and is also much less inconvenient. I shall concentrate attention upon the first of the two conditions.

How are we to know that some suggested generalisation has a finite probability in its favour before we have examined any of the evidence for or against it ? It is this that we must know if Keynes's argument is to give any high degree of probability to a generalisation when we know a great many instances in its favour and none against it. The postulates at which I arrived by an analysis of instances of non-demonstrative inference were intended to be such as would confer this finite *a priori* probability upon certain generalisations and not upon others. It will be observed that, in order that the postulates in question should fulfil their function, it is not necessary that they should be certain; it is only necessary that they should have a finite probability. In this respect they differ very profoundly from the kind of *a priori* principles that idealistic philosophers have sought, for such principles have been supposed by their advocates to possess a certainty greater than that of most empirical knowledge.

The postulates at which I finally arrived were five. I do not lay any stress upon their exact formulation. I think it highly probable that their number could be reduced and that they could be stated with more precision. But, while I am not persuaded that they are all *necessary*, I do think they are *sufficient*. It should be noted that all of them state only probabilities, not certainties, and are designed only to confer that finite antecedent probability which Keynes needs to validate his inductions. I have already said something in a preliminary way about these postulates, but I will now repeat them more exactly and more explicitly.

The first of these I call 'the postulate of quasi-permanence', which may be regarded, in a sense, as replacing Newton's first law of motion. It is in virtue of this postulate that common sense is able to operate more or less successfully with the concept of 'persons' and the concept of 'things'. It is also in virtue of this postulate that science and philosophy were able, for a long time, to make use of the concept of 'substance'. What the postulate states is as follows:

Given any event A, it happens very frequently that, at any neighbouring time, there is at some neighbouring place an event very similar to A.

This very similar event will be regarded by common sense as part of the history of the person or thing to whom the event A happened.

The second postulate is that of separable causal lines. This is perhaps the most important of all the five. It enables us, from partial knowledge, to make a partial probable inference. We believe that everything in the universe has, or may have, *some* effect upon everything else, and since we do not know everything in the universe, we cannot tell exactly and certainly what will happen to anything; but we can tell approximately and with probability; and if we could not, knowledge and scientific laws could never get started. The postulate is as follows:

It is frequently possible to form a series of events such that, from one or two members of the series, something can be inferred as to all the other members.

The most obvious examples are such things as sound waves and light waves. It is owing to the permanence of such waves that hearing and sight can give us information about more or less distant occurrences.

The third postulate is that of spatio-temporal continuity, which is mainly concerned to deny action at a distance. It maintains that, when there is a causal connection between two events that are not contiguous, there must be intermediate links in the causal chain. For example, if A hears what B says, we think that some process must have intervened between A and B. I do not feel sure, however, that this postulate could not be reduced to a tautology, since physical space-time is entirely inferential and the ordering of space-time events is dependent upon causality.

The fourth postulate, which I call 'the structural postulate', is very important and very fruitful. It is concerned with such cases as a number of people hearing the same speech or seeing the same performance in a theatre or, to take an example with wider scope, seeing the same stars in the sky. What the postulate says is as follows:

When a number of structurally similar complex events are ranged about a centre in regions not widely separated, it is usually the case that all belong to causal lines having their origin in an event of the same structure at the centre.

The importance of space-time structure, which I first emphasised in *The Analysis of Matter*, is very great. It explains how one complex event can be causally connected with another complex event, although they are not in any way qualitatively similar. They need only resemble each other in the abstract properties of their space-time structure. It is obvious that the electro-magnetic waves used in broadcasting cause the sensations of the hearers, but do not resemble them except in structural respects. It is because of the importance of structure that theoretical physics is able to content itself with formulae that are about un-experienced occurrences which need not, except in structure, resemble any of the occurrences that we experience.

The last postulate is that of analogy, the most important function of which is to justify the belief in other minds. The postulate is as follows:

Given two classes of events A and B, and given that, whenever both A and B can be observed, there is reason to believe that A causes B, then if, in a given case, A is observed, but there is no way of observing whether B occurs or not, it is probable that B occurs; and similarly if B is observed, but the presence or absence of A cannot be observed.

The above postulates, I repeat, are justified by the fact that they are implied in inferences which we all accept as valid, and that, although they cannot be proved in any formal sense, the whole system of science and everyday knowledge, out of which they have been distilled, is, within limits, self-confirmatory. I do not accept the coherence theory of *truth*, but there is a coherence theory of *probability* which is important and I think valid. Suppose you have two facts and a causal principle which connects them, the probability of all three may be greater than the probability of any one, and the more numerous and complex the inter-connected facts and principles become, the greater is the increase of probability derived from their mutual coherence. It is to be observed that, without the introduction of principles, no suggested collection of facts, or supposed facts, is either coherent or inconsistent, since no two facts can either imply or contradict each other except in virtue of some extralogical principle. I believe that the above five principles, or something analogous to them, can form the basis for the kind of coherence which gives rise to the increased probability with which we have been concerned. Something vaguely called 'causality' or 'the uniformity of nature' appears in many discussions of scientific method. The purpose of my postulates is to substitute something more precise and more effective in place of such rather vague principles. I feel no great confidence in the precise postulates above enumerated, but I feel considerable confidence that something of the same sort is necessary if we are to justify the non-demonstrative inferences concerning which none of us, in fact, can feel any doubt.

Ever since I was engaged on *Principia Mathematica*, I have had a certain method of which at first I was scarcely conscious, but which has gradually become more explicit in my thinking. The method consists in an attempt to build a bridge between the world of sense and the world of science. I accept both as, in broad outline, not to be questioned. As in making a tunnel through an Alpine mountain, work must proceed from both ends in the hope that at last the labour will be crowned by a meeting in the middle.

Let us begin with the analysis of some body of scientific knowledge.

All scientific knowledge uses artificially manufactured entities of which the purpose is to be easily manipulated by the methods of some calculus. The more advanced the science, the more true this is. Among empirical sciences, it is most completely true in physics. In an advanced science, such as physics, there is, for the philosopher, a preliminary labour of exhibiting the science as a deductive system starting with certain principles from which the rest follows logically and with certain real or supposed entities in terms of which everything dealt with by the science in question can, at least theoretically, be defined. If this labour has been adequately performed, the principles and entities, which remain as the residue after analysis, can be taken as hostages for the whole science in question, and the philosopher need no longer concern himself with the rest of the complicated knowledge which constitutes that science.

But no empirical science is intended merely as a coherent fairy-tale. It is intended to consist of statements having application to the real world and believed because of their relation to that world. Even the most abstract parts of science, such, for instance, as the general theory of relativity, are accepted because of observed facts. The philosopher is thus compelled to investigate the relation between observed facts and scientific abstractions. This is a long and arduous task. One of the reasons for its difficulty is that common sense, which is our starting-point, is already infected with theory, though of a crude and primitive kind. What we think that we observe is more than what we in fact observe, the 'more' being added by common-sense metaphysics and science. I am not suggesting that we should wholly reject the metaphysics and science of common sense, but only that it is part of what we have to examine. It does not belong to either of the two poles of formulated science, on the one hand, or unmixed observation, on the other.

I have been much criticised for applying the methods of mathematical logic to the interpretation of physics, but, in this matter, I am wholly unrepentant. It was Whitehead who first showed me what was possible in this field. Mathematical physics works with a space composed of points, a time composed of instants and a matter composed of punctual particles. No modern mathematical physicist supposes that there are such things in nature. But it is possible, given a higgledy-piggledy collection of things destitute of the smooth properties that mathematicians like, to make structures composed of these things and having the properties which are convenient to the mathematician. It is because this is possible that mathematical physics is more than an idle amusement. And it is mathematical logic which shows how such structures are to be made. For this reason, mathematical logic is an essential tool in constructing the bridge between sense and science of which I spoke above.

The method of Cartesian doubt, which appealed to me when I was young and may still serve as a tool in the work of logical dissection, no longer seems to me to have fundamental validity. Universal scepticism cannot be refuted, but also cannot be accepted. I have come to accept the facts of sense and the broad truth of science as things which the philosopher should take as data, since, though their truth is not quite certain, it has a higher degree of probability than anything likely to be achieved in philosophical speculation.

In the transition from crude fact to science, we need forms of inference additional to those of deductive logic. Traditionally, it was supposed that induction would serve this purpose, but this was an error, since it can be shown that the conclusions of inductive inferences from true premisses are more often false than true. The principles of inference required for the transition from sense to science are to be attained by analysis. The analysis involved is that of the kinds of inference which nobody, in fact, questions: as, for example, that if, at one moment, you see your cat on the hearth-rug and, at another, you see it in a doorway, it has passed over intermediate positions although you did not see it doing so. If the work of analysing scientific inference has been properly performed, it will appear that concrete instances of such inference are (*a*) such as no one honestly doubts, and (*b*) such as are essential if, on the basis of sensible facts, we are to believe things which go beyond this basis.

The outcome of such work is to be regarded rather as science than as philosophy. That is to say, the reasons for accepting it are the ordinary reasons applied in scientific work, not remote reasons derived from some metaphysical theory. More especially, there is no such claim to certainty as has, too often and too uselessly, been made by rash philosophers.

Chapter 17

The Retreat from Pythagoras

My philosophical development, since the early years of the present century, may be broadly described as a gradual retreat from Pythagoras. The Pythagoreans had a peculiar form of mysticism which was bound up with mathematics. This form of mysticism greatly affected Plato and had, I think, more influence upon him than is generally acknowledged. I had, for a time, a very similar outlook and found in the nature of mathematical logic, as I then supposed its nature to be, something profoundly satisfying in some important emotional respects.

As a boy, my interest in mathematics was more simple and ordinary: it had more affinity with Thales than with Pythagoras. I was delighted when I found things in the real world obeying mathematical laws. I liked the lever and the pulley and the fact that falling bodies describe parabolas. Although I could not play billiards, I liked the mathematical theory of how billiard balls behave. On one occasion, when I had a new tutor, I spun a penny and he said, 'Why does the penny spin?' I replied, 'Because I make a couple with my fingers.' He was surprised and remarked, 'What do you know about couples?' I replied airily, 'Oh, I know all about couples.' When, on one occasion, I had to mark the tennis court myself, I used the theorem of Pythagoras to make sure that the lines were at right angles with each other. An uncle of mine took me to call on Tyndall, the eminent physicist. While they were talking to each other, I had to find my own amusement. I got hold of two walking-sticks, each with a crook. I balanced them on one finger, inclining them in opposite directions so that they crossed each other at a certain point. Tyndall looked round and asked what I was doing. I replied that I was thinking of a practical way of determining the centre of gravity, because the centre of gravity of each stick must be vertically below my finger and therefore at the point where the sticks crossed each other. Presumably in consequence of this remark, Tyndall gave me one of his books, *The Forms of Water*. I hoped, at that time, that all science could become mathematical, including psychology. The parallelogram of forces shows that a body acted on by two forces simultaneously will pursue a middle course, inclining more towards the stronger force. I hoped that there might be a similar 'parallelogram of motives' – a foolish idea, since a man who comes to a fork in the road and is equally attracted to both roads, does not go across the fields between them. Science had not then arrived at the 'all-or-nothing principle' of which the importance was only discovered during the present century. I thought, when I was young, that two divergent attractions would lead to a Whig compromise, whereas it has appeared since that very often one of them prevails completely. This has justified Dr Johnson in the opinion that the Devil, not the Almighty, was the first Whig.

My interest in the applications of mathematics was gradually replaced by an interest in the principles upon which mathematics is based. This change came about through a wish to refute mathematical scepticism. A great deal of the argumentation that I had been told to accept was obviously fallacious, and I read whatever books I could find that seemed to offer a firmer foundation for mathematical beliefs. This kind of research led me gradually further and further from applied mathematics into more and more abstract regions, and finally into mathematical logic. I came to think of mathematics, not primarily as a tool for understanding and manipulating the sensible world, but as an abstract edifice subsisting in a Platonic heaven and only reaching the world of sense in an impure and degraded form. My general outlook, in the early years of this century, was profoundly ascetic. I disliked the real world and sought refuge in a timeless world, without change or decay or the will-o'-the-wisp of progress. Although this outlook was very serious and sincere, I sometimes expressed it in a frivolous manner. My brother-in-law, Logan Pearsall Smith, had a set of questions that he used to ask people. One of them was, 'What do you particularly like ?' I replied, 'Mathematics and the sea, and theology and heraldry, the two former because they are inhuman, the two latter because they are absurd.' This answer, however, took the form that it did from a desire to win the approval of the questioner.

My attitude to mathematics at this time was expressed in an article called 'The Study of Mathematics', which was printed in *The New Quarterly* in 1907, and reprinted in *Philosophical Essays* (1910). Some quotations from this essay illustrate what I then felt:

'Mathematics, rightly viewed, possesses not only truth, but supreme beauty – a beauty cold and austere, like that of sculpture, without appeal to any part of our weaker nature, without the gorgeous trappings of painting or music, yet sublimely pure, and capable of a stern perfection such as only the greatest art can show. The true spirit of delight, the exaltation, the sense of being more than man, which is the touchstone of the highest excellence, is to be found in mathematics as surely as in poetry. What is best in mathematics deserves not merely to be learnt as a task, but to be assimilated as a part of daily thought, and brought again and again before the mind with ever-renewed encouragement. Real life is, to most men, a long second-best, a perpetual compromise between the ideal and the possible; but the world of pure reason knows no compromise, no practical limitations, no barrier to the creative activity embodying in splendid edifices the passionate aspiration after the perfect from which all great work springs. Remote from human passions, remote even from the pitiful facts of nature, the generations have gradually created an ordered cosmos, where pure thought can dwell as in its natural home, and where one, at least, of our nobler impulses can escape from the dreary exile of the actual world.'

*   *   *

'The contemplation of what is non-human, the discovery that our minds are capable of dealing with material not created by them, above all, the realisation that beauty belongs to the outer world as to the inner, are the chief means of overcoming the terrible sense of impotence, of weakness, of exile amid hostile powers, which is too apt to result from acknowledging the all-but omnipotence of alien forces. To reconcile us, by the exhibition of its awful beauty, to the reign of Fate – which is merely the literary personification of these forces – is the task of tragedy. But mathematics takes us still further from what is human, into the region of absolute necessity, to which not only the actual world, but every possible world must conform; and even here it builds a habitation, or rather finds a habitation eternally standing, where our ideals are fully satisfied and our best hopes are not thwarted.'

*   *   *

'Too often it is said that there is no absolute truth but only opinion and private judgement; that each of us is conditioned, in his view of the world, by his own peculiarities, his own taste and bias; that there is no external kingdom of truth to which, by patience, by discipline, we may at last obtain admittance, but only truth for me, for you, for every separate person. By this habit of mind one of the chief ends of human effort is denied, and the supreme virtue of candour, of fearless acknowledgement of what is, disappears from our moral vision.'

*   *   *

'In a world so full of evil and suffering, retirement into the cloister of contemplation, to the enjoyment of delights which, however noble, must be always be for the few only, cannot but appear as a somewhat selfish refusal to share the burden imposed upon others by accidents in which justice plays no part. Have any of us the right, we ask, to withdraw from present evils, to leave our fellow-men unaided, while we live a life which, though arduous and austere, is yet plainly good in its own nature ?'

All this, though I still remember the pleasure of believing it, has come to seem to me largely nonsense, partly for technical reasons and partly from a change in my general outlook upon the world. Mathematics has ceased to seem to me non-human in its subject-matter. I have come to believe, though very reluctantly, that it consists of tautologies. I fear that, to a mind of sufficient intellectual power, the whole of mathematics would appear trivial, as trivial as the statement that a four-footed animal is an animal. I think that the timelessness of mathematics has none of the sublimity that it once seemed to me to have, but consists merely in the fact that the pure mathematician is not talking about time. I cannot any longer find any mystical satisfaction in the contemplation of mathematical truth.

The aesthetic pleasure to be derived from an elegant piece of mathematical reasoning remains. But here, too, there were disappointments. The solution of the contradictions mentioned in an earlier chapter seemed to be only possible by adopting theories which might be true but were not beautiful. I felt about the contradictions much as an earnest Catholic must feel about wicked Popes. And the splendid certainty which I had always hoped to find in mathematics was lost in a bewildering maze. All this would have made me sad but for the fact that the ascetic mood had begun to fade. It had had so strong a hold upon me that Dante's *Vita Nuova* appeared to me psychologically quite natural, and its strange symbolism appealed to me as emotionally satisfying. But this mood began to pass, and was finally dispelled by the First World War.

One effect of that War was to make it impossible for me to go on living in a world of abstraction. I used to watch young men embarking in troop trains to be slaughtered on the Somme because generals were stupid. I felt an aching compassion for these young men, and found myself united to the actual world in a strange marriage of pain. All the high-flown thoughts that I had had about the abstract world of ideas seemed to me thin and rather trivial in view of the vast suffering that surrounded me. The non-human world remained as an occasional refuge, but not as a country in which to build one's permanent habitation.

In this change of mood, something was lost, though something also was gained. What was lost was the hope of finding perfection and finality and certainty. What was gained was a new submission to some truths which were to me repugnant. My abandonment of former beliefs was, however, never complete. Some things remained with me, and still remain: I still think that truth depends upon a relation to fact, and that facts in general are non-human; I still think that man is cosmically unimportant, and that a Being, if there were one, who could view the universe impartially, without the bias of *here* and *now*, would hardly mention man, except perhaps in a footnote near the end of the volume; but I no longer have the wish to thrust out human elements from regions where they belong; I have no longer the feeling that intellect is superior to sense, and that only Plato's world of ideas gives access to the 'real' world. I used to think of sense, and of thought which is built on sense, as a prison from which we can be freed by thought which is emancipated from sense. I now have no such feelings. I think of sense, and of thoughts built on sense, as windows, not as prison bars. I think that we can, however imperfectly, mirror the world, like Leibniz's monads; and I think it is the duty of the philosopher to make himself as undistorting a mirror as he can. But it is also his duty to recognise such distortions as are inevitable from our very nature. Of these, the most fundamental is that we view the world from the point of view of the *here* and *now*, not with that large impartiality which theists attribute to the Deity. To achieve such impartiality is impossible for us, but we can travel a certain distance towards it. To show the road to this end is the supreme duty of the philosopher.

Chapter 18

Some Replies to Criticism

It is not an altogether pleasant experience to find oneself regarded as antiquated after having been, for a time, in the fashion. It is difficult to accept this experience gracefully. When Leibniz, in old age, heard the praises of Berkeley, he remarked: 'The young man in Ireland who disputes the reality of bodies seems neither to explain himself sufficiently nor to produce adequate arguments. I suspect him of wishing to be known for his paradoxes.' I could not say quite the same of Wittgenstein, by whom I was superseded in the opinion of many British philosophers. It was not by paradoxes that *he* wished to be known, but by a suave evasion of paradoxes. He was a very singular man, and I doubt whether his disciples knew what manner of man he was.

There are two great men in history whom he somewhat resembles. One was Pascal, the other was Tolstoy. Pascal was a mathematician of genius, but abandoned mathematics for piety. Tolstoy sacrificed his genius as a writer to a kind of bogus humility which made him prefer peasants to educated men and *Uncle Tom's Cabin* to all other works of fiction. Wittgenstein, who could play with metaphysical intricacies as cleverly as Pascal with hexagons or Tolstoy with emperors, threw away this talent and debased himself before common sense as Tolstoy debased himself before the peasants – in each case from an impulse of pride. I admired Wittgenstein's *Tractatus* but not his later work, which seemed to me to involve an abnegation of his own best talent very similar to those of Pascal and Tolstoy.

His followers, without (so far as I can discover) undergoing the mental torments which make him and Pascal and Tolstoy pardonable in spite of their treachery to their own greatness, have produced a number of works which, I am told, have merit, and in these works they have set forth a number of arguments against my views and methods. I have been unable, in spite of serious efforts, to see any validity in their criticisms of me. I do not know whether this is due to blindness on my part or whether it has some more justifiable grounds. I hope the reader will be helped to form a judgement on this point by four polemical articles which have already been published in learned journals but which are here reprinted. The four articles in question are: (1) on 'Philosophical Analysis' which is a review of a book by Mr Urmson; (2) 'Logic and Ontology', which is an examination of a chapter by Mr Warnock called 'Metaphysics in Logic'; (3) 'Mr Strawson on Referring', which is a rebuttal of his criticism of my theory of descriptions; and (4) 'What is Mind?' which is a review of Professor Ryle's book *The Concept of Mind*.

I   PHILOSOPHICAL ANALYSIS[1]

Mr Urmson's book *Philosophical Analysis* serves a very useful purpose. It gives within a comparatively small compass the reasons which have led Wittgenstein and his disciples to reject both my philosophy and that of the Logical Positivists and to substitute a new philosophy which they firmly believe to be better than any of its predecessors. Mr Urmson states very fairly such earlier views as he discusses, and I suppose that the arguments which he advances in favour of the newer views are such as seem cogent to their adherents. I find myself totally unable to see any cogency whatever in the arguments that Mr Urmson advances. And there is one important respect in which, from his own point of view, his book must be judged defective. He avowedly does not notice any writings of the schools which he is criticising that have appeared during the last twenty years. The Logical Positivists and I have in various respects tried to remedy what seemed to us defects in our doctrines, but such attempts are not noticed by Mr Urmson. In this he is only following the practice of the whole school to which he belongs.

In reading the works of this school I have a curious feeling such as Descartes might have had if he had been miraculously restored to life in the time of Leibniz and Locke. Ever since 1914 I have given a large part of my time and energy to matters other than philosophy. During the period since 1914 three philosophies have successively dominated the British philosophical world: first that of Wittgenstein's *Tractatus*, second that of the Logical Positivists, and third that of Wittgenstein's *Philosophical Investigations*. Of these, the first had very considerable influence upon my own thinking, though I do not now think that this influence was wholly good. The second school, that of the Local Positivists, had my general sympathy though I disagreed with some of its most distinctive doctrines. The third school, which for convenience I shall designate as WII to distinguish it from the doctrines of the *Tractatus* which I shall call WI, remains to me completely unintelligible. Its positive doctrines seem to me trivial and its negative doctrines,

[1] *Philosophical Analysis: Its Development Between the Two World Wars.* J. O. Urmson. Oxford at the Clarendon Press. 1956.

unfounded. I have not found in Wittgenstein's *Philosophical Investigations* anything that seemed to me interesting and I do not understand why a whole school finds important wisdom in its pages. Psychologically this is surprising. The earlier Wittgenstein, whom I knew intimately, was a man addicted to passionately intense thinking, profoundly aware of difficult problems of which I, like him, felt the importance, and possessed (or at least so I thought) of true philosophical genius. The later Wittgenstein, on the contrary, seems to have grown tired of serious thinking and to have invented a doctrine which would make such an activity unnecessary. I do not for one moment believe that the doctrine which has these lazy consequences is true. I realise, however, that I have an overpoweringly strong bias against it, for, if it is true, philosophy is, at best, a slight help to lexicographers, and at worst, an idle tea-table amusement.

Mr Urmson's criticisms of me are in part due to misunderstandings and in part to genuine philosophical disagreement. In order to clear away the former kind, I will try to state as concisely as I can the purpose and methods which have guided my work in philosophy.

In common with all philosophers before WII, my fundamental aim has been to understand the world as well as may be, and to separate what may count as knowledge from what must be rejected as unfounded opinion. But for WII I should not have thought it worth while to state this aim, which I should have supposed could be taken for granted. But we are now told that it is not the world that we are to try to understand but only sentences, and it is assumed that all sentences can count as true except those uttered by philosophers. This, however, is perhaps an overstatement. Adherents of WII are fond of pointing out, as if it were a discovery, that sentences may be interrogative, imperative or optative as well as indicative. This, however, does not take us beyond the realm of sentences. There is a curious suggestion, already to be found among some Logical Positivists, that the world of language can be quite divorced from the world of fact. If you mention that a spoken sentence is a physical occurrence consisting of certain movements of matter and that a written sentence consists of marks of one colour on a background of another colour, you will be thought vulgar. You are supposed to forget that the things people say have non-linguistic causes and non-linguistic effects and that language is just as much a bodily activity as walking or eating. Some Logical Positivists – notably Neurath and Hempel, and Carnap at one time – maintained explicitly that sentences must not be confronted with fact. They maintain that assertions are compared with assertions, not with experiences, and that we can never compare reality with propositions. Hempel maintains that the system which we call true 'may only be characterised by the historical fact, that it is the system which is actually adopted by mankind, and especially by the scientists of our culture circle'. I have criticised this view in *An Inquiry into Meaning and Truth*, page 142ff., and will here only repeat the gist of the criticism, which is that what the scientists of your 'culture circle' say is a fact and therefore it does not matter what they say but only what other members of your culture circle say they say. It does not seem to have occurred to these authors that when I see a printed statement on a page I am confronted with a sensible fact and that, if they are right, the truth as to what is printed on the page is not to be ascertained by looking at the page but by asking our friends what they *say* is printed there. We may illustrate Hempel's position by a fable: at a certain period, when his finances were not very flourishing (so the fable avers), he entered a cheap restaurant in Paris. He asked for the menu. He read it, and he ordered beef. All this since entering the restaurant was language. The food came and he took a mouthful. This was confrontation with facts. He summoned the restaurateur and said, 'this is horse-flesh, not beef'. The restaurateur replied, 'Pardon me, but the scientists of my culture circle include the sentence "this is beef" among those that they accept.' Hempel on his own showing would be obliged to accept this with equanimity. This is absurd, as Carnap in due course came to realise. But the adherents of WII go a step further. There had been two views about empirical statements: one that they were justified by some relation to facts; the other that they were justified by conformity to syntactical rules. But the adherents of WII do not bother with any kind of justification, and thus secure for language an untrammelled freedom which it has never hitherto enjoyed. The desire to understand the world is, they think, an outdated folly. This is my most fundamental point of disagreement with them.

What I myself have had to say, whether about mathematics or about physics or about perception or about the relation of language to fact, has proceeded always by a certain method. Taking it for granted that, broadly speaking, science and common sense are capable of being interpreted so as to be true in the main, the question arises: what are the minimum hypotheses from which this broad measure of truth will result? This is a technical question and it has no unique answer. A body of propositions, such as those of pure mathematics or theoretical physics, can be deduced from a certain apparatus of initial assumptions concerning initial undefined terms. Any reduction in the number of undefined terms and unproved premisses is an improvement since it diminishes the range of possible error and provides a smaller assemblage of hostages for the truth of the whole system. It was for this reason that I was glad to find mathematics reducible to logic. Kronecker said that God created the natural numbers and the mathematicians created the rest: viz. fractions, real numbers, imaginary numbers and complex numbers. But the natural numbers themselves, on this view, remained at an infinite set of mysterious entities. It was comforting to find that they could all be swept into limbo, leaving Divine Creation confined to such purely logical concepts as *or* and *not* and *all* and *some*. It is true that when this analysis had been effected, philosophical problems remained as regards the residue, but the problems were fewer and more manageable. It had formerly been necessary to give some kind of Platonic being to all the natural numbers. It was not now necessary to *deny* being to them, but only to abstain from *asserting* it, that is to say one could maintain the truth of pure mathematics with fewer assumptions than were formerly necessary.

In regard to the empirical sciences, various questions arise which do not arise in relation to pure mathematics. It is still possible in the most advanced empirical sciences such as theoretical physics to arrive at a minimum of undefined terms and unproved premisses. But such a minimum, when arrived at, does not give the reasons for which we believe the system to be true. Truth in pure mathematics is syntactical as some Logical Positivists believe all truth to be, but truth in empirical matters has a different basis. I should have supposed it incredible that there could be philosophers who would deny that an empirical proposition must owe whatever claim to truth it deserves to some relation to one or more *facts*. The nature of the relation may be difficult to define, but that some relation is involved can only be denied by those who have got themselves so befogged in philosophy that they have forgotten even what is completely evident. Let us take some quite everyday illustration, say: 'Professor Z goes for a walk every afternoon unless it is raining.' How does one come to know the truth of such a statement? Let us try to forget that we are doing philosophy and think of the matter in a common-sense way. You may know the sentence to be true because you have been told it by Professor Z or by Mrs Z, for the moral character of both of whom you have the highest respect. Or you may live next door to Professor Z and observe him passing your window except in bad weather. So far, I suppose, the matter is un-controversial; but it becomes controversial as soon as we take account of Mr Urmson's objections to analysis. I myself fail completely to see the force of Mr Urmson's anti-analytic theories. Suppose you believe the sentence because you have heard Professor Z pronounce it. Can it reasonably be denied that you have heard a number of sounds one after another while he was speaking? The matter is even clearer if you have arrived at the sentence by your own observations. On fine days, you have had the experience which you call 'seeing Professor Z walk past my house'. On wet days you have not had this experience. I cannot see the justification for denying complexity in the experiences which led to your statement. I dare say Mr Urmson and those who agree with him would not dispute what I have said so far, but would grow uneasy if I carried the analysis a stage further. They would say, 'we all know what you mean by saying that you saw Professor Z pass your window. If you pretend to analyse this statement any further, you are falling into metaphysics.' The accusation of metaphysics has become in philosophy something like the accusation of being a security risk in the public service. I do not for my part know what is meant by the word 'metaphysics'. The only definition I have found that fits all cases is: 'a philosophical opinion not held by the present author'. However that may be, when I wish to analyse further the experience which is called 'seeing Professor Z walk past my window', I am not talking philosophy but science. It is quite obvious, both to science and to common sense, that a series of visual impressions is involved, and that each of the visual impressions concerned has parts corresponding to Professor Z's head and body and legs. It is quite clear also that a series of separate pictures such as is involved in making a film for the cinema can reproduce an experience closely resembling that which you have when you see Professor Z walking.

Mr Urmson, however, raises two different kinds of objections. He urges, on the one hand, that however far you may carry your analysis you will never reach simples, and, on the other hand, that the collection of statements that you reach by analysing is not equivalent to the original unanalysed statement. Let us consider these two objections in turn. As regards simples, I can see no reason either to assert or to deny that they may be reached by analysis. Wittgenstein in the *Tractatus* and I on occasion spoke of 'atomic facts' as the final residue in analysis, but it was never an essential part of the analytic philosophy which Mr Urmson is criticising to suppose that such facts were attainable. In a discussion in 1918 quoted in *The Philosophy of Logical Atomism* reproduced by the Department of Philosophy of the University of Minnesota, you will find the following questions and answers (page 16): 'MR CARR: You think there are simple facts that are not complex. Are complexes all composed of simples ? Are not the simples that go into complexes themselves complex ? MR RUSSELL: No facts are simple. As to your second question, that is, of course, a question that might be argued – whether when a thing is complex it is necessary that it should in analysis have constituents that are simple. I think it is perfectly possible to suppose that complex things are capable of analysis *ad infinitum*, and that you never reach the simple. I do not think it is true, but it is a thing that one might argue, certainly. I do myself think that complexes – I do not like to talk of complexes – but that facts are composed of simples, but I admit that there is a difficult argument, and it might be that analysis could go on forever. MR CARR: You do not mean that in calling the thing complex, you have asserted that there really are simples ? MR RUSSELL: No, I do not think that is *necessarily* implied.' I have since become more convinced than I was then that there is no reason to expect analysis to arrive at simples. On this subject I will quote a paragraph from *Human Knowledge* (pages 268–9): 'The analysis of structure usually proceeds

by successive stages. ... What are taken as unanalysed units in one
stage are themselves exhibited as complex structures in the next
stage. The skeleton is composed of bones, the bones of cells, the cells
of molecules, the molecules of atoms, the atoms of electrons, positrons,
and neutrons; further analysis is as yet conjectural. Bones, molecules,
atoms, and electrons may each be treated, for certain purposes, as if
they were unanalysable units devoid of structure, but at no stage is
there any positive reason to suppose that this is in fact the case. The
ultimate units so far reached may at any moment turn out to be capable
of analysis. Whether there must be units incapable of analysis because
they are destitute of parts, is a question which there seems no way of
deciding. Nor is it important, since there is nothing erroneous in an
account of structure which starts from units that are afterwards
found to be themselves complex. For example, points may be defined
as classes of events, but that does not falsify anything in traditional
geometry, which treated points as simples. Every account of structure
is relative to certain units which are, for the time being, treated as
if they were devoid of structure, but it must never be assumed that
these units will not, in another context, have a structure which it is
important to recognise.'

In not asserting atomic *facts*, we do not necessarily cease to admit
atomic *sentences*. Whether a sentence is atomic is a purely syntactical
question. It is so if it does not contain the word 'all' or 'some' and has
no parts that are sentences.

For the above reasons what Mr Urmson has to say against atomic
facts is irrelevant.

I come now to the second point, that complex statements are not
equivalent to any collection of simpler statements. His stock example is
'England declared war in 1939' (one infers that he is not a Scot). I
cannot understand his position about this proposition, for he maintains
two things which seem to me incompatible. On the one hand he says
that it is not equivalent to a number of statements about what various
English people did, and on the other hand he contends that it nevertheless does not involve admitting that there is such an entity as 'England'.
He reconciles these two parts of his position by a resolute refusal to
analyse at all. You must not suppose that the statement is about something called 'England' or (may we add) about something called 'war'.
And yet it certainly is not a mere collection of empty words. It is
about something momentous having innumerable effects. He never
attempts to *prove* that the statement is not equivalent to a number of
statements about what English people did and I am at a loss to imagine
how he would prove it. The number of statements involved would
of course be very great. One might begin with a dictaphone reproducing
the Cabinet discussion which ended in the decision to declare war.
But one would have to proceed to the relations of the Cabinet to the

individual English people who admitted its authority. He points out that the Cabinet decision could conceivably have been met by a revolution repudiating its authority and that in that case 'England' would not have declared war. But this only shows that the statement 'England declared war' involves statements about the attitude of English people to their Government. I cannot see that he has in any way proved that, given a sufficient number of such statements, they would not logically imply the statement 'England declared war'.

In this connection there is another confusion which must be cleared up, which is as to the perfect logical language. If you are engaged in the work of logical dissection, you need a language differing considerably from that of daily life, but you need it for this purpose only. This is explained emphatically on page 2 of *Principia Mathematica:* 'The grammatical structure of language is adapted to a wide variety of usages. Thus it possesses no unique simplicity in representing the few simple, though highly abstract, processes and ideas arising in the deductive trains of reasoning employed here. In fact the very abstract simplicity of the ideas of this work defeats language. Language can represent complex ideas more easily. The proposition "a whale is big" represents language at its best, giving terse expression to a complicated fact; while the true analysis of "one is a number" leads, in language, to an intolerable prolixity. Accordingly terseness is gained by using a symbolism especially designed to represent the ideas and processes of deduction which occur in this work.' Those who advocate a peculiar language for purposes of logical analysis do not mean to suggest that such words as 'Whale' or 'England' should cease to be employed. What they do suggest is that, given sufficient time and sufficient knowledge, all the facts asserted by the use of such words could be asserted without the use either of these words or of any synonyms. No logician imagines that such a language would have practical utility. He is only concerned to say that it is possible, and that its possibility is due to the nature of world-structure.

One of the matters which the new philosophy does not like to see submitted to analytic treatment is the nature of empirical evidence. I think part of the difficulty arises from the fact that when people start to do philosophy they think they must forget common sense. We all of us believe in the existence of the things which we see, such as tables and chairs and houses and the sun and moon, but we know also, if we stop to think, that we are sometimes mistaken in such beliefs. Common sense enables us, as a rule, to correct such mistakes, for example, when we wake up from a dream. But the methods of common sense, though valid as a rule, are not infallible and depend upon the nature of a man's experience. If you had no experience of broadcasting and you heard a man's voice coming from the next room, you would have no doubt that there was a man there. Some restaurants produce an impression of vastness by means of mirrors and, if you do not look carefully, you may easily think that the reflections are 'real'. When you are tired you may hear a buzzing noise exactly like that of telegraph wires in a wind, and when you are mad you may hear voices uttering whole sentences in the imperative. The problem of illusions of sense is an ancient one which has come down to us from Greek times. Up to a point, I repeat, it can be decided by common sense. And up to this point, the new philosophy would raise no objections. But if you attempt to be a little more precise and to arrive at principles for the avoidance of illusion, you will be told that you are indulging in metaphysics. In fact, it is regarded as a sin to think seriously about the problem of perception. There is a great body of scientific work by physicists, physiologists, and psychologists tracing out the causal chains which intervene between an object and the perceiving of it. Although this work is done in the name of science and not of philosophy, many philosophers who profess to reject philosophy in favour of science choose to ignore it. By ignoring it they fall into errors which are only concealed from them by their resolute refusal to analyse.

There is one argument in particular which has a certain plausibility but cannot survive careful scrutiny. It is said that you cannot know a proposition of the form 'all A is B' except through experience of As which are Bs. This view is due to a false analysis of general propositions. No particular A is a constituent of the proposition 'all A is B' and the proposition can therefore be understood if you know the meaning of the word 'A' even if you have never seen an 'A'. Not only can you know the meaning of the proposition, but you may even know that it is true. Take for example: 'All the whole numbers which no one will have thought of before the end of the present century are greater than 1,000.' I do not see how anybody can deny this proposition although it is clearly impossible to give an instance of its truth until the present century comes to an end. It is not however strictly necessary to confine oneself to such an elaborate illustration. Every statement about the future which is generally agreed to be true will illustrate the same principle. The Nautical Almanack at the time of its publication contains a large number of very precise prophecies, but sailors do not on that account consider it a work of questionable metaphysics.

The whole relation of experience to empirical propositions is habitually misconceived. It is misconceived in two opposite ways: on the one hand, crude experience tells us less than we think it does, and, on the other hand, inferences from what is experienced to what is not experienced and even to what cannot be experienced are essential if we are to retain common-sense beliefs in spite of the assaults of science. I will say something about each of these two points.

The word 'experience' is used very loosely in philosophy, and hardly any philosophers have taken the trouble to assign a definite meaning to it. The relation of empirical knowledge to experience is one of those problems best treated by beginning with something vague but indubitable and proceeding by scrutiny to prove that the vague something involves something much more precise but *prima facie* much less indubitable. Let us begin by what is vague but indubitable. We all believe without hesitation a host of propositions which we have come to believe in virtue of things that have happened to us. We believe that there is such a place as Cape Horn and that the Norman Conquest occurred in 1066. Why do we believe these things? We believe them because we have heard or seen them asserted. If we had never heard or seen these assertions, we should not know what they assert. But hearing and seeing are kinds of sensations. Thus, even in regard to what is distant in time or space, what we consider ourselves to know depends, not for its truth but for our knowing of it, upon sensations of our own. I think it may be said without any exception or qualification that every piece of empirical knowledge that a given person possesses, he would not possess but for some sensation or sensations in his own life. This, I should say, is the essential truth upon which empiricists rely.

We must here make a distinction. I do not mean to say that when I see a table I say to myself: 'I have a certain visual sensation and I believe this sensation to have an external cause, namely what I call a table.' This, of course, is not what happens. I believe in the table as an external object at the moment when I have the sensation. The sensation is an indispensable part of the *cause* of my belief, but need be no part of what I am believing. Owing, however, to experience of the illusions of sense I may come to know that what I am believing as an effect of my present sensation is sometimes mistaken. I think I could agree with the philosophers whom I am criticising in rejecting that sort of wholesale and indiscriminating scepticism which, because of occasional illusions of sense, rejects sensation wholly as a source of knowledge about things other than itself. Where I disagree with the new philosophy is that I think it worth while to find out when and in what respects sensation is likely for scientific reasons to prove misleading, and, further, what general principles are implied in our common rejection of wholesale scepticism as to the knowledge of the external world to be derived from our own sensations.

This brings me to the second of the points that I mentioned a moment ago. Physics and physiology make it plain that if we know anything of the external world we know of it only because of causal chains proceeding from it to our own nerves and brain. We know of it, that is to say, as the unexperienced cause of experienced effects. To this theory it is objected that a kind of cause which must be unexperienced can never be validly inferred. Those who say this incur, in my opinion, two kinds of error: on the one hand, the error already noted of supposing that we cannot know a proposition of the form 'all A is B' except through experience of As; the other, of failing to note the absolutely devastating consequences of denying the possibility of inference to what cannot be experienced. I do not find in the new philosophy any awareness of the problems which thus arise. It is possible that the new philosophy might be able to find an answer, but so far it has made no attempt to do so. Indeed, whenever it comes up against a difficulty, it seems to deal with it as the March Hare did by saying, 'I'm tired of this. Suppose we change the subject.'

It is perhaps regrettable that Mr Urmson's discussion of logical atomism is conducted (so far as one can discover) in ignorance of its later developments. There is, for example, in his book a discussion of proper names which concludes (page 85): 'The doctrine of proper names was an important part of the view of language which was the major cause of disaster to logical atomism, and it must not be thought to be of minor importance.' In my *Human Knowledge* I have discussed proper names at considerable length and in a number of passages. I do not think that what I say in that book is open to any of Mr Urmson's criticisms or is an abandonment of the doctrine of philosophical analysis. I should be glad to see a criticism of what is said in that book from the point of view that Mr Urmson favours.

In conclusion, there are some general observations to be made about the point of view which Mr Urmson advocates. There have always been those who objected to analysis. They have been the same people as those who opposed every scientific advance. If Mr Urmson had lived when people were beginning to question the belief that earth, air, fire and water are the four elements, he would have deprecated, as contrary to common sense and common usage, every scientific approach to a more adequate analysis of matter. All the advances of modern physics have consisted in a more and more minute analysis of the material world. Atoms at first were considered almost unbelievably small, but to the modern physicist each atom is a complicated world like the solar system. No man of science would dream of questioning the propriety of analysis. At the very beginning of the first chapter of a book just published, I find the sentence: 'What is the nature of the prime materials of the simple bricks of which all matter is built ?'[1] It is not only in relation to matter that analysis is the road to understanding. A person without musical training, if he hears a symphony, acquires a vague general impression of a whole, whereas the conductor, as you may see from his gestures, is hearing a total which he minutely analyses into its several parts. The merit of analysis is that it gives knowledge not otherwise obtainable. When you learn that water

[1] *Atoms and the Universe*, by G. O. Jones, J. Rotblat, G. J. Whitrow. London. Eyre & Spottiswoode. 1956.

consists of two parts of hydrogen to one of oxygen, you do not cease to know anything that you knew before about water, but you do acquire the power to know many things that an un-analytic observation could not teach you. If Mr Urmson had been brought up to use Chinese ideograms, he would have vehemently opposed the phonetic analysis which led to the invention of the alphabet. To advance such considerations in defence of philosophical analysis is not, of course, to say that this or that philosopher has analysed rightly. It is only to say that he was right to attempt an analysis.

Although I feel strongly about the importance of analysis, this is not the most serious of my objections to the new philosophy. The most serious of my objections is that the new philosophy seems to me to have abandoned, without necessity, that grave and important task which philosophy throughout the ages has hitherto pursued. Philosophers from Thales onwards have tried to understand the world. Most of them have been unduly optimistic as regards their own successes. But even when they have failed, they have supplied material to their successors and an incentive to new effort. I cannot feel that the new philosophy is carrying on this tradition. It seems to concern itself, not with the world and our relation to it, but only with the different ways in which silly people can say silly things. If this is all that philosophy has to offer, I cannot think that it is a worthy subject of study. The only reason that I can imagine for the restriction of philosophy to such triviality is the desire to separate it sharply from empirical science. I do not think such a separation can be usefully made. A philosophy which is to have any value should be built upon a wide and firm foundation of knowledge that is not specifically philosophical. Such knowledge is the soil from which the tree of philosophy derives its vigour. Philosophy which does not draw nourishment from this soil will soon wither and cease to grow, and this, I think, will be the fate of the philosophy that Mr Urmson champions with an ability worthy of a better cause.

II LOGIC AND ONTOLOGY

My purpose in this article is first to discuss G. F. Warnock's 'Metaphysics in Logic', published in *Essays in Conceptual Analysis*, edited by Professor Antony Flew, and then to say what little I have to say on my own account on the same subject. I will begin with a few general remarks. Mr Warnock belongs to the 'Philosophy-Without-Tears' School, so named because it makes philosophy very much easier than it has ever been before: in order to be a competent philosopher, it is only necessary to study Fowler's *Modern English Usage*; post-graduates may advance to *The King's English*, but this book is to be used with caution for, as its title shows, it is somewhat archaic. Mr Warnock states that we should not 'impose the neat simplicities of logic upon the troublesome complexities of language'. He is concerned to discuss the existential quantifier, and thinks it important to point out that a number of assertions, which the logician would represent by the one symbol ∃, would be represented in common speech by a variety of phrases, and on this ground he assumes that the general concept represented by ∃ is unimportant or spurious. This seems to me a totally absurd inference. Perhaps I can illustrate the absurdity by means of a fable.

One upon a time, a very long while ago, there was a tribe which lived upon the banks of a river. Some say that the river was called 'The Isis', and those who lived beside it, 'The Isidians', but perhaps this is a later accretion to the original legend. The language of the tribe contained the words 'minnow', 'trout', 'perch' and 'pike', but did not contain the word 'fish'. A party of Isidians, proceeding down the river rather further than usual, caught what we call a salmon.[1] Immediately, a furious debate broke out: one party maintained that the creature was a sort of pike; the other party maintained that it was obscene and horrible, and that anybody who mentioned it should be banished from the tribe. At this juncture, a stranger arrived from the banks of another stream which was despised because it went footing slow. 'In our tribe,' he said, 'we have the word "fish" which applies equally to minnows, trout, perch and pike, and also to this creature which is causing so much debate.' The Isidians were indignant. 'What is the use,' they said, 'of such new-fangled words? Whatever we get out of the river can be named in our language, since it is always a minnow or a trout or a perch or a pike. You may advance against this view the supposed recent occurrence in the lower reaches of our sacred stream, but we think it a linguistic economy to make a law that this occurrence shall not be mentioned. We therefore regard your word "fish" as a piece of useless pedantry.'

This fable is scarcely a parody of Mr Warnock's argument about the existential quantifier. 'Existential quantifier' is a general concept analogous to 'fish'. Applied to names, it is analogous to minnows; applied to predicates, it is analogous to trout; applied to relations, it is analogous to perch; and so on. The fact that in ordinary talk people use different words for different occasions when the logician uses the existential quantifier is due to the fact that people who have not studied logic have not arrived at the very general idea represented by ∃, just as the Isidians in the fable had not arrived at the general idea 'fish'. Mr Warnock says that the existential quantifier confuses things that common speech distinguishes. This is exactly as if the Isidians had complained that a man who uses the word 'fish' confuses minnows with pike. Mr Warnock speaks of the 'invaluable non-simplicity of

---

[1] See *Crotchet Castle*, Chapter IV

ordinary speech'. I do not deny that there are distinctions in ordinary speech which are not made in logic. In ordinary speech we include the expression of our own emotions. If we say that So-and-so is an un-mitigated scoundrel, or that unfortunately So-and-so had not invariably acted in accordance with the moral law, the element of fact in the two statements is the same, but our emotional attitude towards the one fact is different in the two cases.

Mr Warnock deliberately and consciously ignores all that logicians have done to clarify the problems with which he professes to deal. He makes play with the statement 'Valhalla is mythological'. He does not mention the somewhat careful theory according to which state-ments that seem to be about Valhalla are really about 'Valhalla'. This theory may be right or wrong, but I cannot see the justification for pretending that there is no such theory. He tells us at the beginning of his article that the central question with which he is concerned is: are there abstract entities ? He then proceeds to object to the logician's interpretation of the words 'there are', and on this ground (at least, I can find no other in his article) he leaves his central question un-answered and, apparently, in his view unanswerable. He points out, quite truly, that the use of the word 'something' does not, in ordinary speech imply that there is such a thing. He instances the statement 'something is a prime number', which, as he says, 'is odd and mystify-ing'. It does not occur to him that the language of mathematical logic surpasses common language both in precision, and in generality. If you have twelve things and twelve names, it may easily happen that com-mon speech applies all twelve names to all twelve things. Common speech has two opposite defects: it has often one word with many meanings and many words with one meaning. The former defect may be illustrated by the following sentence: 'Whether Romulus existed is doubtful, since reasons exist for questioning the reliability of existing legends as to the first century of Rome's existence.' The opposite de-fect of having several expressions for the same meaning is illustrated by Mr Warnock's discussion of when we should say 'There are primes', 'Lions still exist in Africa', 'There are shadows on the moon' – which last, he seems to think, does not imply that shadows exist, a phrase which he rejects solely on the ground that most people would not use it. The logician thinks that a language is preferable in which there is one name for one thing. And when I say 'preferable', I do not mean 'preferable' for everyday use, but 'preferable' in an attempt to make precise statements about the world.

I come now to the particular question of 'existence'. I maintain – and I think that this has great importance in avoiding muddles – that the word 'existence' as ordinarily used gives rise to syntactical con-fusion and has been a source of a great deal of metaphysical confusion. Take, for example, the following piece of reasoning: 'my present sensation exists; this is my present sensation; therefore this exists'. I maintain that the two premisses may be true, but the conclusion is nonsense. It is impossible to make this clear in common language. This is an argument against common language. I maintain that the legitimate concept involved is that of ∃. This concept may be defined as follows: given an expression fx containing a variable, x, and becoming a proposition when a value is assigned to the variable, we say that the expression $(\exists x).fx$ is to mean that there is at least one value of x for which fx is true. I should prefer, myself, to regard this as a definition of 'there is', but, if I did, I could not make myself understood.

When we say 'there is' or 'there are', it does not follow from the truth of our statement that what we say there is or there are is part of the furniture of the world, to use a deliberately vague phrase. Mathematical logic admits the statement 'there are numbers' and metalogic admits the statement 'numbers are logical fictions or symbolic conveniences'. Numbers are classes of classes, and classes are symbolic conveniences. An attempt to translate ∃ into ordinary language is bound to land one in trouble, because the notion to be conveyed is one which has been unknown to those who have framed ordinary speech. The statement 'there are numbers' has to be interpreted by a rather elaborate process. We have first to start with some propositional function, say fx, then to define 'the number of things having the property f', then to define 'number' as 'whatever is the number of things having some property or other'. In this way we get a definition of the propositional function 'n is a number', and we find that if we substitute for n what we have defined as '1', we have a true statement. This is the sort of thing that is meant by saying there is at least one number, but it is very difficult, in common language, to make clear that we are not making a platonic assertion of the reality of numbers.

The relation of logic to ontology is, in fact, very complex. We can in some degree separate linguistic aspects of this problem from those that have a bearing on ontology. The linguistic problems are capable, at least in theory, of a precise solution, but the ontological problems remain much more obscure. The purely linguistic problems, however, have an ontological background, though a somewhat vague one. Sentences are composed of words, and, if they are to be able to assert facts, some, at least, of the words must have that kind of relation to something else which is called 'meaning'. If a waiter in a restaurant tells me, 'We have some very nice fresh asparagus', I shall be justly incensed if he explains that his remark was purely linguistic and bore no reference to any actual asparagus. This degree of ontological commitment is involved in all ordinary speech. But the relation of words to objects other than words varies according to the kind of word concerned, and this gives rise to a logical form of the doctrine of parts of speech. If a sentence is to have significance, unless it is a sentence of pure logic, some of its words must point to something, but others need not. A sentence could not significantly contain the phrase 'The Queen of England' unless there were something in the world that was pointed to by the word 'Queen' and by the word 'England', but there need not be anything pointed to by the word 'the' or the word 'of'. A large part of the bearing of mathematical logic upon ontology consists in diminishing the number of objects required in order to make sense of statements which we feel to be intelligible. The only reason for this process of whittling away is to avoid rash and unwarranted assumptions. If our ordinary empirical statements are to be significant, they must (if they are not linguistic) point to something outside words. The purely technical question thus arises: what is the smallest vocabulary which will enable us to assert what we believe to be fact ?

Presuming this problem solved, we are left with the ontological problem: what relations must subsist between our words and sentences, on the one hand, and fact, on the other, if our words are to have meaning and our sentences are to be significant ? We can, to begin with, exclude from our vocabulary all words that have a verbal definition, since we can always substitute the definition for the words. Sometimes (omitting niceties) the relation of a word to an object is fairly clear: we know the object indicated by the name 'Dwight D. Eisenhower'; we know what we mean by the names of colours; and so on. But there are other words about which we feel more difficulty: if we say 'Alexander preceded Caesar', we feel (perhaps mistakenly) that Alexander and Caesar are solid. But what about the word 'preceded' ? We could, at a pinch, imagine a universe consisting only of Alexander or only of Caesar or only of the pair of them. But we cannot imagine a universe consisting only of 'preceded'. It is this sort of thing that has led to belief in substance and to doubt about universals. Here, again, the needs of language are clear, but the metaphysical implications of these needs are obscure. We cannot do without such words as 'precede', but such words do not seem to point at one of the bricks of the universe in the kind of way in which proper names can do.

The question 'Are there universals ?' can be interpreted in various ways. In the first place, it can be interpreted in the sense of the existential quantifier. We can say: 'There are sentences containing two names and a relation-word, and without such sentences many assertions of facts which we believe ourselves to know would be impossible.' We can go on to say that, just as the names in such sentences point to objects, so the relation-words must point to something extra-linguistic. It is a fact that Alexander preceded Caesar, and this fact does not consist merely of Alexander and Caesar. Relation-words, it is clear, serve a purpose in enabling us to assert facts which would otherwise be unstatable. So far, I think, we are on firm ground. But I do not think it follows that there is, in any sense whatever, a 'thing' called 'preceding'. A relation-word is only used correctly when relata are supplied.

This applies equally to predicates. Quine finds a special difficulty when predicates or relation-words appear as apparent variables. Take, for example, the statement 'Napoleon had all the qualities of a great general'. This will have to be interpreted as follows: 'whatever *f* may be, if "*x* was a great general" implies *fx*, whatever *x* may be, then *f* (Napoleon)'. This seems to imply giving a substantiality to *f* which we should like to avoid if we could. I think the difficulty real, and I do not know the answer. We certainly cannot do without variables that represent predicates or relation-words, but my feeling is that a technical device should be possible which would preserve the differences of ontological status between what is meant by names on the one hand, and predicates and relation-words on the other.

What mathematical logic does is not to establish ontological status where it might be doubted, but rather to diminish the number of words which have the straightforward meaning of pointing to an object. It used to be a common view that all the integers were entities, and those who would not go so far as this were at least persuaded that the number 1 is an entity. We cannot prove that this is not the case, but we can prove that mathematics affords no evidence for it.

Finally, the question 'Are there universals?' is ambiguous. In some interpretations, the answer is certainly 'yes'; in others no decisive answer seems possible at present. What I have to say about the ontological status of universals is contained in the last chapter of *An Inquiry into Meaning and Truth*.

III   MR STRAWSON ON REFERRING

Mr P. F. Strawson published in *Mind* of 1950 an article called 'On Referring'. This article is reprinted in *Essays in Conceptual Analysis*, selected and edited by Professor Antony Flew. The references that follow are to this reprint. The main purpose of the article is to refute my theory of descriptions. As I find that some philosophers whom I respect consider that it has achieved its purpose successfully, I have come to the conclusion that a polemical reply is called for. I may say, to begin with, that I am totally unable to see any validity whatever in any of Mr Strawson's arguments. Whether this inability is due to senility on my part or to some other cause, I must leave readers to judge.

The gist of Mr Strawson's argument consists in identifying two problems which I have regarded as quite distinct – namely, the problem of descriptions and the problem of egocentricity. I have dealt with both these problems at considerable length, but as I have considered them to be different problems, I have not dealt with the one when I was considering the other. This enables Mr Strawson to pretend that I have overlooked the problem of egocentricity.

He is helped in this pretence by a careful selection of material. In the article in which I first set forth the theory of descriptions, I dealt specially with two examples: 'The present King of France is bald' and 'Scott is the author of *Waverley*'. The latter example does not suit Mr Strawson, and he therefore entirely ignores it except for one quite perfunctory reference. As regards 'the present King of France', he fastens upon the egocentric word 'present' and does not seem able to grasp that, if for the word 'present' I had substituted the words 'in 1905', the whole of his argument would have collapsed.

Or perhaps not quite the whole, for reasons which I had set forth before Mr Strawson wrote. It is, however, not difficult to give other examples of the use of descriptive phrases from which egocentricity is wholly absent. I should like to see him apply his doctrine to such sentences as the following: 'the square-root of minus one is half the square-root of minus four', or 'the cube of three is the integer immediately preceding the second perfect number'. There are no egocentric words in either of these two sentences, but the problem of interpreting the descriptive phrases is exactly the same as if there were.

There is not a word in Mr Strawson's article to suggest that I ever considered egocentric words, still less that the theory which he advocates in regard to them is the very one which I had set forth at great length and in considerable detail.[1] The gist of what he has to say about such words is the entirely correct statement that what they refer to depends upon when and where they are used. As to this, I need only quote one paragraph from *Human Knowledge* (page 107):

'"This" denotes whatever, at the moment when the word is used, occupies the centre of attention. With words which are not egocentric, what is constant is something about the object indicated, but "this" denotes a different object on each occasion of its use: what is constant is not the object denoted, but its relation to the particular use of the word. Whenever the word is used, the person using it is attending to something, and the word indicates this something. When a word is not egocentric, there is no need to distinguish between different occasions when it is used, but we must make this distinction with egocentric words, since what they indicate is something having a given relation to the particular use of the word.'

I must refer, also, to the case that I discuss (page 101ff.) in which I am walking with a friend on a dark night. We lose touch with each

[1] cf. *An Inquiry into Meaning and Truth*, Chapter VII, and *Human Knowledge*, Part II, Chapter IV.

other and he calls 'Where are you?' and I reply 'Here I am!' It is of
the essence of a scientific account of the world to reduce to a minimum
the egocentric element in an assertion, but success in this attempt is a
matter of degree, and is never complete where empirical material is
concerned. This is due to the fact that the meanings of all empirical
words depend ultimately upon ostensive definitions, that ostensive
definitions depend upon experience, and that experience is egocentric.
We can, however, by means of egocentric words, *describe* something
which is not egocentric; it is this that enables us to use a common
language.

All this may be right or wrong, but, whichever it is, Mr Strawson
should not expound it as if it were a theory that he had invented,
whereas, in fact, I had set it forth before he wrote, though perhaps he
did not grasp the purport of what I said. I shall say no more about
egocentricity since, for the reasons I have already given, I think Mr
Strawson completely mistaken in connecting it with the problem of
descriptions.

I am at a loss to understand Mr Strawson's position on the subject
of names. When he is writing about me, he says: 'There are no logically
proper names and there are no descriptions (in this sense)' (page 26).
But when he is writing about Quine, in *Mind*, October 1956, he takes a
quite different line. Quine has a theory that names are unnecessary
and can always be replaced by descriptions. This theory shocks Mr
Strawson for reasons which, to me, remain obscure. However, I will
leave the defence of Quine to Quine, who is quite capable of looking
after himself. What is important for my purposes is to elucidate the
meaning of the words 'in this sense' which Mr Strawson puts in
brackets. So far as I can discover from the context, what he objects to
is the belief that there are words which are only significant because
there is something that they mean, and if there were not this something,
they would be empty noises, not words. For my part, I think that there
must be such words if language is to have any relation to fact. The
necessity for such words is made obvious by the process of ostensive
definition. How do we know what is meant by such words as 'red' and
'blue'? We cannot know what these words mean unless we have seen
red and seen blue. If there were no red and no blue in our experience,
we might, perhaps, invent some elaborate description which we could
substitute for the word 'red' or for the word 'blue'. For example, if
you were dealing with a blind man, you could hold a red-hot poker
near enough for him to feel the heat, and you could tell him that red is
what he would see if he could see – but of course for the word 'see'
you would have to substitute another elaborate description. Any
description which the blind man could understand would have to be
in terms of words expressing experiences which he had had. Unless
fundamental words in the individual's vocabulary had this kind of

direct relation to fact, language in general would have no such relation. I defy Mr Strawson to give the usual meaning to the word 'red' unless there is something which the word designates.

This brings me to a further point. 'Red' is usually regarded as a predicate and as designating a universal. I prefer for purposes of philosophical analysis a language in which 'red' is a subject, and, while I should not say that it is a positive error to call it a universal, I should say that calling it so invites confusion. This is connected with what Mr Strawson calls my 'logically disastrous theory of names' (page 39). He does not deign to mention why he considers this theory 'logically disastrous'. I hope that on some future occasions he will enlighten me on this point.

This brings me to a fundamental divergence between myself and many philosophers with whom Mr Strawson appears to be in general agreement. They are persuaded that common speech is good enough, not only for daily life, but also for philosophy. I, on the contrary, am persuaded that common speech is full of vagueness and inaccuracy, and that any attempt to be precise and accurate requires modification of common speech both as regards vocabulary and as regards syntax. Everybody admits that physics and chemistry and medicine each require a language which is not that of everyday life. I fail to see why philosophy, alone, should be forbidden to make a similar approach towards precision and accuracy. Let us take, in illustration, one of the commonest words of everyday speech: namely, the word 'day'. The most august use of this word is in the first chapter of Genesis and in the Ten Commandments. The desire to keep holy the Sabbath 'day' has led orthodox Jews to give a precision to the word 'day' which it does not have in common speech: they have defined it as the period from one sunset to the next. Astronomers, with other reasons for seeking precision, have three sorts of day: the true solar day; the mean solar day; and the sidereal day. These have different uses: the true solar day is relevant if you are considering lighting-up time; the mean solar day is relevant if you are sentenced to fourteen days without the option; and the sidereal day is relevant if you are trying to estimate the influence of the tides in retarding the earth's rotation. All these four kinds of day – decalogical, true, mean and sidereal – are more precise than the common use of the word 'day'. If astronomers were subject to the prohibition of precision which some recent philosophers apparently favour, the whole science of astronomy would be impossible.

For technical purposes, technical languages differing from those of daily life are indispensable. I feel that those who object to linguistic novelties, if they had lived a hundred and fifty years ago, would have stuck to feet and ounces, and would have maintained that centimetres and grammes savour of the guillotine.

In philosophy, it is syntax, even more than vocabulary, that needs to be corrected. The subject-predicate logic to which we are accustomed depends for its convenience upon the fact that at the usual temperatures of the earth there are approximately permanent 'things'. This would not be true at the temperature of the sun, and is only roughly true at the temperatures to which we are accustomed.

My theory of descriptions was never intended as an analysis of the state of mind of those who utter sentences containing descriptions. Mr Strawson gives the name 'S' to the sentence 'The King of France is wise', and he says of me 'The way in which he arrived at the analysis was clearly by asking himself what would be the circumstances in which we would say that anyone who uttered the sentence S had made a true assertion'. This does not seem to me a correct account of what I was doing. Suppose (which God forbid) Mr Strawson were so rash as to accuse his charlady of thieving: she would reply indignantly, 'I ain't never done no harm to no one.' Assuming her a pattern of virtue, I should say that she was making a true assertion, although, according to the rules of syntax which Mr Strawson would adopt in his own speech, what she said should have meant: 'there was at least one moment when I was injuring the whole human race'. Mr Strawson would not have supposed that this was what she meant to assert, although he would not have used her words to express the same sentiment. Similarly, I was concerned to find a more accurate and analysed thought to replace the somewhat confused thoughts which most people at most times have in their heads.

Mr Strawson objects to my saying that 'the King of France is wise' is false if there is no King of France. He admits that the sentence is significant and not true, but not that it is false. This is a mere question of verbal convenience. He considers that the word 'false' has an unalterable meaning which it would be sinful to regard as adjustable, though he prudently avoids telling us what this meaning is. For my part, I find it more convenient to define the word 'false' so that every significant sentence is either true or false. This is a purely verbal question; and although I have no wish to claim the support of common usage, I do not think that he can claim it either. Suppose, for example, that in some country there was a law that no person could hold public office if he considered it false that the Ruler of the Universe is wise. I think an avowed atheist who took advantage of Mr Strawson's doctrine to say that he did not hold this proposition false, would be regarded as a somewhat shifty character.

It is not only as to names and as to falsehood that Mr Strawson shows his conviction that there is an unalterably right way of using words and that no change is to be tolerated however convenient it may be. He shows the same feeling as regards universal affirmatives – i.e. sentences of the form 'All A is B'. Traditionally, such sentences are supposed to imply that there are As, but it is much more convenient in mathematical logic to drop this implication and to consider that 'All A is B' is true if there are no As. This is wholly and solely a question of convenience. For some purposes the one convention is more convenient, and for others, the other. We shall prefer the one convention or the other according to the purpose we have in view. I agree, however, with Mr Strawson's statement (page 52) that ordinary language has no exact logic.

Mr Strawson, in spite of his very real logical competence, has a curious prejudice against logic. On page 43, he has a sudden dithyrambic outburst, to the effect that life is greater than logic, which he uses to give a quite false interpretation of my doctrines.

Leaving detail aside, I think we may sum up Mr Strawson's argument and my reply to it as follows:

There are two problems, that of descriptions and that of egocentricity. Mr Strawson thinks they are one and the same problem, but it is obvious from his discussion that he has not considered as many kinds of descriptive phrases as are relevant to the argument. Having confused the two problems, he asserts dogmatically that it is only the egocentric problem that needs to be solved, and he offers a solution of this problem which he seems to believe to be new, but which in fact was familiar before he wrote. He then thinks that he has offered an adequate theory of descriptions, and announces his supposed achievement with astonishing dogmatic certainty. Perhaps I am doing him an injustice, but I am unable to see in what respect this is the case.

IV WHAT IS MIND ?

Professor Ryle's book *The Concept of Mind* has a thesis which is very original and, if true, very important. I find myself unable to accept his thesis, and I propose to give my reasons in what follows.

I will begin, however, with certain points as to which I had already expressed opinions similar to his, although he does not seem to be aware of this fact.

The first point as to which I agree with him is the rejection of Cartesian dualism, which he sets forth in his opening chapter. I was somewhat surprised by his emphasis upon this point. Cartesian dualism was rejected by Malebranche, Leibniz, Berkeley, Hegel and William James. I cannot think of any philosophers of repute who accept it in the present day, except Marxists and Catholic theologians, who are compelled to be old-fashioned by the rigidities of their respective creeds. I imagine, however, that Professor Ryle would defend his emphasis on the ground that many who reject Descartes's doctrine in words nevertheless retain a number of beliefs which are logically connected with it. I think this is true of Professor Ryle himself on one important point, as I shall argue presently.

A second point upon which I am in agreement with him is the rejection of sense-data. I believed in these at one time, but emphatically abandoned them in 1921.[1]

A third matter, which is one of considerable importance, is the rejection of sensation as a form of knowledge. It is not denied, either by him or by me, that sensation is an indispensable part of the *causes* of our knowledge as to matters of fact; what is denied is that it is itself knowledge. There must be added what Professor Ryle calls 'observation' and I call 'noticing'.[2]

Since we agree on these points, I shall say no more about them.

I come now to Professor Ryle's main thesis. I think his thesis may be stated as follows: the adjective 'mental' is not applicable to any special kind of 'stuff', but only to certain organisations and dispositions illustrated by patterns composed of elements which it is not significant to call 'mental'. He gives a great many examples of the kind of adjective or noun that he has in mind. Cricket, he points out, is not another 'thing' side by side with particular matches and particular players, but is something of a logically higher order. Another example is the British Constitution. The House of Commons, as he remarks, is one of the constituents of which the British Constitution is composed, but when you have visited both Houses of Parliament, the Law Courts, Downing Street and Buckingham Palace there does not remain another place for you to visit which is the British Constitution. He contends that the word 'mental' is only applicable to objects having the kind of logical status belonging to cricket or the British Constitution. His favourite examples of 'mental' adjectives are such words as 'intelligent', 'lazy', 'good-natured', which denote dispositions. I will quote a summary which seems to me to state his thesis very clearly:

'One of the central negative motives of this book is to show that "mental" does not denote a status, such that one can sensibly ask of a given thing or event whether it is mental or physical, "in the mind" or "in the outside world". To talk of a person's mind is not to talk of a repository which is permitted to house objects that something called "the physical world" is forbidden to house; it is to talk of the person's abilities, liabilities and inclinations to do and undergo certain sorts of things, and of the doing and undergoing of these things in the ordinary world. Indeed, it makes no sense to speak as if there could be two or eleven worlds. Nothing but confusion is achieved by labelling worlds after particular avocations. Even the solemn phrase "the physical world" is as philosophically pointless as would be the phrase "the numismatic world", "the haberdashery world", or "the botanical world"' (page 199).

[1] *Analysis of Mind*, page 141.
[2] See *An Inquiry into Meaning and Truth*, page 51.

I have failed to understand why other adjectives having a similar logical status are not considered by Professor Ryle to be 'mental'. One of his favourite examples is the adjective 'brittle'. When you say that a piece of glass is brittle, you do not say that it *will* break, but only that in certain circumstances it *would* break, just as you may call a man 'intelligent' even though he happens to be asleep at the moment, if he would exhibit intelligence in suitable circumstances. But Professor Ryle never explains, or seems to think it necessary to explain, what is the difference between 'brittle' and 'intelligent' that makes the latter mental and the former not. A plain man would say that 'brittle' denotes a disposition of bodies and 'intelligent' denotes a disposition of minds – in fact, that the two adjectives apply to different kinds of 'stuff'. But it is not open to Professor Ryle to say this, and I do not quite know what he would say.

Professor Ryle backs up his rejection of all mental 'stuff' by denying that, in principle, there is anything that a man can know about himself which another cannot know unless he is told. He does not, of course, mean that in fact everything is known to observers as well as to the patient. You may hear a clap of thunder when you are alone in the desert and when no one else hears it, but this may be called an accidental privacy. What he means to deny is that there are occurrences which are *essentially* private, which are known to one person but are such as others could not possibly know except through testimony. On this point, as on a good many others, I find that he is astonishingly slap-dash and is content to let dogmatic assertion take the place of refutation of adverse theories. I will take one quite obvious example: dreams. Except in the Book of Exodus it is generally accepted that one man cannot know what another dreams unless he is told. But Professor Ryle has nothing to say about dreams. They do not occur in the index and his few allusions to them are entirely perfunctory. It is singular that, although he goes out of his way to praise Freud, he does not allude to Freud's work on dreams and no one could guess that he even knows of it. He does deal, after a fashion, with such things as stomach-aches and toothaches, but such things, he maintains, become known to the observer through the patient's groans. Evidently none of his friends are Stoics.

Some difficulties in his denial of private data he does deal with, more or less. He has a whole chapter on imagination, but I entirely fail to understand how he can be satisfied by what he says. He says that operations of imagining are exercises of mental powers, but what we imagine exists nowhere. Let us examine this for a moment. In its obvious sense, it is, of course, a truism. If I shut my eyes and imagine a horse, there is no horse in the room. But it is one thing to imagine a horse and another to imagine a hippopotamus. Something happens when I imagine the one, and something else happens when I imagine the other. What can it be that is happening in these two cases? Professor Ryle states explicitly (page 161) that there are no such things as mental happenings. Where perception is concerned, he contents himself with naïve realism: I perceive a horse, and the horse is out there. It is not a 'mental' horse. But when I imagine a horse, it is not out there, and yet the occurrence is not the same as imagining a hippopotamus. I should have thought it as obvious as anything can be that something is happening in me and cannot be known to anybody else unless I do something overt to let it be known what it is that I am imagining.

I should have thought that the same sort of thing might be said about pleasure and unpleasure (Professor Ryle agrees with most psychologists in pointing out that 'pain' is not the opposite of 'pleasure'). A man may exhibit overt signs of pleasure, but it is quite possible for him to conceal pleasure, for example, if he hears of a misfortune to a man whom he hates but pretends to love. It is difficult to suppose that sticks and stones feel either pleasure or unpleasure, but it would be an impossible paradox to maintain that human beings do not. I should have regarded this as one of the most important differences between what is mental and what is not. I should not give this position to intelligence, because calculating machines are, in some ways, more intelligent than any human being. But I should not favour a campaign to give votes to calculating machines, because I do not believe that they experience either pleasure or unpleasure.

Professor Ryle's denial of introspection as a source of knowledge links him with the Behaviourists. He ends his book with a discussion of Behaviourism in which he says that the only point on which he disagrees with its advocates is that they believe in mechanistic explanations and he does not. Mechanism is another of the matters that he treats with cavalier dogmatism. When he speaks of it, he seems to be thinking of the old-fashioned billiard-ball mechanism and to think that since physicists have abandoned this, they have abandoned mechanism. He never gives any reason for rejecting mechanism in the modern sense of the word. The question that deserves to be discussed is this: do the equations of physics, combined with data as to the distribution of energy at some given time, suffice to determine what has happened and will happen to portions of matter not below a certain minimum size? To make the question concrete: since speaking involves macroscopic movements of matter, could an ideally competent physicist calculate what So-and-so will say throughout the rest of his life? I do not profess to know the answer to this question, but Professor Ryle does. I wish he had condescended to give us his reasons.

Professor Ryle's attitude to science is curious. He no doubt knows that scientists say things which they believe to be relevant to the problems he is discussing, but he is quite persuaded that the philosopher need pay no attention to science. He seems to believe that a philosopher need not know anything scientific beyond what was known in the time of our ancestors when they dyed themselves with woad. It is this attitude that enables him to think that the philosopher should pay attention to the way in which uneducated people speak and should treat with contempt the sophisticated language of the learned. To this principle, however, there is, in his opinion, one exception: common people think that thoughts and ideas are in people's heads. As Goldsmith says,

> Still the wonder grew
> That one small head could carry all he knew.

On this point, Professor Ryle rejects common usage. He cannot believe that thoughts and feelings are in our heads, and tries to make out that on this point the plain man agrees with him. He offers no argument of any sort or kind to show that thoughts are not in people's heads, and I fear – though I say this with trepidation – that he has allowed himself to be influenced on this matter by the Cartesian dualism, which makes it seem preposterous to assign a spatial location to anything mental. Granted his thesis as to the sorts of structure that can be called mental, it would, of course, follow that what is to be called mental is not in space. Cricket is not located on the cricket field and cleverness is not located in clever people. But if his thesis is rejected, as I believe it should be, there remains only a dualistic prejudice to prevent us from locating mental occurrences in brains.

The problem of perception has troubled philosophers from a very early date. My own belief is that the problem is scientific not philosophical, or, rather, no longer philosophical. A great many philosophical questions are, in fact, scientific questions with which science is not yet ready to deal. Both sensation and perception were in this class of problems, but are now, so I should contend, amenable to scientific treatment and not capable of being fruitfully handled by anyone who chooses to ignore what science has to say about them.

Professor Ryle ties himself in knots in struggles to maintain naïve realism. He almost denies that a round plate tilted away from the observer looks elliptical. He says:

'A person without a theory feels no qualms in saying that the round plate might look elliptical. Nor would he feel any qualms in saying that the round plate looks as if it were elliptical. But he would feel qualms in following the recommendation to say that he is seeing an elliptical look of a round plate' (page 216).

I cannot understand what, exactly, he is maintaining. In the case of the plate, you know that it is round because that is the way plates are made. But suppose it is an object in the sky which you cannot touch. You will be at a loss to know whether it is 'really' circular or elliptical, and you will be confined to saying what it 'looks like'. The essential point is that a given thing looks different from different points of view, and that differing things may look alike from different points of view, and, further, that what things look like is essential to our knowledge of what they 'really' are, although, for the above reasons, it does not by itself afford conclusive evidence. It is quite unnecessary, in considering this problem, to bring in minds or sensations: the whole thing is physical. A number of cameras photographing a given object produce results which differ in just the same way as our visual perceptions do.

The same sort of considerations apply to colours. Professor Ryle says:

'When I describe a common object as green or bitter, I am not reporting a fact about my present sensation, though I am saying something about how it looks or tastes. I am saying that it would look or taste so and so to anyone who was in a condition and position to see or taste properly. Hence I do not contradict myself if I say that the field is green, though at the moment it looks greyish-blue to me' (page 220).

I am particularly puzzled by the word 'properly'. Birds, whose eyes look in opposite directions, presumably see things quite differently from the way in which we see them. Flies, which have five eyes of two different sorts, must see things even more differently. A bird or a fly would say that it sees 'properly' and that Professor Ryle's way of seeing is eccentric and peculiar. Seeing that there are more flies than human beings in the world, democratic principles should lead us to agree with the fly.

The complications into which Professor Ryle is led by his desire to uphold naïve realism remind me of the complications into which upholders of the Ptolemaic theory were driven by their opposition to the Copernican system. The Copernican system demanded one considerable effort of imagination, namely, to entertain the possibility that the earth, which seems so immovable, can be conceived as rotating and revolving. By means of this initial effort of imagination, an immense simplification was effected in astronomy. An equal simplification is effected in the theory of perception if we can learn to imagine what is called 'perceiving an object' as a remote effect of the object, which resembles it only approximately and only in certain respects. It is only in regard to everyday objects in our neighbourhood that this theory offers serious imaginative difficulties. Nobody can suppose that the Pleiades, if you got near to one of them, would look at all the way they look to us. The difference between the Pleiades and the furniture of our room is only one of degree.

Professor Ryle shares with the school that he adorns a passionate determination to give a linguistic form to the problems that arise. He says, for example, in regard to our perception of visual objects:

'The questions, that is, are not questions of the para-mechanical form "How do we see robins ?" but questions of the form, "How do we use such descriptions as 'he saw a robin' ?"' (page 225).

This seems to me to involve dismissing important scientific knowledge in favour of verbal trivialities. The question, 'How do we see robins ?' is one to which physics and physiology, combined, have given an answer which is interesting and important, and has somewhat curious consequences. It appears that certain processes in the optic nerve will cause you 'to see a robin' even if these processes have not been caused, as they usually are, by something outside the body of the percipient. I have been taken to task for saying that what a physiologist sees when he examines another man's brain is in his own brain, and not in the other man's. To justify this statement fully would require a long discussion of the word 'see' and the word 'in'. This latter word, in particular, is much more complicated and ambiguous than is usually supposed. But I will not go into these questions here as I have dealt with them elsewhere.[1]

I suppose Professor Ryle might agree that the main purpose of his book is to give a new definition of the adjective 'mental'. This, of course, is a linguistic question, and, in so far as it is purely linguistic, it is proper to give weight to common usage in arriving at a definition. But the ways in which it is convenient to use words change with changes in our knowledge. At one time, it was not convenient to speak of the earth as a planet, but this has become convenient since the adoption of the Copernican system. If there were, as Descartes contended, two radically different kinds of substance, one approximately co-extensive with what common sense regards as bodies, and the other approximately co-extensive with what common sense regards as minds, then it would be convenient to divide mind from matter as Descartes did, even if this involved some departure from the way in which these words had been used until Descartes's time. But, if as Professor Ryle contends, and as I agree, there is not this fundamental dualism, then we are compelled, if we wish to continue distinguishing mind from matter, to seek some other basis for our distinction. Professor Ryle finds the distinction in syntax: mental adjectives are of a higher type than those which may still be called physical. For the reasons given

[1] See, e.g. *Human Knowledge*, pages 224–5.

above, I do not think that such a usage is useful, and I also do not think that Professor Ryle has made his own thought clear since he has not explained why he does not consider 'brittle' a mental adjective. My own belief is that the distinction between what is mental and what is physical does not lie in any intrinsic character of either, but in the way in which we acquire knowledge of them. I should call an event 'mental' if it is one that somebody can notice or, as Professor Ryle would say, observe. I should regard all events as physical, but I should regard as *only* physical those which no one knows except by inference. Although it might seem as if my disagreement with Professor Ryle were linguistic, this is only superficially true. It is from differences as to the constitution of the world that he and I are led to different views as to the most convenient definitions of the words 'mental' and 'physical'.

One very general conclusion to which I have been led by reading Professor Ryle's book is that philosophy cannot be fruitful if divorced from empirical science. And by this I do not mean only that the philosopher should 'get up' some science as a holiday task. I mean something much more intimate: that his imagination should be impregnated with the scientific outlook and that he should feel that science has presented us with a new world, new concepts and new methods, not known in earlier times, but proved by experience to be fruitful where the older concepts and methods proved barren.

Russell's Philosophy

A Study of its Development

by ALAN WOOD

Query 64. Whether mathematicians, who are so delicate on religious points, are strictly scrupulous in their own science? Whether they do not submit to authority, take things on trust, and believe points inconceivable? Whether they have not their mysteries, and, what is more, their repugnances and contradictions?

BERKELEY

'The case,' said Sherlock Holmes, as we chatted over our cigars that night in our rooms at Baker Street, 'is one where . . . we have been compelled to reason backwards from effects to causes.'

CONAN DOYLE

Preface

Russell's work covers so many different subjects that there is probably no single living person equipped with a sufficiently thorough knowledge of them all to write an adequate commentary – with the exception, of course, of Russell himself. The present author makes no claim to be so equipped. It is therefore requisite in any comments as to Russell to have the judgement to select the right aspects to advise him on different specialist subjects. Any complete record of Russell's work by any single hand must be based to a certain extent on knowledge by description as well as knowledge by acquaintance. And it is the duty of any writer on Russell to be explicit about the limits he places on the scope of his inquiry, in order that his own limitations should not be mistaken for any limitations in his subject, and to make it plain how much work remains for others to do in the same field.

So far as possible, I have tried to indicate the limitations of the present work by its title. I am concerned with the origin and development of Russell's own ideas; not their continuation by others. Unless this is borne in mind, a false impression may be given of Russell's stature; I believe there is little of importance in present-day philosophising which is not derived from him. The post-Russellians are all propter-Russellians. (I indicate some grounds for this statement in the text.) Any adequate commentary on Russell must take account of his influences on subsequent philosophy; which means that it may be many centuries before it can be written.

For the purpose of this essay I interpret 'Russell's philosophy' in a rather strict sense; almost the sense in which he himself once said that logic is not part of philosophy. He always believed, of course, that logic is the essential prerequisite of philosophy; and it is obvious enough that the foundations of most of his philosophical ideas are to be found in *The Principles of Mathematics* and *Principia Mathematica*. But I only concern myself with those aspects of these works which have been important for Russell as a philosopher, and thus leave on one side a vast amount of material of first-rate importance for the mathematician and the technical logician. In discussing the contradictions and the Theory of Types, for instance, my main concern is not with the controversial questions which still surround them, but with a fact which is beyond controversy – that, with the Theory of Types,

Russell brought into philosophy a new idea of cardinal importance.

My purpose is almost solely expository, not critical; for I believe that Russell's philosophy leaves little scope for criticism on orthodox lines. Napoleon told the inn-keeper, in Bernard Shaw's play, that 'You will never be hanged. There is no satisfaction in hanging a man who does not object to it.' Something of the same difficulty faces the would-be critic of Russell. There are few faults and weak points in his work which he has not pointed out with the utmost candour himself; each advance he made constituted a criticism of his previous position. I have come across few present-day critics of Russell who do not either unwittingly repeat points he himself has made, or else show ignorance of his true views. (It must be remembered that his books are already becoming classics; and a classic may be defined as a book which people think they know about without having read it.)

The need at the moment, therefore, is not to criticise Russell, but to understand him. The present work is intended to serve as an introduction to this purpose. It may be compared to a guide book to a cathedral which exemplifies many different architectural styles and periods; it is essential, when reading any book by Russell, to know its place in the development of his thought.

I hope that it may also, however, add to the understanding of Russell in another way. It is often the case that the easiest way to explain Russell's views is to trace in detail the steps by which he reached them. Here again, I have a quite modest object in mind. There are some obvious questions which puzzle anyone who first attempts the reading of Russell. Why should a book on *The Principles of Mathematics* contain a chapter on 'Proper Names, Adjectives and Verbs'? Why should an *Introduction to Mathematic Philosophy* devote two chapters to the word 'the'? I do not know of any commentary on Russell which sets out to answer any questions so simple as these. Russell apparently regarded his *Introduction to Mathematic Philosophy* as a book suitable for a 'beginner'; but few beginners can honestly say that they agree with him. I think the easiest approach is to explain how Russell followed a chain of thought which began with a problem in Dynamics, and led him in turn to Geometry, Analysis, Symbolic Logic and Grammar. His order of exposition in *The Principles of Mathematics* is just the reverse of this; the reader begins with Logic and ends with Dynamics. The easiest way to the understanding of it, as of some other books by Russell, is to know it backwards; and in what follows I have outlined its ideas from back to front in this way.

I

Summary and
Introduction

Bertrand Russell is a philosopher without a philosophy. The same point might be made by saying that he is a philosopher of all the philosophies.

There is hardly any philosophical viewpoint of importance today which cannot be found reflected in his writings at some period.

Whitehead once described Russell as a Platonic dialogue in himself.[1] Lytton Strachey compared Russell's mind to a circular saw.[2] The metaphor is particularly apt. The teeth on opposite sides of a circular saw move in opposite directions; in fact the teeth are moving in every different direction at once. But the saw itself cuts straight forward.

In spite of all the apparently conflicting statements to be found in the total of Russell's philosophical writings, in spite of the number of cases where he champions different opinions at different times, there is throughout a consistency of purpose and direction, and a consistency of method.

'I wanted certainty,' Russell wrote in retrospect, 'in the kind of way in which people want religious faith.'[3] I believe the underlying purpose behind all Russell's work was an almost religious passion for some truth that was more than human, independent of the minds of men, and even of the existence of men. It is well to be brought face to face, at the start, with one of the problems of conflicting quotations which faces any student of Russell. For we can also quote him as calling on us, in the context of a popular essay, 'to recognise that the non-human world is unworthy of worship'.

We are discussing here a matter of motive. I can therefore only appeal to evidence of the strength of Russell's feelings to support my contention that, while seeing two sides to the question, his overriding motive was yearning for absolutely certain impersonal knowledge.

We can cite, for instance, the way he would speak of Kant's allegation of a subjective element in mathematics: the tone of his voice can

[1] Conversation between Whitehead and B. R., reported to Alan Wood.
[2] Lytton Strachey to Virginia Woolf, 27th May, 1919.
[3] 'Reflections on My Eightieth Birthday', in *Portraits from Memory*.

only be described as one of disgust, like a Fundamentalist confronted with the suggestion that Moses had made up the Ten Commandments himself. 'Kant made me *sick*.'[1]

There was his contempt for 'the grovelling microscopic vision of those philosophers whose serious attention is confined to this petty planet and the grovelling animalcules that crawl upon its surface'. There was his complaint of 'cosmic impiety' against Dewey.[2] In later years, there were his criticisms of some Oxford philosophers for being too much concerned with 'the different ways in which silly people can say silly things',[3] and not with trying to understand the world.

The view I am advocating provides the reconciliation of the apparent contradiction that he could have a passion for mathematics and also a sympathetic understanding of mysticism; the attraction of both was that they aimed at truths independent of passing human experience.

But the strongest evidence is to be found in his letters. For instance, he wrote in 1918: 'I *must*, before I die, find *some* way to say the essential thing that is in me, that I have never said yet – a thing that is not love or hate or pity or scorn, but the very breath of life, fierce and coming from far away, bringing into human life the vastness and the fearful passionless force of non-human things . . .'[4]

I take, therefore, the following passage for my main text:

'When I was young I hoped to find religious satisfaction in philosophy; even after I had abandoned Hegel, the eternal Platonic world gave me something non-human to admire . . . I thought of mathematics with reverence. . . .

'I have always ardently desired to find some justification for the emotions inspired by certain things that seemed to stand outside human life and to deserve feelings of awe . . . the starry heavens . . . the vastness of the scientific universe . . . the edifice of impersonal truth which, like that of mathematics, does not merely describe the world that happens to exist.

'Those who attempt to make a religion of humanism, which recognises nothing greater than man, do not satisfy my emotions. And yet I am unable to believe that, in the world as known, there is anything that I can value outside human beings. . . . Impersonal non-human truth appears to be a delusion.

'And so my intellect goes with the humanists, though my emotions violently rebel.'[5]

---

[1] B. R. in conversation with Alan Wood.
[2] *History of Western Philosophy*, page 856.
[3] Review of Urmson's *Philosophical Analysis* in *The Hibbert Journal*, July 1956. cf. 'The Cult of "Common Usage",' in *Portraits from Memory*.
[4] Letter from B. R. to Constance Malleson.
[5] 'My Mental Development' in *The Philosophy of Bertrand Russell* (Evanston and Cambridge, 1944).

This conflict is the main connecting thread in the exposition of the development of Russell's philosophy which follows.

One might sum up his public career as a philosopher, briefly and crudely, as: From Kant to Kant.[1] In the *Foundations of Geometry*, published in 1897, he wrote that his viewpoint 'can be obtained by a certain limitation and interpretation of Kant's classic arguments'.[2] In *Human Knowledge*, published in 1948, he recurred to ideas and nomenclature with a Kantian affinity. But he was still glad to be able to claim that the synthetic *a priori* of *Human Knowledge* was not so subjective as Kant: just as he was not so subjective as Kant in the *Foundations of Geometry*.[3] Russell's intellectual life was devoted to three main quests. He sought impersonal objective truth successively in Religion, Mathematics and Science.

Not in philosophy.[4] In his heart he usually thought of philosophy as an inferior pursuit compared with mathematics and science. One of the most often repeated notes in his writings is the continued gibery at 'the philosophers' for being too lazy to undertake the study of mathematics, or too stupid to understand it.[5] He expressed regret more than once (for instance, to Beatrice Webb in 1936) that he had not been a scientist instead of a philosopher.[6]

The key to understanding Russell's philosophy is that it was essentially a by-product. To treat it as though it were an end in itself, though a natural enough mistake for philosophers to make, is liable to render it meaningless. But in fact there is a sense in which *any* worthwhile philosophy is a by-product. As Russell himself wrote, 'A philosophy which is to have any value should be built upon a wide and firm foundation of knowledge that is not specifically philosophical.'[7]

Russell's primary objects were to establish the truth of religion, the truth of mathematics and the truth of science. He himself stated this

[1] I cannot subscribe to this formula. My final views are less Kantian than Alan Wood supposes. I will mention two points. First: though the external world is probably not quite like the world of perception, it is connected with the world of perception by correlations, which are impossible in a philosophy which regards time and space as subjective. Second: the principles of non-deductive inference which I advocate are not put forward as certain or *a priori*, but as scientific hypotheses. – B. R.

[2] *Foundations of Geometry*, page 179.

[3] B. R. to Alan Wood.

[4] For one thing, he never made up his mind exactly what he meant by philosophy.

[5] e.g. in *Principles of Mathematics* (passim), *Mysticism and Logic*, page 80, *Introduction to Mathematical Philosophy*, page 11, and *Sceptical Essays*, page 72.

[6] Letter to Beatrice Webb.

[7] Review of Urmson's *Philosophical Analysis* in *The Hibbert Journal*, July, 1956.

explicitly in the case of religion and mathematics. 'I hoped to find religious satisfaction in philosophy. . . .'[1] . . . 'I came to philosophy through mathematics, or rather through the wish to find some reason to believe in the truth of mathematics.'[2]

With science the feeling was perhaps not quite so strong: after all, science merely deals with 'the world that happens to exist'. But Professor Weitz, one of the ablest of commentators on Russell, declares that 'Russell's primary interest, it seems to me, has been the attempt to justify science'.[3] In a sense, therefore, it could be said that Russell's career was a threefold failure.

(*a*) He not only had to abandon religion, but objective ethical knowledge as well. (*b*) He was not fully satisfied with the system of *Principia Mathematica*, and Wittgenstein convinced him – or almost convinced him – that in any case mathematical knowledge was only tautological.[4] (*c*) His defence of scientific knowledge in *Human Knowledge* was not in accordance with the kind of standards he had hoped to satisfy earlier.[5]

All philosophers are failures. But Russell was one of the few with enough integrity to admit it. Therein lies his supreme importance. One might write of him, as he himself wrote in praise of Kant, that:

'A candid philosopher should acknowledge that he is not very likely to have arrived at ultimate truth, but, in view of the incurable tendency to discipleship in human nature, he will be thought to have done so unless he makes his failures very evident. The duty of making this evident was one which Kant's candour led him to perform better than most other philosophers.' His philosophical ideas were the by-products of his quests for certain knowledge, and these quests ended in failure. How then could his failures prove so fruitful? Broadly speaking, this came about in two different ways.

(*a*) It is a solution to a philosophical problem to show that it has no solution: just as it was an advance in mathematics when Lindemann showed that it is impossible to square the circle.

(*b*) In his quests Russell developed a distinctive philosophical method which added to knowledge, even though it could not confer certainty. 'Every truly philosophical problem', he said, 'is a problem of analysis; and in problems of analysis the best method is that which sets out from results and arrives at the premisses.'[6]

To put it crudely, Russell saw the role of a philosopher as analogous

---

[1] *Philosophy of Bertrand Russell* ('My Mental Development').

[2] 'Logical Atomism' in *Contemporary British Philosophy*, Vol. I (Ed. J. H Muirhead: George Allen & Unwin, London).

[3] *Philosophy of Bertrand Russell*, page 102.

[4] 'Reflections on My Eightieth Birthday' in *Portraits from Memory*.

[5] *Introduction to Mathematical Philosophy*, page 71.

[6] 'Philosophical Importance of Mathematical Logic' (*Monist*, October 1913); cf. *Our Knowledge of the External World*, page 211.

to that of a detective in a detective story; he had to start from results, and work backwards by analysing the evidence. (The extent to which the crudity of this analogy is misleading will emerge later.)

It is perhaps unfortunate that attention has usually been focused on what was only the first part of Russell's description, as given above, of his philosophical procedure. The emphasis has been placed on his methods of 'analysis', and in fact no better single word could be chosen; but 'analysis' has now been used and abused with so many different meanings that it has become almost meaningless. I think it possible that the idea of starting from results and arriving at premisses is prior to that of 'analysis'; and it gives a more fundamental picture of the underlying unity of Russell's work. He started from results and arrived at premisses in the *Principles of Mathematics*. He did exactly the same thing, over forty years later, in *Human Knowledge*, where his main argument for his 'Postulates' of Scientific Inference was the same as his defence of the Axiom of Reducibility in *Principia Mathematica*.[1] His work on epistemology was not a kind of subsidiary supplement to his work on mathematical philosophy. It came from the same workshop and was made with the same tools.

He said: 'The inferring of premisses from consequences is the essence of induction; thus the method in investigating the principles of mathematics is really an inductive method, and is substantially the same as the method of discovering general laws in any other sciences.'

He wrote in 1924 that, both in pure mathematics and in any science arranged as a deductive system: 'Some of the premisses are much less obvious than some of their consequences, and are believed chiefly because of their consequences.'[2]

Why did Russell adopt this philosophical method? Why did he want to find the premisses for a given body of knowledge? Because at first he hoped that, by going far enough back, he could arrive at premisses which were absolutely certain. Why should he want to reduce the number of premisses to the fewest possible? One reason was to reduce the risk of error: hence Occam's Razor. What was the purpose of analysis? To increase knowledge. Russell's philosophical method would never, I believe, have been developed if he had not at first been inspired by the hope of arriving at knowledge which was certain. Had he realised from the start that certainty was unattainable, he might have abandoned philosophy and devoted himself to economics, or history. His work is thus a classic example of what can be achieved as a result of attempting the impossible.

Certain consequences follow from Russell's view that the proper

[1] Vol. I, page 59.
[2] *Logic and Knowledge*, page 325; cf. *Human Knowledge*.

philosophical procedure is not deductive, from premises to conclusions, but exactly the reverse.

The only decisive weapon in philosophical controversy is the *reductio
ad absurdum*; the premises reached can be shown to lead to contradictions. True, in philosophy it is possible to *disprove* something,
but never possible to *prove* anything. Thus: 'Philosophical argument,
strictly speaking, consists mainly of an endeavour to cause the reader
to perceive what has been perceived by the author. The argument, in
short, is not of the nature of proof, but of exhortation.'[1]

The way to clarify controversial questions is by 'a more careful
scrutiny of the premises that are apt to be employed unconsciously,
and a more prolonged attention to fundamentals'. After that a philosophical argument can only take the form of saying, 'Look, can't you
see what I see?' (These are not Russell's words.) A philosophical
advance consists in suddenly seeing a new way of looking at something.

Philosophical advances are achieved by analysis, together with
something which Russell refers to variously as (*a*) 'insight',[2] (*b*)
'intuition',[3] (*c*) 'instinct',[4] (*d*) 'vision'.[5]

And though he often stressed the fallibility of 'insight' and 'instinct' into what we believe obvious, he recognised that in the last
resort our instinctive belief could only be rejected because it conflicted
with another instinctive belief. The best aim philosophy could hope to
achieve was, (1) to arrange our instinctive beliefs in a kind of hierarchy
from more to less certain; (2) to arrive at a system of beliefs which was
internally consistent.[6]

These views of Russell on philosophy are worth stressing. Because
he wrote at times as though he rigidly excluded appeals to 'intuition'
and 'instinct' (and many other things) from his philosophy, this did
not mean that he did not realise their importance. There are many
things excluded from his philosophy, to which critics point as evidence
of a lack of 'profundity', which are to be found in his way of *doing*
philosophy. (And to be found in what he did in other fields.)

---

[1] Russell prefaced these remarks, in the *Principles of Mathematics*, by
saying they arose from the consideration of mathematical philosophy, and
were 'not necessarily' applicable to other branches of philosophy. In view of
the underlying unity of his philosophical method, referred to earlier, I do
not think this qualification is now necessary, pages 129, 130.

[2] *Principles of Mathematics*, page 129; cf. *Our Knowledge of the External
World.*

[3] *Our Knowledge of the External World*, page 31; cf. *Philosophy of Leibniz*,
page 171.

[4] Letter from B. R. to F. H. Bradley.

[5] *Our Knowledge of the External World*, page 241.

[6] *Problems of Philosophy.*

The fact that philosophical argument consists of 'exhortation' accounts for much of the informal flavour of his writing, and the use of different popular illustrations of his ideas, in which critics can find contradictions. It is as though Russell were saying 'if *that* way of putting it won't convince you, perhaps *this* will'.[1]

Since Russell reached the above views on philosophy over fifty years ago, there has been time for them to be forgotten, and they have been presented again in recent years as though they were new discoveries due to Wittgenstein and his school. (For instance, Dr Waismann in the latest volume of *Contemporary British Philosophy*: 'There is a notion that philosophical questions can be settled by argument, and conclusively if one only knew how to set about it. . . . I incline to come to a new and somewhat shocking conclusion: that the thing cannot be done. No philosopher has ever proved anything . . . (because) philosophical arguments are not deductive.')[2]

I have referred above to Occam's Razor as a part of Russell's philosophical method inspired by his passion for certain knowledge. This was how Russell himself justified its use. ('That is the advantage of Occam's Razor, that it diminishes your risk of error.')[3] But much more was involved than this; and we must beware of Russell's habit of describing his own work in terms of belittlement.

What he would not say about himself he said about Einstein. He gave a better clue to his real feelings when he wrote that the Theory of Relativity 'is possessed by that sort of grandeur that is felt in vast results achieved with the very minimum of material'.

Occam's Razor is not just a kind of philosophical economy campaign; that is like describing a sculptor as a man who gets rid of unnecessary chips of marble. It is not, as suggested by Wittgenstein, a rule of symbolism. It is not even merely a rule for securing a greater chance of accuracy in philosophical calculations. Russell's use of Occam's Razor was not only a means to an end but part of something which was a motive in itself; a passion which had almost as much force in Russell's mind as his passion for impersonal truth.

It is a passion known to every writer who whittles away unnecessary words from his manuscript, and to every mathematician and scientist in search for the most elegant proofs and most general laws. It is easier to give illustrations of it than to attempt to define or explain it.[4]

Russell wrote in 1906 that, when choosing among the different alternative systems of primitive propositions for mathematical logic,

[1] Perhaps it is of interest to note that A. D. Lindsay made a similar remark about Kant.
[2] Vol. III, page 471.
[3] 'Philosophy of Logical Atomism' (*Logic and Knowledge*).
[4] cf. *Mysticism and Logic*, page 70.

'that one is to be preferred, *aesthetically*, in which the primitive propositions are fewest and most general; exactly as the Law of Gravitation is to be preferred to Kepler's three Laws' (my italics).[1] He recalled that he had 'a sense almost of intoxication' when he first studied Newton's deduction of Kepler's Second Law from the Law of Gravitation.[2] He told of his delight when he discovered for himself, as a boy, the formula for the sum of an arithmetic progression, and his delight in such a concise formula as $E^{i\pi} = -1$. In such instances he gave a much truer picture, but when he wrote, for example, 'then the justification for the utmost generalisation in mathematics was not to "waste our time" proving in a particular case what can be proved generally'.[3]

What is involved might variously be described as love of aesthetic elegance, love of unity, love of system, or profundity. (In the only sense of the word 'profundity' which I think has any meaning.) It was a passion partly connected with, and partly at variance with, his passion for impersonal and certain truth. And it proved just as impossible to attain.

In an early article he described how, in the greatest mathematical works, 'unity and inevitability are felt as in the unfolding of a drama. . . . The love of system, of interconnection . . . is perhaps the inmost essence of the intellectual impulse'.[4] He was later forced to the conclusion that the love of system was the greatest barrier to honest thinking in philosophy; just as he decided that 'the demand for certainty is one which is natural to man, but is nevertheless an intellectual vice'.[5]

He put his conclusions in their most extreme form when he wrote in 1931:

'Academic philosophers, ever since the time of Parmenides, have believed that the world is a unity. . . . The most fundamental of my intellectual beliefs is that this is rubbish. I think the universe is all spots and jumps, without unity, without continuity, without coherence of orderliness or any of the other properties that governesses love. Indeed, there is little but prejudice and habit to be said for the view that there is a world at all. . . .[6]

'The external world may be an illusion, but if it exists, it consists of events, short, small and haphazard. Order, unity and continuity

[1] *Philosophy of Leibniz*, page 8.

[2] *On Education*, page 203.

[3] *Introduction to Mathematical Philosophy*, pages 197–8.

[4] *Mysticism and Logic*, page 66; cf. *Our Knowledge of the External World*, page 238.

[5] *Unpopular Essays*, page 42.

[6] *The Scientific Outlook*, page 98.

are human inventions, just as truly as are catalogues and encyclo-paedias.'[1]

To appreciate the force of such a passage, it must not be regarded as simply a sweeping attack on most 'academic philosophers'. It was an attack on a position which Russell held himself; and one which he always, in a sense, wanted to hold as intellectually possible.

It may now be easier to understand why Russell's writings are so complex, subtle and intricate, and why Whitehead called him a Platonic dialogue in himself. In fact there is no great philosopher since Plato whose ideas are harder to sum up in a short space. His philos-ophy was a battleground on which he fought a losing battle against himself; sometimes going one way, sometimes another; and he covered the whole field before reaching conclusions usually diametrically opposed to those which he had hoped for.

It is very difficult to sum up the main point at issue, between Russell and his earliest philosophical opponent, without making it appear that both sides were, in a sense, right. But I think the fundamental point at issue, in Russell's controversy with Bradley over internal relations, was some sort of assumption, on Bradley's part, that an entity *must* have the relations which it has. Perhaps we can best sum up Russell's dilemma by saying that for the most part he *wanted* to believe in a Law of Sufficient Reason; his intellectual integrity made him reject it; and he was therefore left with the problem of explaining how scientific knowledge could be possible.

Paradoxically enough, the very clarity of Russell's usual style has obscured the continual subtlety and originality of his arguments. The polemic overstatements and sweeping epigrams which anyone can understand have been quoted again and again; the books where he is painfully working his way from one position to another, or arguing with himself, often remain unread. According to a modern commen-tator of some repute, Russell 'even on the most difficult topics is always simple, easy'; from which it would seem a fair deduction that the com-mentator in question has never read *The Principles of Mathematics*, nor even *Human Knowledge*.

As Russell himself said in criticism of Santayana, a smooth literary form is rarely compatible with original ideas, which are more likely to be marked – at least in their first expression – by 'uncouth jargon'. Russell himself kept remarkably free from 'uncouth jargon'; but his philosophy was far from 'simple'.[2] It is right that any study of a philosopher should be prefaced by a statement of the author's own views, so that the reader can allow for any unconscious bias.

By temperament I am a mystic Bergsonian; I cannot be satisfied

[1] *ibid.*, page 101.
[2] B. R. on George Santayana.

with the static analytic approach of Russell. In fact my main aim, in studying his philosophy, was to find some way of getting round his conclusions; but in this, so far, I have been completely unsuccessful; and I do not believe that anyone else has produced any answer to his philosophy which can be accepted with intellectual integrity.

As I have said, it is hard to be sure about exactly what point is at issue between Russell and the monists. Russell could hardly quarrel with Bradley's statement that 'Since what I start with in fact is this, and what analysis leaves to me instead is that – I therefore cannot but reject, at least in part, the result of analysis.'[1] To the question 'Does analysis mean falsification ?' I believe the only correct answer is 'Yes, if you don't know what you are doing.' A physicist is obviously wrong if he thinks that, after carrying out the electrolysis of water, he can still get a cooling drink from the products of his analysis; but the fact remains that analysis is the proper method of increasing our knowledge of water. A physiologist who dissects a living body cannot expect to be able to put the body together again, or (I believe) to discover what makes the body live and breathe. But most major advances in medicine have come from accepting the materialistic view of the human body as a working hypothesis; even though some doctors in recent years have tended to go astray through regarding the materialistic view as sufficient in itself. In the same way, I believe that Russell was right, as a method of increasing knowledge, in pushing the philosophy of analysis as far as it will go; in his case he came up against its furthest present-day limits, and could not really feel satisfied with his conclusions, when he came to ethical theory.

The philosopher has the choice today of advancing precise thinking as far as possible, while recognising spheres remaining separate outside it, or else attempting a grand synthesis in which his emotions and his mystic yearnings are brought in to muddle up his thinking. Russell followed in the first course.

In short, I believe that analysis is abundantly justified as a method, but can be misleading if it comes to be regarded as a metaphysic. There are hints in Russell's writings that he himself may have felt this: for instance (my italics): 'Speaking generally, scientific progress has been made by analysis and *artificial* isolation.'[2]

In at least one passage he emphasised the distinction I have in mind between a metaphysic and a method. He wrote of Meinong (in 1904):

'Although empiricism as a philosophy does not appear to be tenable, there is an empirical method of investigating, which should be applied in every subject-matter.'

[1] F. H. Bradley: *Philosophy of Logic*, page 693.
[2] *Human Knowledge*, page 49.

Cautionary Notes

Some preliminary notes are necessary before beginning to discuss the development of Russell's ideas.

I may often have occasion to write that his thoughts were impelled in a certain direction because of his desire to reach such-and-such a conclusion. This must never be taken as implying that this motive, consciously or unconsciously, affected the *results* of his thinking: the distinction must be kept absolutely clear cut throughout. It has already been pointed out that the general trend of this thought led to results directly opposite to those he hoped to reach; but the distinction also applies to other motives I may mention incidentally.

There is a danger that, in tracing connections between Russell's ideas and those of his predecessors and contemporaries, an impression may be given that his thought was not so original as it was. This impression may also be fostered by his own over-generosity in acknowledging his debts to others; he once wrote that a philosopher who claimed priority for a discovery was descending to the level of a stock-jobber.

Russell probably read more widely than any other contemporary philosopher, with the possible exception of Whitehead. Some of his greatest contributions to philosophy arose through his ability to take a multitude of ideas from many sources and combine them into a fully-wrought system; in the same way that Newton's *Principia* brought together a number of fundamental concepts originated by Galileo.[1] But even when ideas were suggested in the first place by others, Russell wrote nothing which was not the product of his own mind. The most obvious evidence is in the number of cases (for instance, with neutral monism) where there was a long time-lag before he came to accept another philosopher's point of view.

There were also many cases of pure coincidence, where Russell reached his conclusion in ignorance of similar conclusions by others; like the discovery of the calculus by Leibniz and Newton, or like the four identical bars in Verdi's *Otello* and Gounod's *Romeo et Juliette*. In Russell's case, of course, the most obvious example is the theory of

---

[1] Russell's remark (in conversation with Alan Wood) that he owed his achievements to 'pertinacity and obstinacy' can be compated with Newton's: 'I had no special sagacity – only the power of patient thought.'

mathematics which he and Frege arrived at completely independently.

It may also be noticed that Russell did not acquire much knowledge of philosophy – in the usual academic sense of studying the writings of other philosophers – until comparatively late in life. He did not read philosophy officially until his fourth year at Cambridge, and his course of study at Cambridge had some important gaps. As a boy, Russell arrived at something like Descartian dualism before he read Descartes; he had Humean doubts before he read Hume.[1] I am inclined to think that his lack of systematic philosophical education was an advantage, and that nothing can do more to stultify original thinking than a thorough knowledge of past philosophers acquired too early in life; because it brings with it the deadening discouragement of realising that most of the ideas one thinks up have been thought of by someone else before. (Perhaps the classic example of the advantages of ignorance was Wittgenstein.)

Some knowledge of Russell's method of working is essential to understanding his writings.[2] There were successive periods of intense thinking, each of which culminated in a book which, in the end, was written rapidly. Russell hardly ever revised anything he had written, and almost never re-read a book after it had been published. (There is sufficient evidence for this in the number of small misprints which survived edition after edition of his work.) When he began each new advance in his thinking he did so with a fresh mind. He rarely concerned himself with the relation between his new ideas and what he had said the last time; in the way that Wittgenstein, for instance, always had the *Tractatus* in mind when writing his *Philosophical Investigations*.

The result is to give an impression of greater inconsistency than really existed between earlier and later years. There are apparent contradictions because he is discussing a problem from a completely different point of view, or arguing against a different opponent. There was no inconsistency in Russell facing in different ways when defending the same ground against attacks from opposite directions. I believe this polemic aspect of many of Russell's writings is of great importance, and that it is often impossible to understand his position without knowing what his opponents were saying.

Another result of Russell's refusal to work backwards is that apparent inconsistencies can arise through his use of words in slightly different senses in different books, without his being explicit about how one usage differs from the other. Any hostile critic can collect an easy crop of verbal inconsistencies in this way.

---

[1] *Philosophy of Bertrand Russell* ('My Mental Development'), page 7, and 'Logical Atomism' in *Contemporary British Philosophy*, page 323.

[2] *Portraits from Memory*, pages 195-6.

It might be said that it was the duty of a commentator to remove such purely verbal confusion by providing a kind of dictionary, whereby Russell's use of a word at one time can be translated in terms of his use of it at another. Such lexicography has appeared an obvious first step in philosophical scholarship ever since Moore's *Principia Ethica*; and Russell himself frequently prefaces a philosophical discussion with an attempt to define his terms. But I do not think this is the best way of trying to avoid the kind of vagueness which, as Russell rightly insisted, is unavoidable in ordinary language.[1]

There are obvious dangers in using words without being sure what we mean by them. But there is another danger, though less obvious, in trying to provide exact definitions. The danger is that we may think we have succeeded.

I do not believe the correct procedure in philosophy is to begin with an apparatus of indefinables, and other words defined in terms of them. I believe that, in philosophy, any statement of indefinables and definitions must come at the end, rather than at the beginning. Philosophy is a subject in which we use such words as idealist and realist, *a priori* and empirical, necessary and contingent, universal and particular; and we are inspired by the hope (never fully realised) that we will end up by knowing what we are talking about.

It may be necessary to indicate various places where Russell's different uses of different words may lead to misunderstandings. But, in general, if we wish to know what Russell means by a particular word in a particular context, the best procedure is to look at the context.

For an illustration, we may consider the word 'philosophy' itself, which Russell finally gave up the attempt to define: 'I don't know what a philosopher is.' Broadly speaking he had two different ways of looking at philosophy:

(*a*) 'In the special sciences . . . the movement is . . . from the simple to the more complex.[2] But in philosophy . . . we proceed towards the simple and abstract by means of analysis, seeking, in the process, to eliminate the particularity of the original subject-matter, and to confine our attention entirely to the logical *form* of the facts concerned.'

'The new realism . . . aims only at clarifying the fundamental ideas of the sciences, and synthesising the different sciences in a single comprehensive view.'[3]

(*b*) 'Philosophy . . . is something intermediate between theology and science . . . a No Man's Land.'[4]

'Science is what you know, philosophy is what you don't know.'[5]

[1] e.g. *Philosophy of Bertrand Russell*, page 690.
[2] *Our Knowledge of the External World*, pages 189–90.
[3] *Sceptical Essays*, page 79; cf. *Problems of Philosophy*, page 233.
[4] *History of Western Philosophy*, page 10.
[5] cf. *Logic and Knowledge*, page 281.

When he was thinking of philosophy in the first way, (*a*), he wrote that logic was 'the essence of philosophy'. In the other way, (*b*), he made such startlingly contradictory statements as that 'Logic, I maintain, is no part of philosophy', and that 'Nine-tenths of what is regarded as philosophy is humbug. The only part that is at all definite is logic, and since it is logic, it is not philosophy.'

This example will give us an excellent preliminary exercise in the art of not being misled by verbal contradictions in Russell. In these apparently conflicting statements about logic and philosophy, he was using 'philosophy' in a different sense; there may also have been some difference in the sense in which he was using 'logic'; and there was a different context.

It is true that logic – in one sense – does not feature in Russell's later philosophy to the extent that it did in 1914. But there was no such complete reversal of his views as might appear at first reading. One can imagine someone writing in one context that 'You cannot read without knowing your ABC', and in another context that 'A knowledge of the ABC has nothing to do with appreciating literature'.

As Russell himself once put it: 'Logic and mathematics . . . are the alphabet of the book of nature, not the book itself.'

(*The essay remained unfinished at this point.*)

INDEX OF NAMES

1896 *German Social Democracy*
1897 *An Essay on the Foundations of Geometry* (Constable)
1900 *The Philosophy of Leibniz*
1903 *The Principles of Mathematics*
1910 *Philosophical Essays*
1912 *Problems of Philosophy* (Oxford U.P.)
1910–13 *Principia Mathematica* 3 vols. (with A. N. Whitehead) (Cambridge U.P.)
1914 *Our Knowledge of the External World*
1916 *Justice in Wartime* (out of print)
1916 *Principles of Social Reconstruction*
1917 *Political Ideals*
1918 *Roads to Freedom*
1918 *Mysticism and Logic*
1919 *Introduction to Mathematical Philosophy*
1920 *The Practice and Theory of Bolshevism*
1921 *The Analysis of Mind*
1922 *The Problem of China*
1923 *Prospects of Industrial Civilization* (with Dora Russell)
1923 *The ABC of Atoms* (out of print)
1924 *Icarus or the Future of Science* (USA only)
1925 *The ABC of Relativity*
1925 *What I Believe*
1926 *On Education*
1927 *An Outline of Philosophy*
1927 *The Analysis of Matter*
1928 *Sceptical Essays*
1929 *Marriage and Morals*
1930 *The Conquest of Happiness*
1931 *The Scientific Outlook*
1932 *Education and the Social Order*
1934 *Freedom and Organization: 1814–1914*
1935 *In Praise of Idleness*
1935 *Religion and Science* (Oxford U.P.)
1936 *Which Way to Peace* (out of print)
1937 *The Amberley Papers* (with Patricia Russell)
1938 *Power*
1940 *An Inquiry into Meaning and Truth*
1945 *History of Western Philosophy*

1948 *Human Knowledge: Its Scope and Limits*
1949 *Authority and the Individual*
1950 *Unpopular Essays*
1951 *New Hopes for a Changing World*
1952 *The Impact of Science on Society*
1953 *The Good Citizen's Alphabet* (Gabberbochus)
1953 *Satan in the Suburbs*
1954 *Nightmares of Eminent Persons*
1954 *Human Society in Ethics and Politics*
1956 *Logic and Knowledge* (ed. by R. C. Marsh)
1956 *Portraits from Memory*
1957 *Why I am not a Christian* (ed. by Paul Edwards)
1957 *Understanding History and other essays* (USA only)
1958 *Vital Letters of Russell, Khrushchev and Dulles* (Macgibbon & Kee)
1958 *Bertrand Russell's Best* (ed. by Robert Egner)
1959 *Common Sense and Nuclear Warfare*
1959 *Wisdom of the West* (ed. by Paul Foulkes) (Macdonald)
1959 *My Philosophical Development*
1960 *Bertrand Russell Speaks his Mind* (USA only)
1961 *Fact and Fiction*
1961 *Has Man a Future?*
1961 *The Basic Writings of Bertrand Russell* (ed. by R. E. Egner & L. Dennon)
1963 *Unarmed Victory*
1967 *War Crimes in Vietnam*
1967 *The Archives of Bertrand Russell* (ed. by B. Feinberg, Continuum) (out of print)
1967 *Autobiography 1872–1914*
1968 *Autobiography 1914–1944*
1969 *Autobiography 1944–1967*
1969 *Dear Bertrand Russell . . .* (ed. by B. Feinberg & R. Kasrils)
1972 *The Collected Stories of Bertrand Russell* (ed. by B. Feinberg)
1973 *Bertrand Russell's America* (ed. by B. Feinberg and R. Kasrils)